CITY
MONSTER

ALSO BY REZA FARAZMAND

Poorly Drawn Lines

Comics for a Strange World

Poorlier Drawn Lines

CITY MONSTER

A GRAPHIC NOVEL

REZA FARAZMAND

PLUME

PLUME

An imprint of Penguin Random House LLC
penguinrandomhouse.com

Plume is a registered trademark and its colophon is a trademark of Penguin Random House LLC.

LIBRARY OF CONGRESS CATALOGING-IN-PUBLICATION DATA

Names: Farazmand, Reza, author, artist.
Title: City Monster / Reza Farazmand.
Description: New York: Plume, Penguin Random House LLC, 2020.
Identifiers: LCCN 2020030482 (print) | LCCN 2020030483 (ebook) | ISBN 9780593087794 (paperback) | ISBN 9780593087800 (ebook)
Subjects: LCSH: Graphic novels.
Classification: LCC PN6727.F355 C58 2020 (print) | LCC PN6727.F355 (ebook) | DDC 741.5/973—dc23
LC record available at https://lccn.loc.gov/2020030482
LC ebook record available at https://lccn.loc.gov/2020030483

Printed in the United States of America
10 9 8 7 6 5 4 3 2 1

BOOK DESIGN BY TIFFANY ESTREICHER

CITY
MONSTER

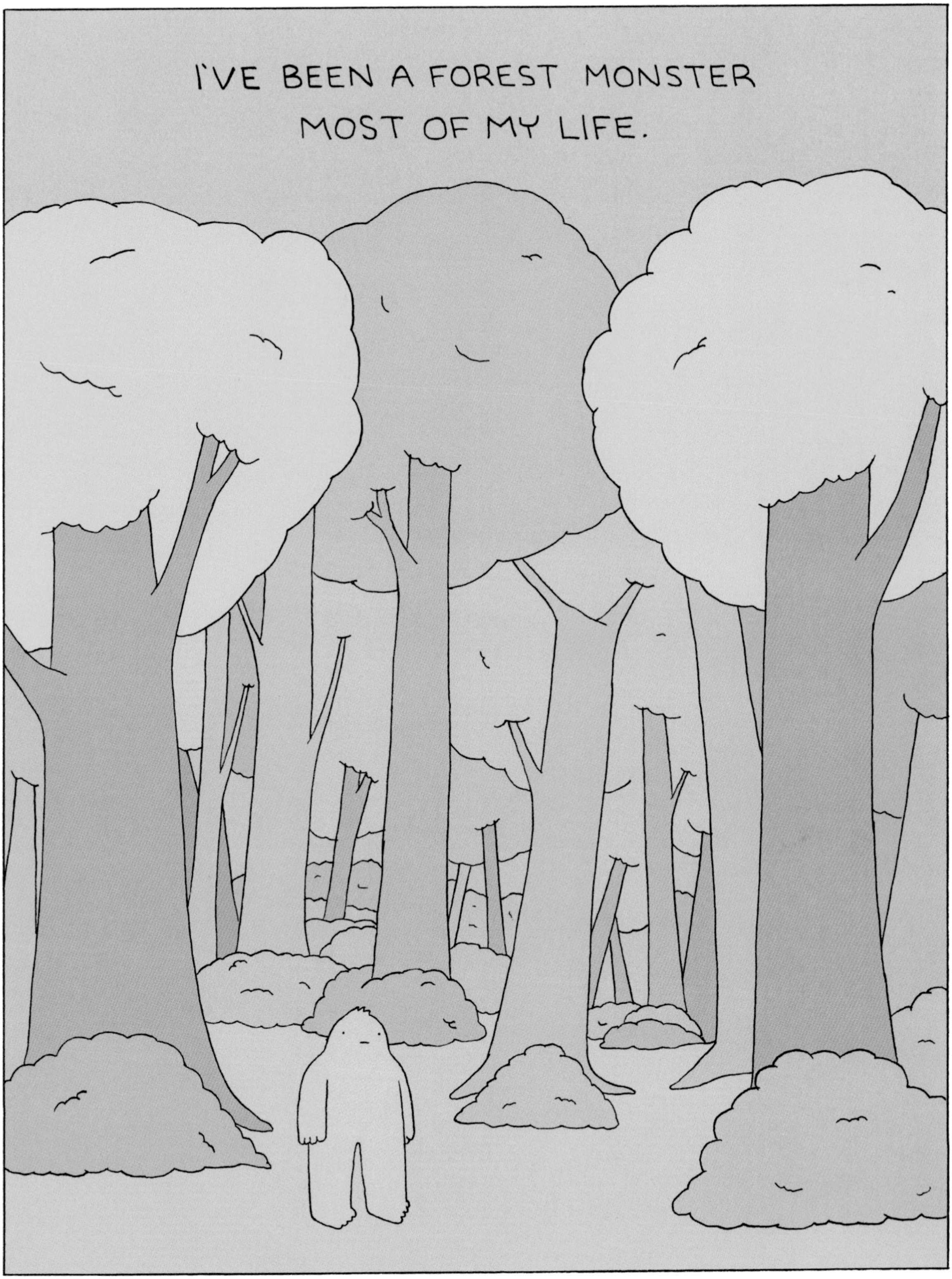
I'VE BEEN A FOREST MONSTER MOST OF MY LIFE.

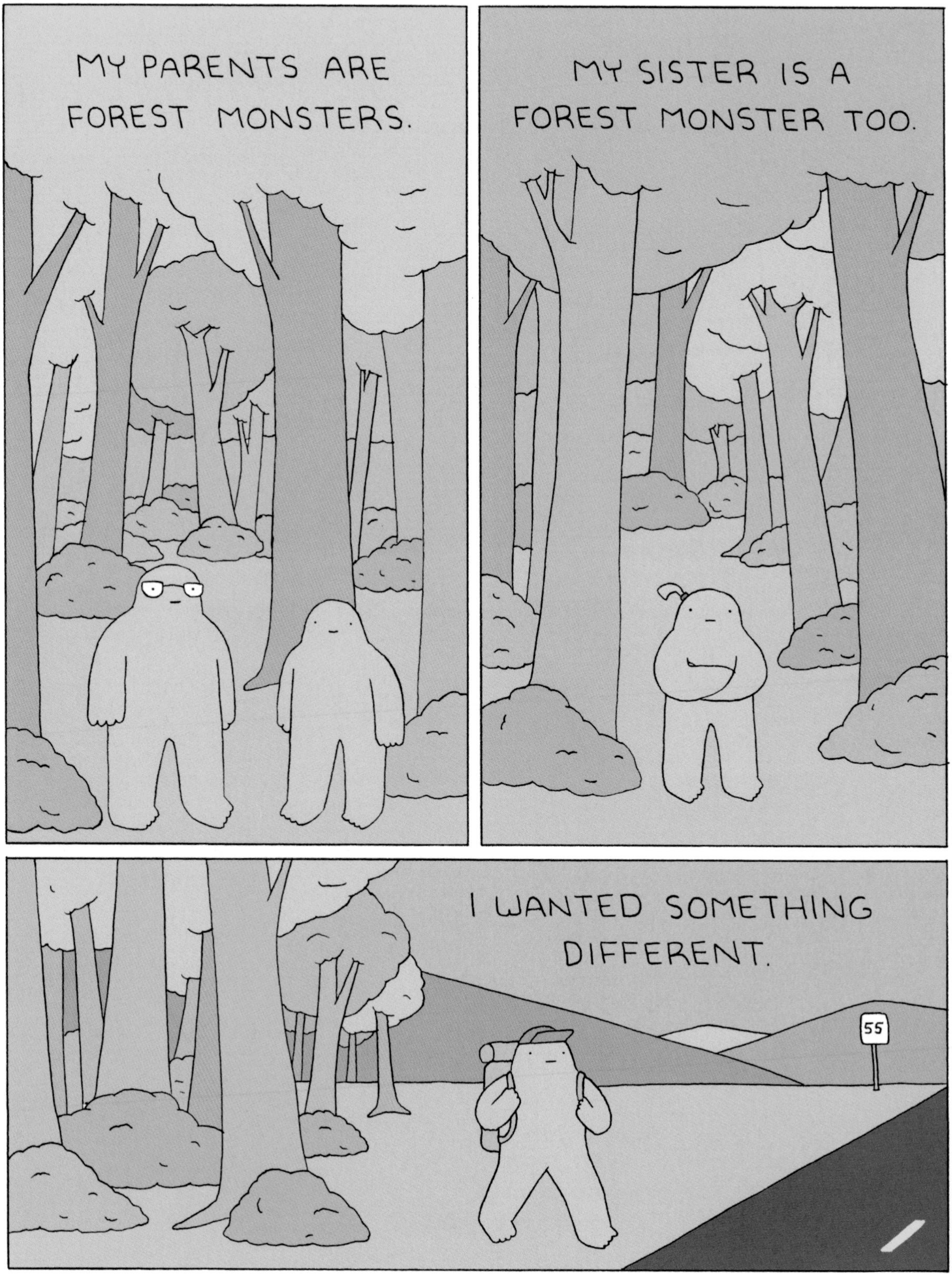
MY PARENTS ARE FOREST MONSTERS.
MY SISTER IS A FOREST MONSTER TOO.
I WANTED SOMETHING DIFFERENT.
55

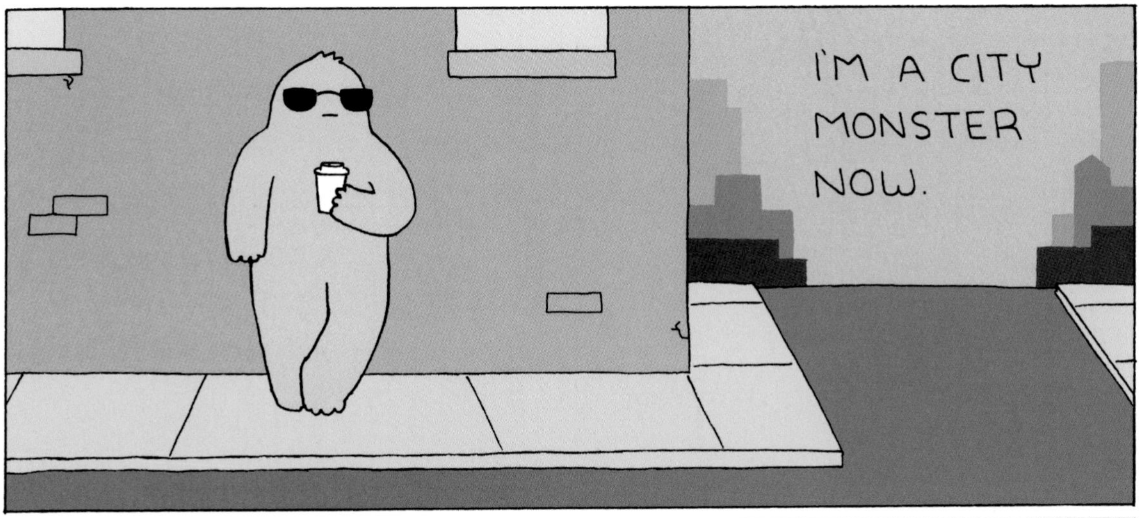
I'M A CITY MONSTER NOW.

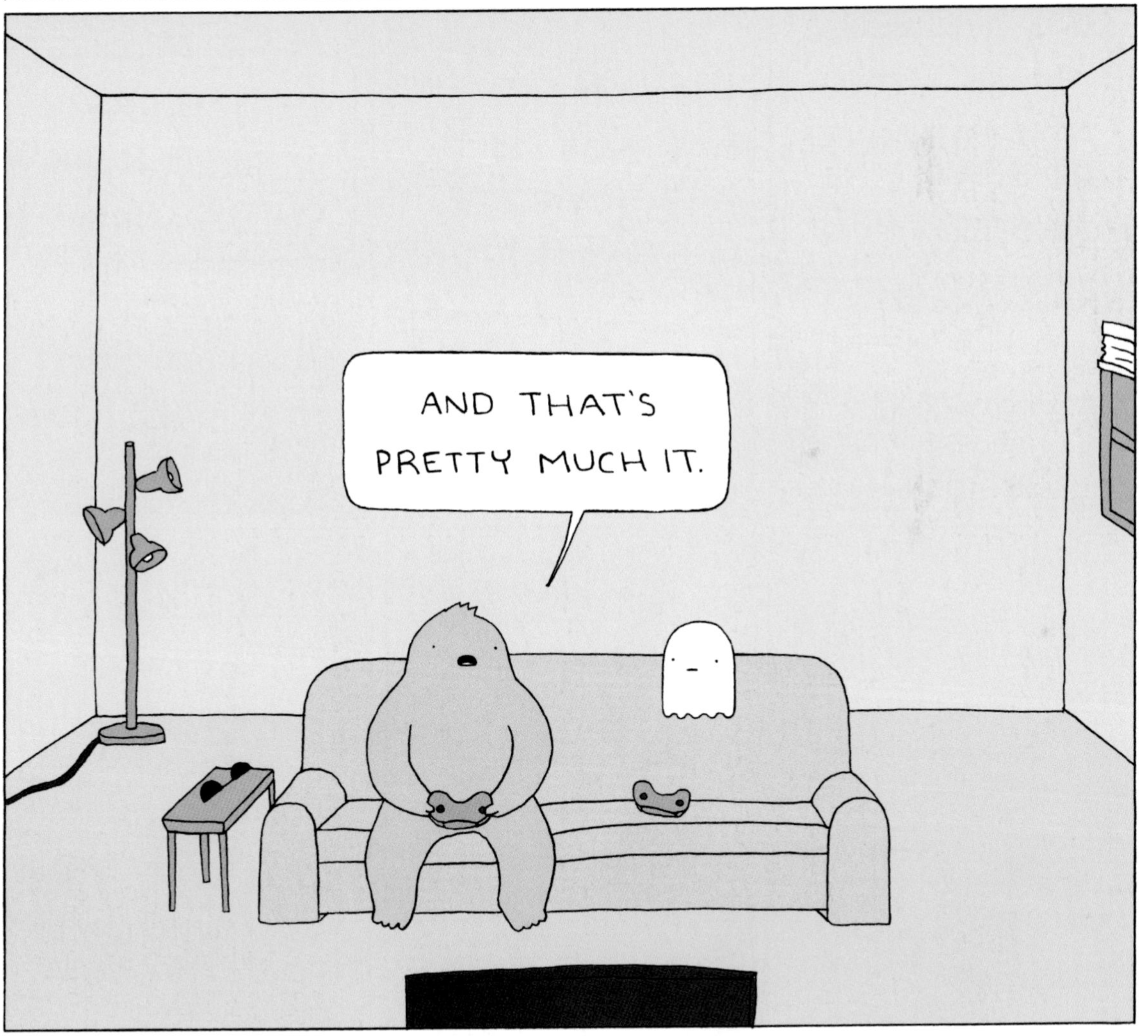
AND THAT'S PRETTY MUCH IT.

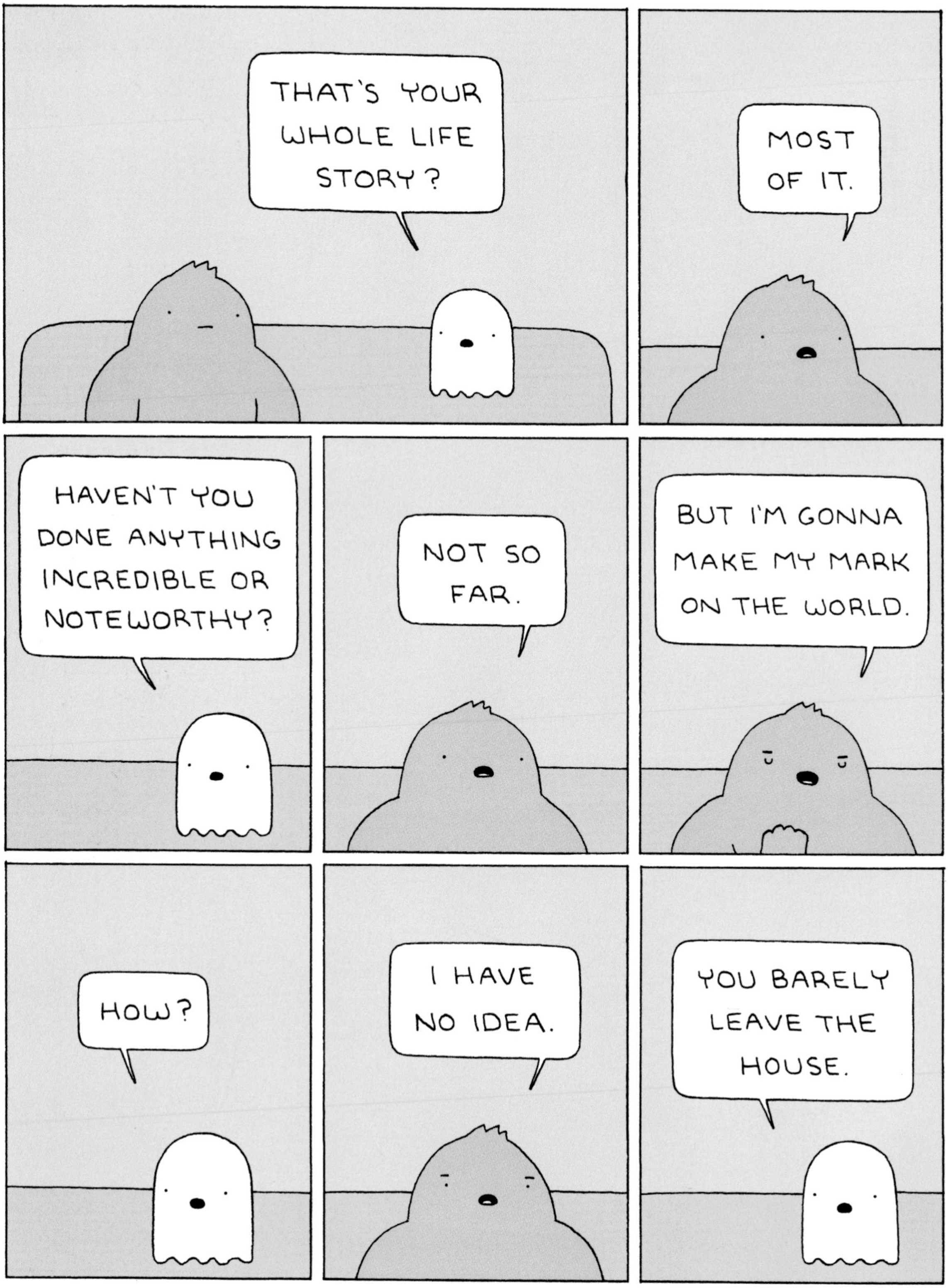
THAT'S YOUR WHOLE LIFE STORY?
MOST OF IT.
HAVEN'T YOU DONE ANYTHING INCREDIBLE OR NOTEWORTHY?
NOT SO FAR.
BUT I'M GONNA MAKE MY MARK ON THE WORLD.
HOW?
I HAVE NO IDEA.
YOU BARELY LEAVE THE HOUSE.

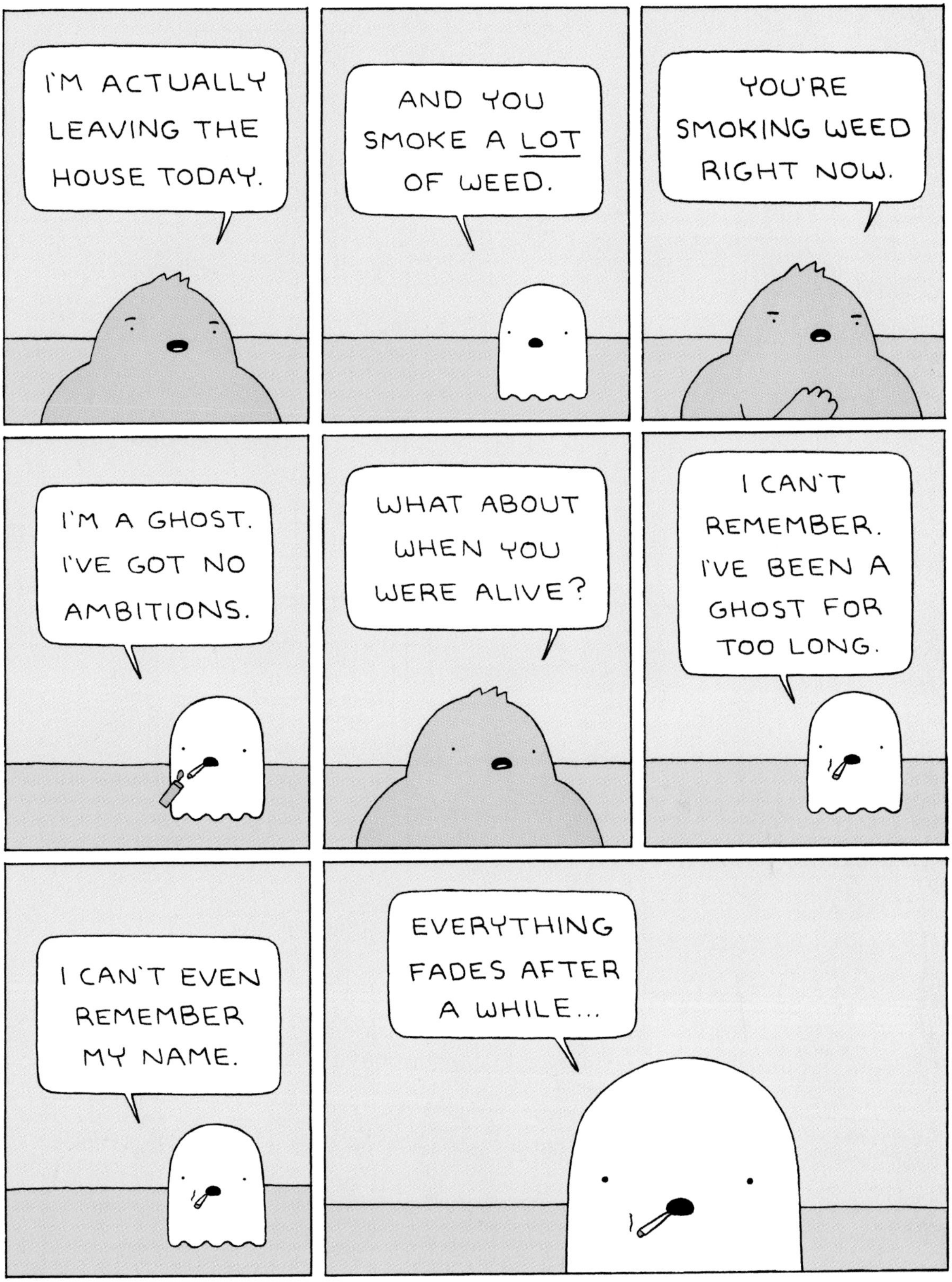
I'M ACTUALLY LEAVING THE HOUSE TODAY.
AND YOU SMOKE A LOT OF WEED.
YOU'RE SMOKING WEED RIGHT NOW.
I'M A GHOST. I'VE GOT NO AMBITIONS.
WHAT ABOUT WHEN YOU WERE ALIVE?
I CAN'T REMEMBER. I'VE BEEN A GHOST FOR TOO LONG.
I CAN'T EVEN REMEMBER MY NAME.
EVERYTHING FADES AFTER A WHILE...

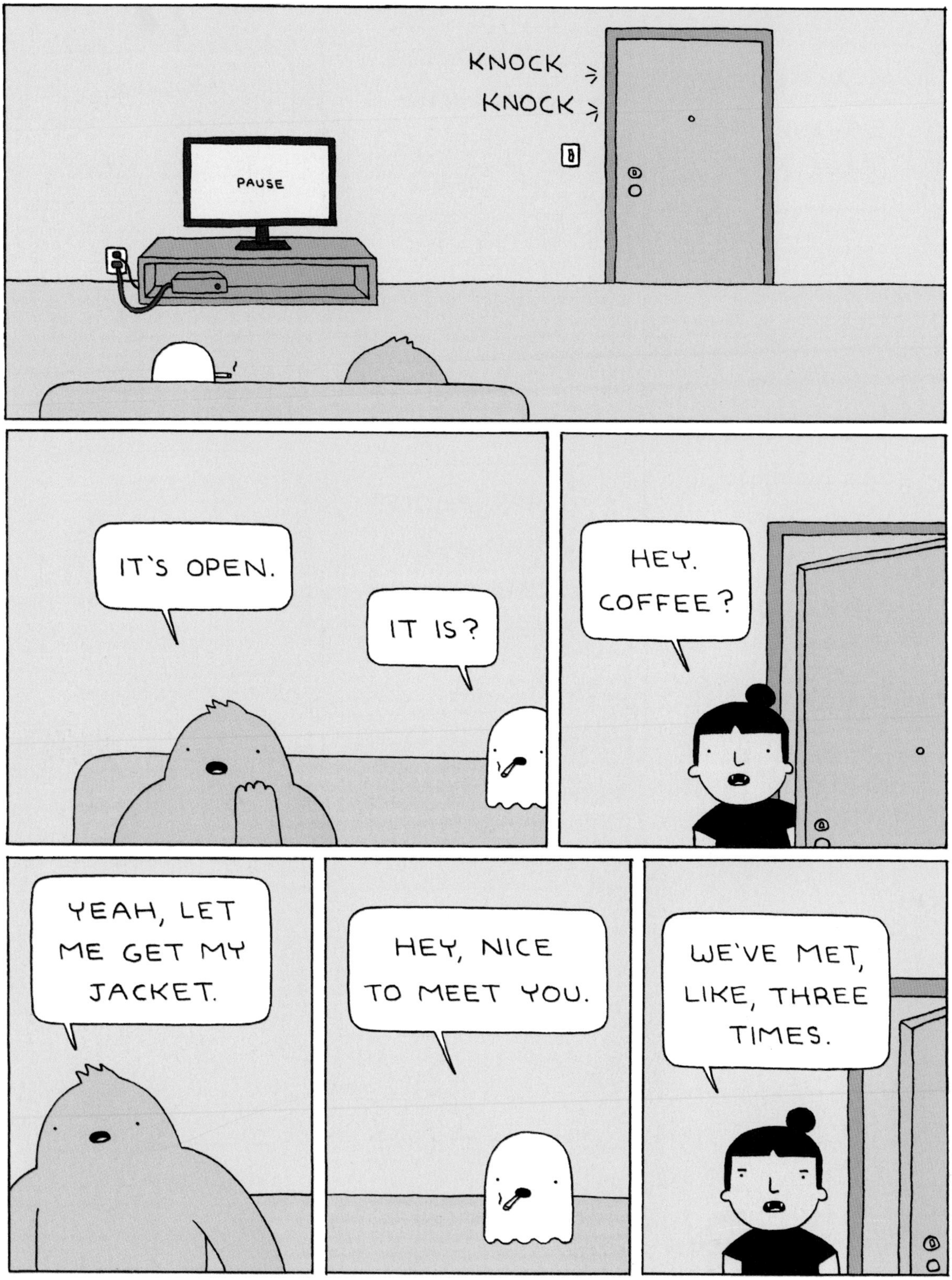
KNOCK
KNOCK
PAUSE
IT'S OPEN.
IT IS?
HEY. COFFEE?
YEAH, LET ME GET MY JACKET.
HEY, NICE TO MEET YOU.
WE'VE MET, LIKE, THREE TIMES.

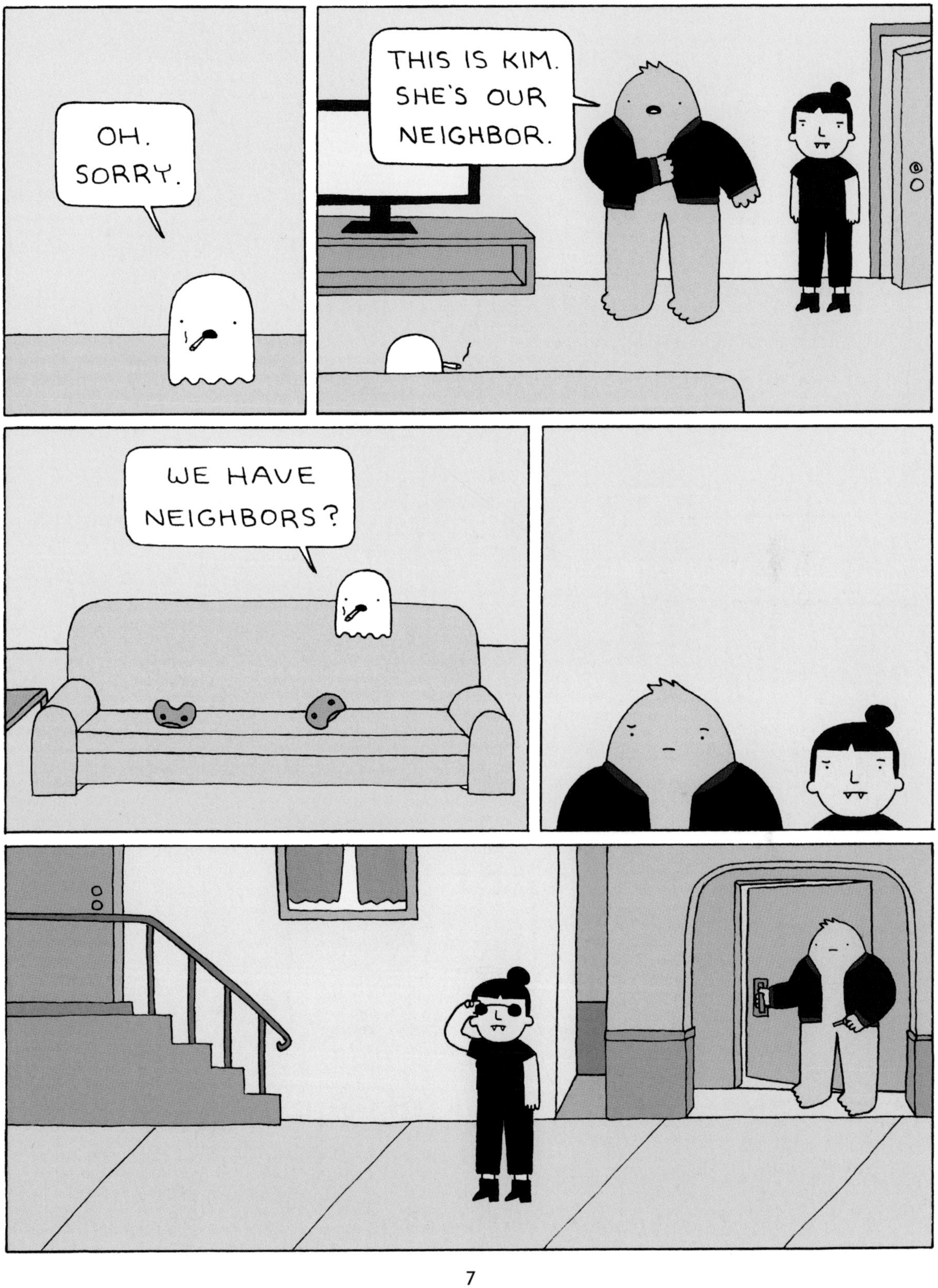
OH. SORRY.
THIS IS KIM. SHE'S OUR NEIGHBOR.
WE HAVE NEIGHBORS?

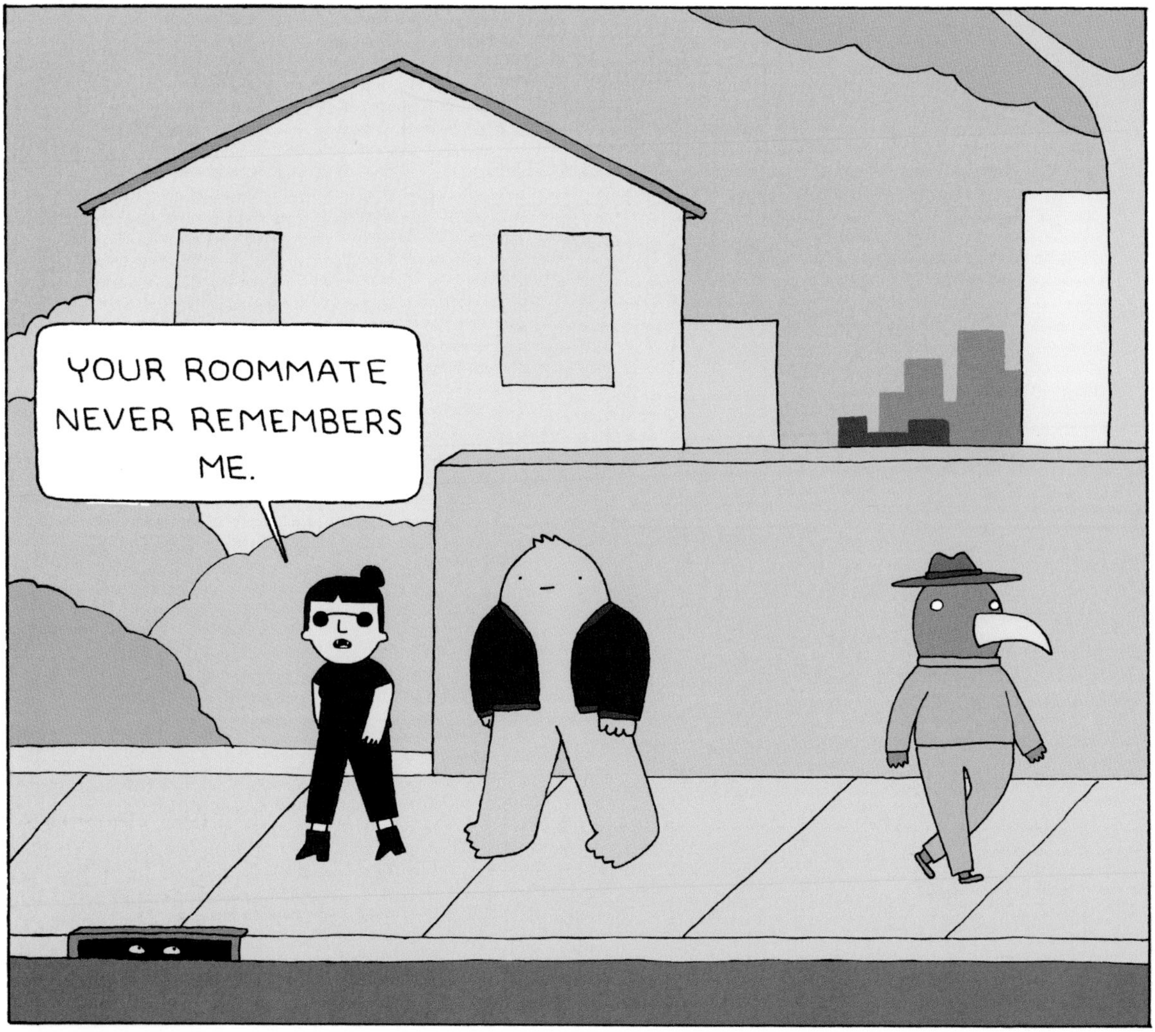
YOUR ROOMMATE NEVER REMEMBERS ME.

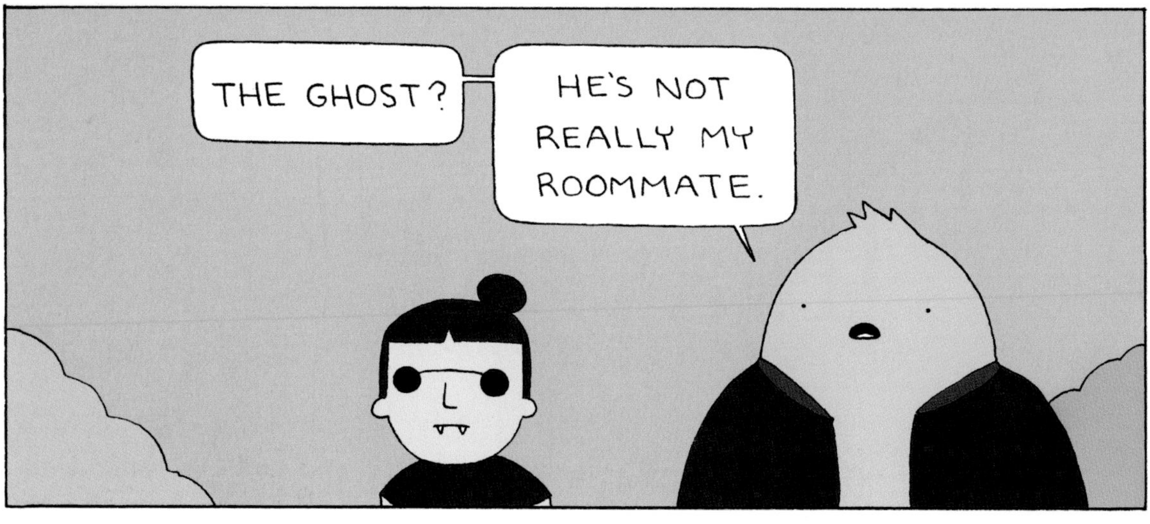
THE GHOST?
HE'S NOT REALLY MY ROOMMATE.

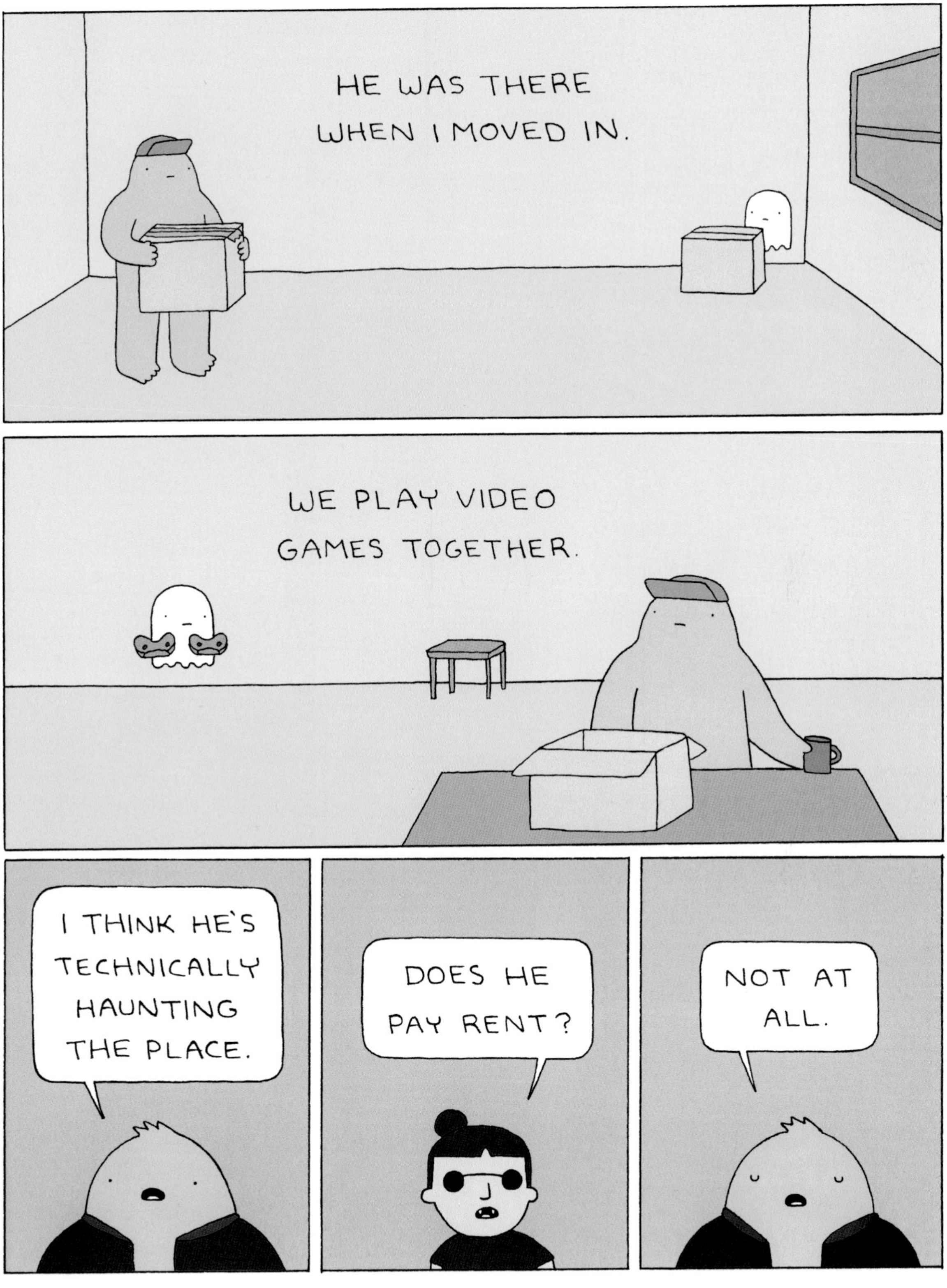
HE WAS THERE WHEN I MOVED IN.
WE PLAY VIDEO GAMES TOGETHER.
I THINK HE'S TECHNICALLY HAUNTING THE PLACE.
DOES HE PAY RENT?
NOT AT ALL.

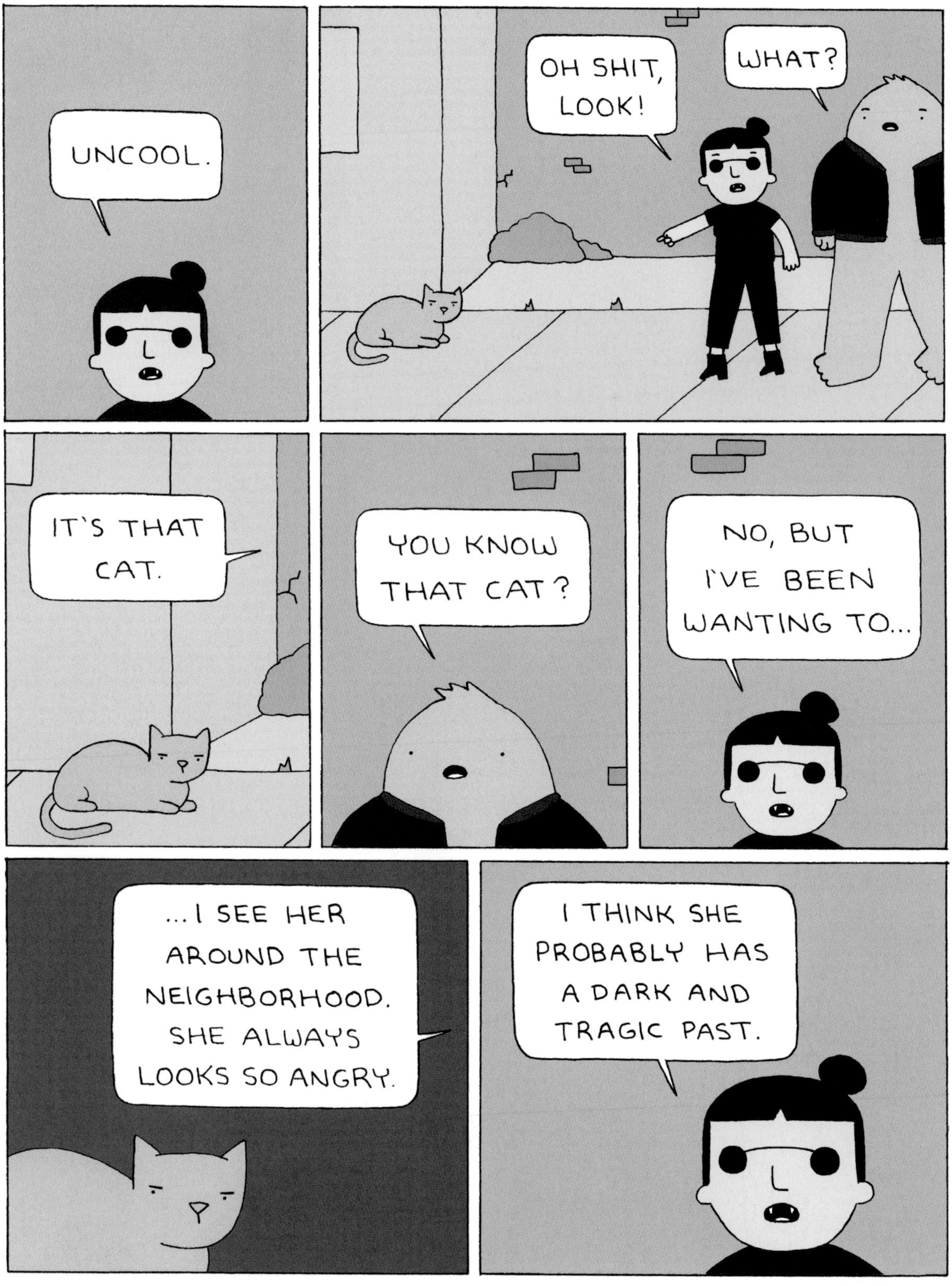
UNCOOL.
OH SHIT, LOOK!
WHAT?
IT'S THAT CAT.
YOU KNOW THAT CAT?
NO, BUT I'VE BEEN WANTING TO...
...I SEE HER AROUND THE NEIGHBORHOOD. SHE ALWAYS LOOKS SO ANGRY.
I THINK SHE PROBABLY HAS A DARK AND TRAGIC PAST.

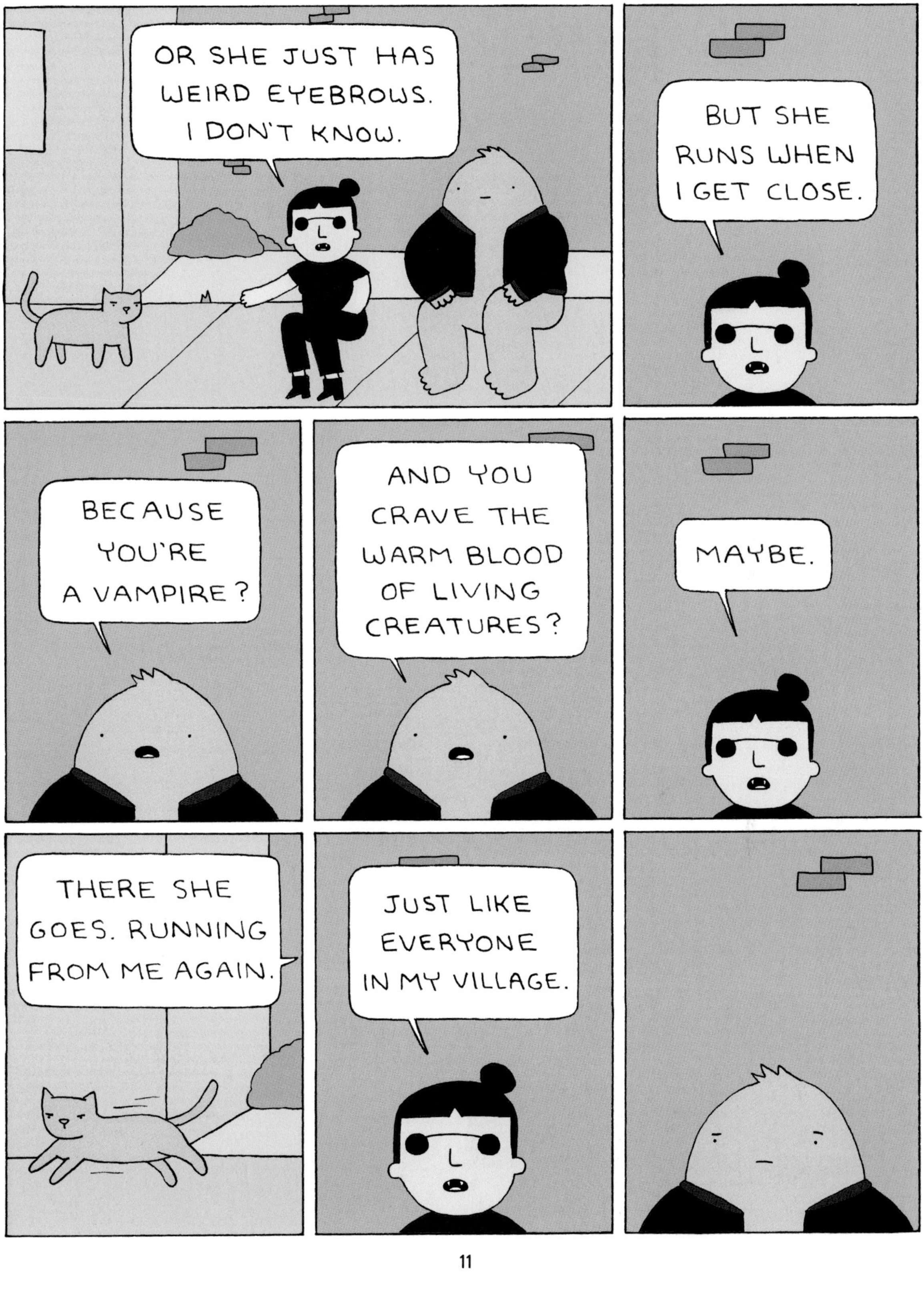
OR SHE JUST HAS WEIRD EYEBROWS. I DON'T KNOW.
BUT SHE RUNS WHEN I GET CLOSE.
BECAUSE YOU'RE A VAMPIRE?
AND YOU CRAVE THE WARM BLOOD OF LIVING CREATURES?
MAYBE.
THERE SHE GOES. RUNNING FROM ME AGAIN.
JUST LIKE EVERYONE IN MY VILLAGE.

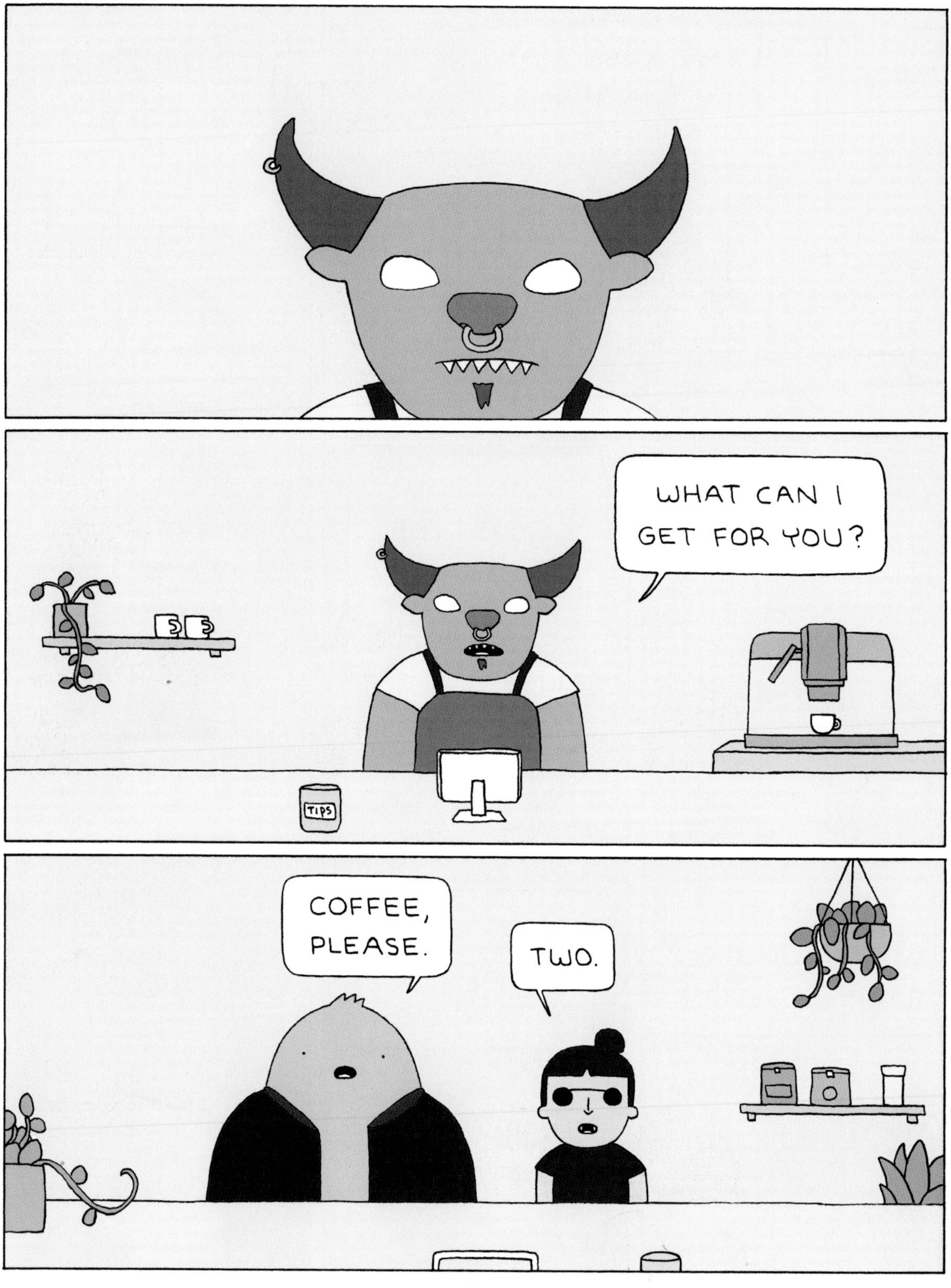
WHAT CAN I GET FOR YOU?
TIPS
COFFEE, PLEASE.
TWO.

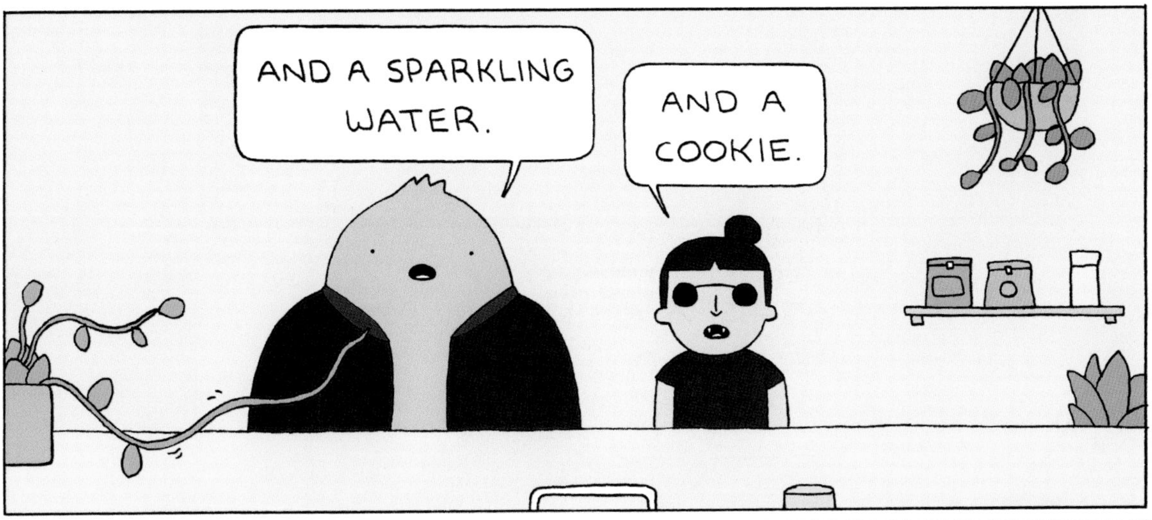
AND A SPARKLING WATER.
AND A COOKIE.

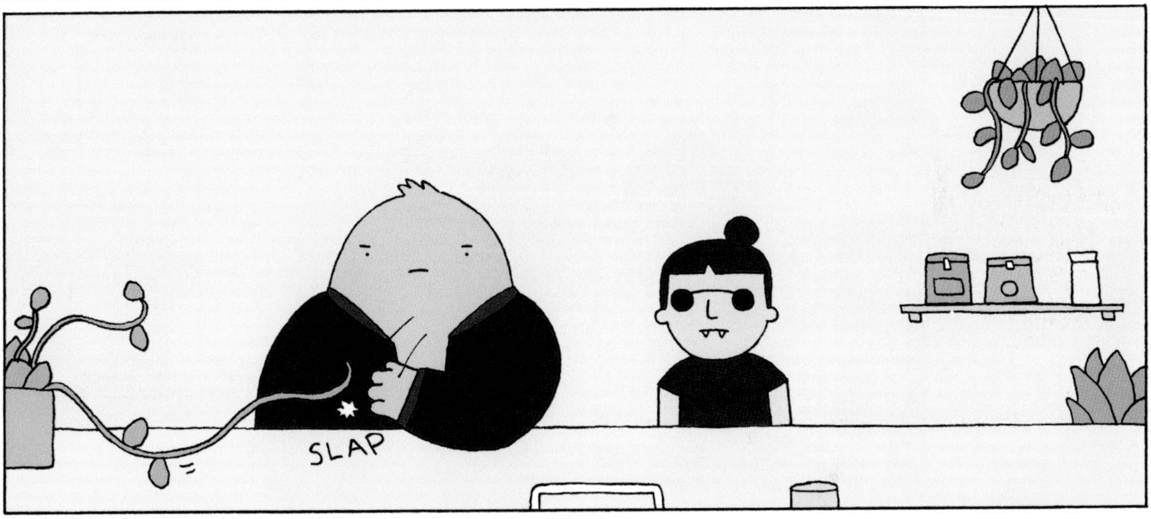
SLAP

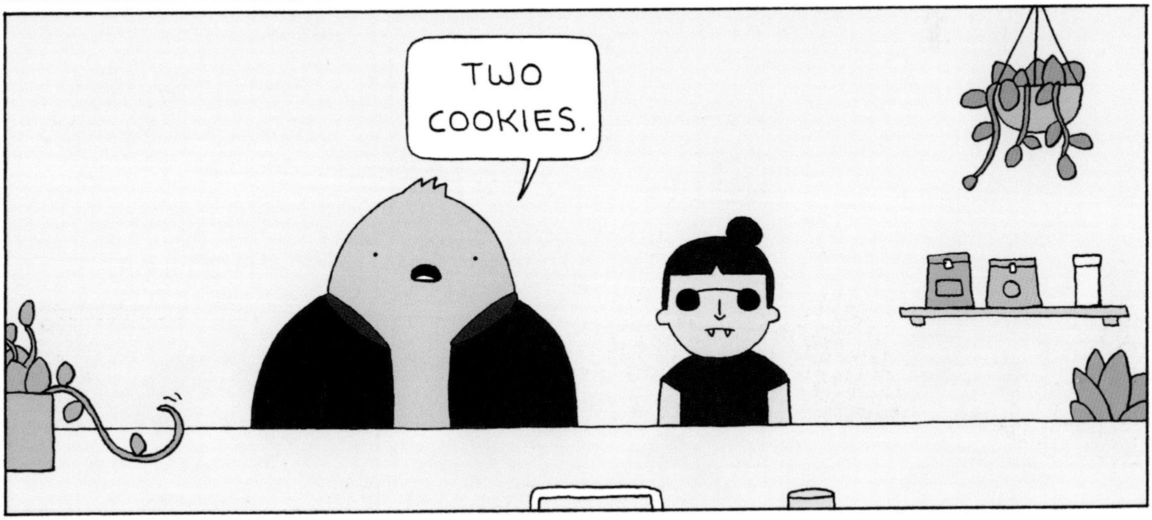
TWO COOKIES.

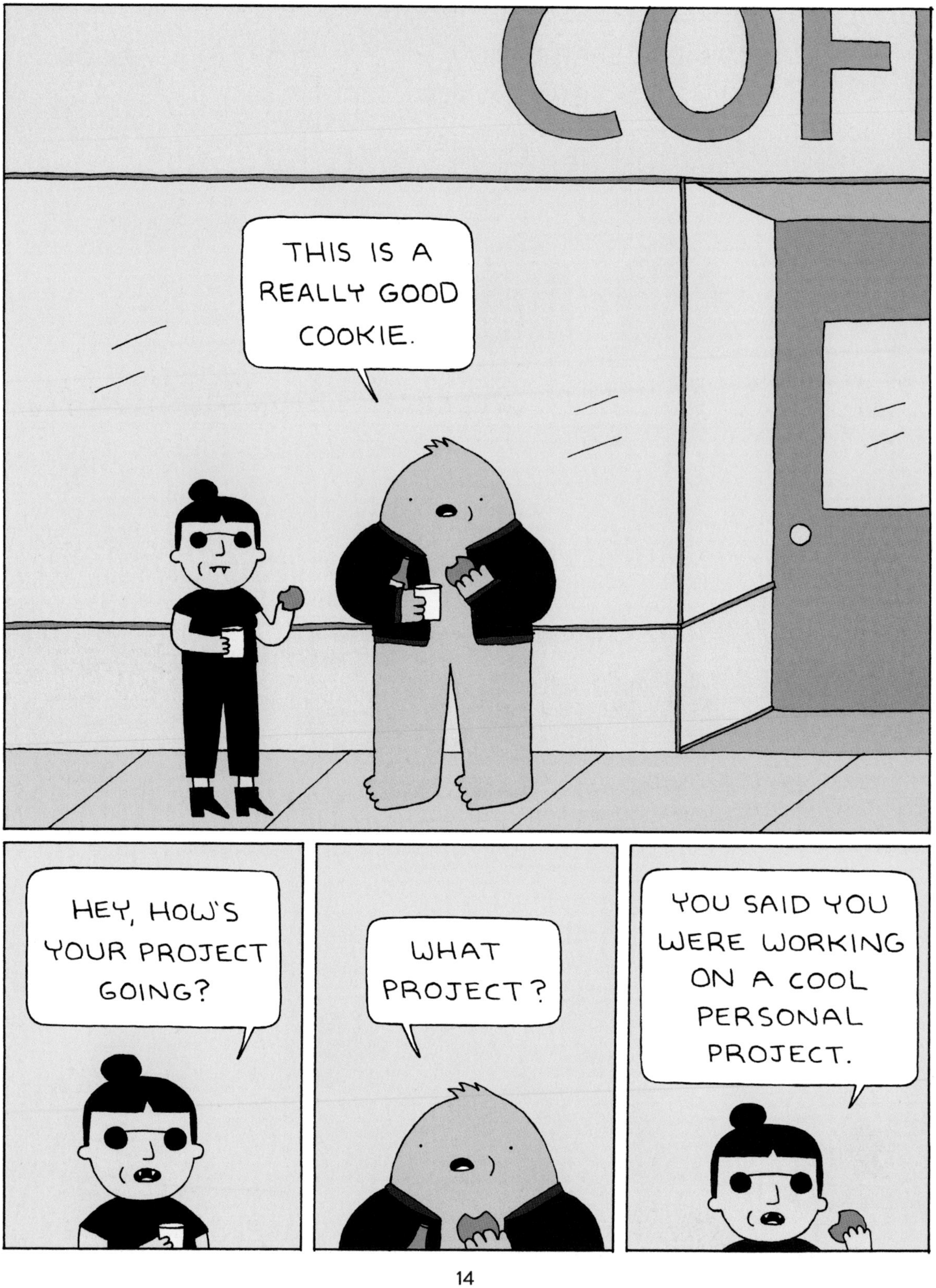
COF
THIS IS A REALLY GOOD COOKIE.
HEY, HOW'S YOUR PROJECT GOING?
WHAT PROJECT?
YOU SAID YOU WERE WORKING ON A COOL PERSONAL PROJECT.

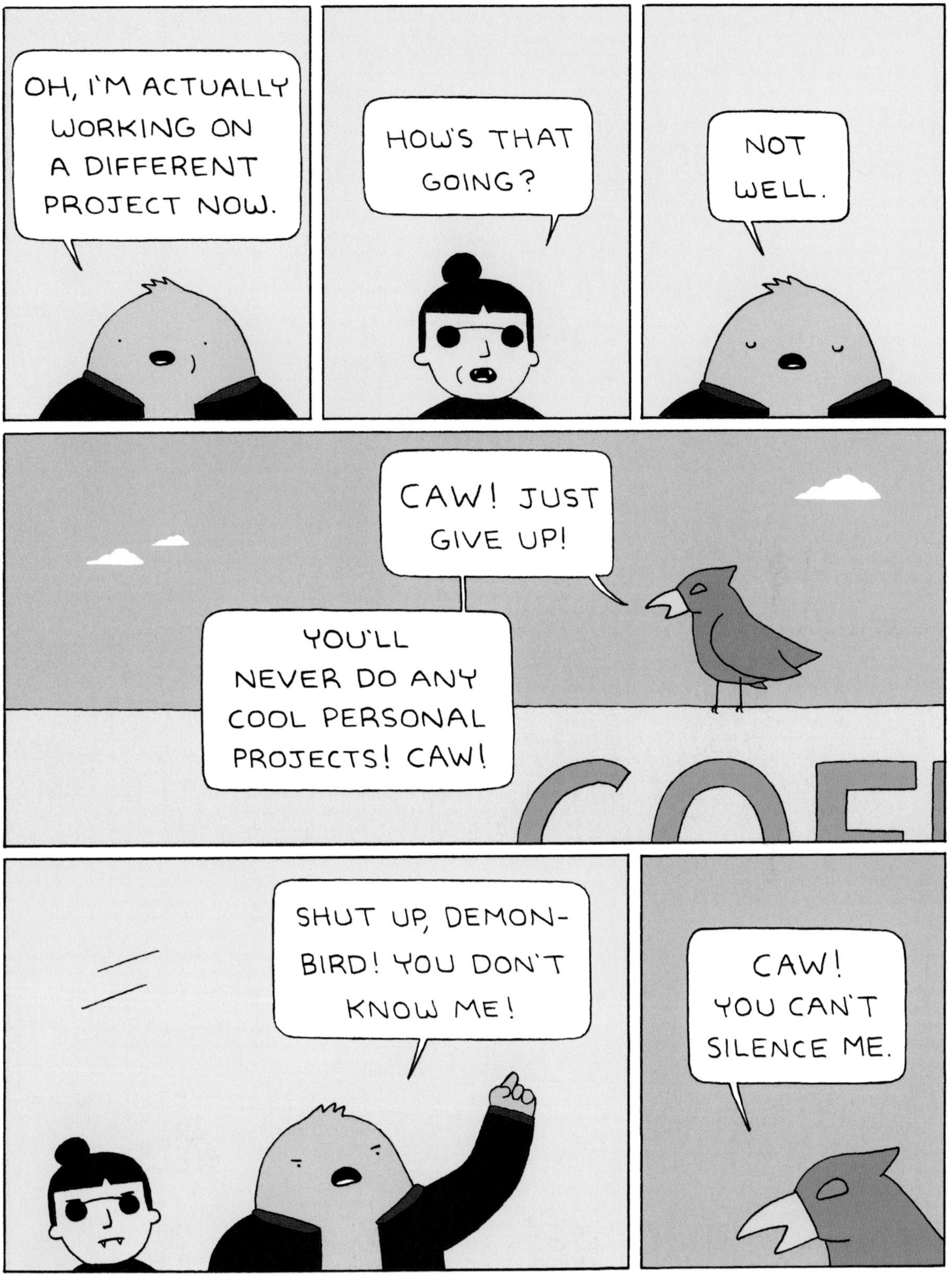
OH, I'M ACTUALLY WORKING ON A DIFFERENT PROJECT NOW.
HOW'S THAT GOING?
NOT WELL.
CAW! JUST GIVE UP!
YOU'LL NEVER DO ANY COOL PERSONAL PROJECTS! CAW!
SHUT UP, DEMON-BIRD! YOU DON'T KNOW ME!
CAW! YOU CAN'T SILENCE ME.

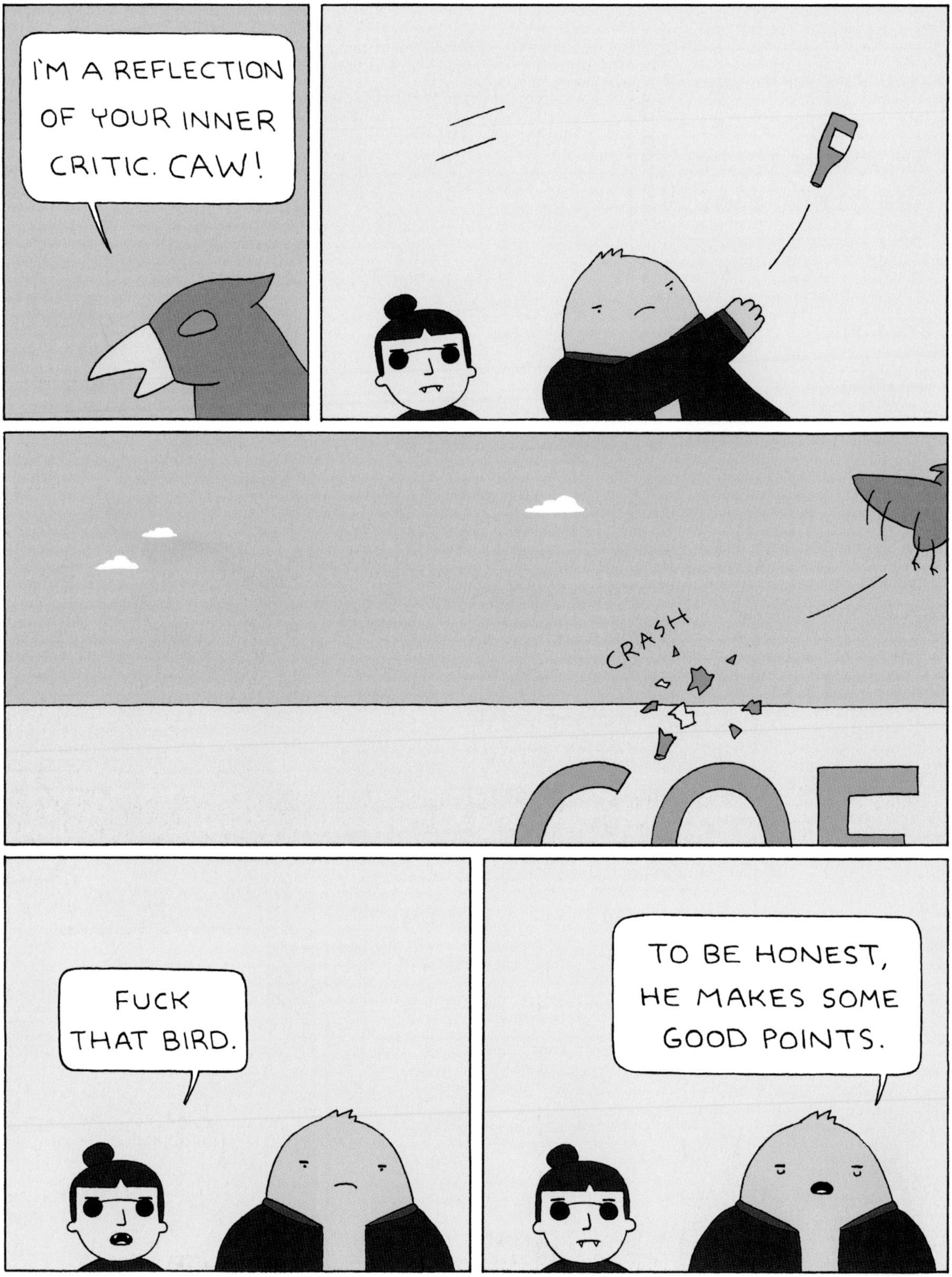
I'M A REFLECTION OF YOUR INNER CRITIC. CAW!
CRASH
FUCK THAT BIRD.
TO BE HONEST, HE MAKES SOME GOOD POINTS.

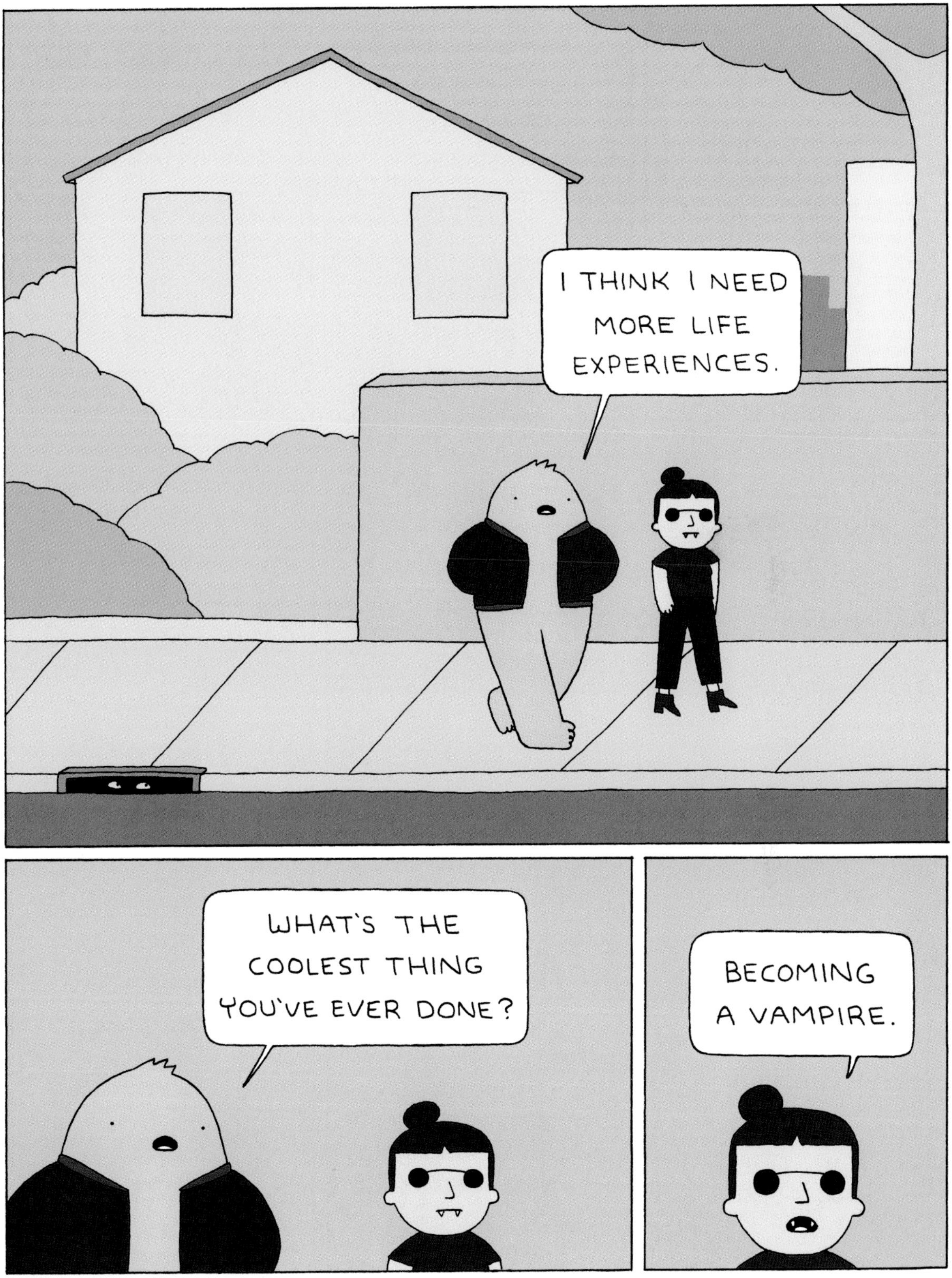
I THINK I NEED MORE LIFE EXPERIENCES.
WHAT'S THE COOLEST THING YOU'VE EVER DONE?
BECOMING A VAMPIRE.

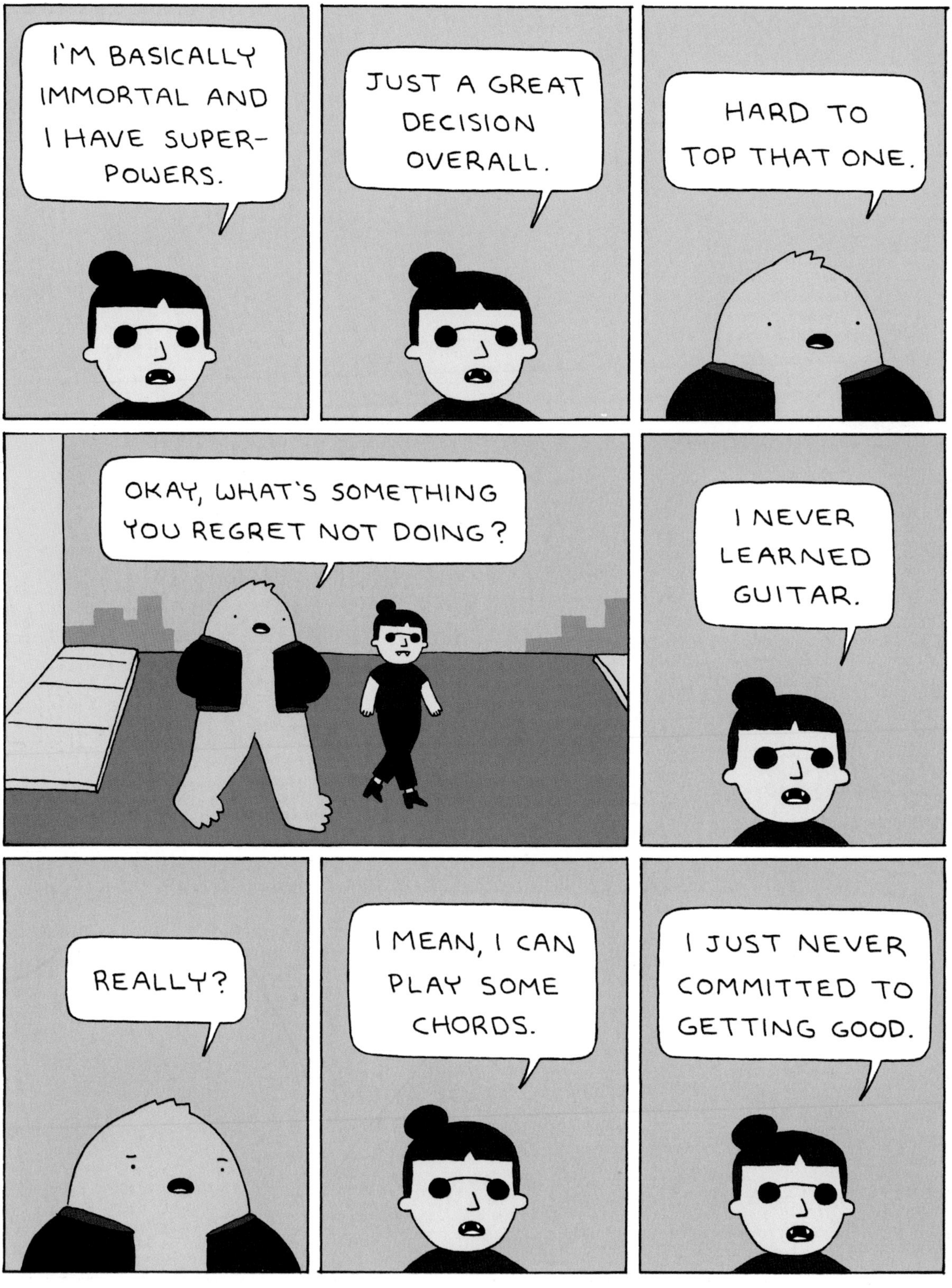
I'M BASICALLY IMMORTAL AND I HAVE SUPER-POWERS.
JUST A GREAT DECISION OVERALL.
HARD TO TOP THAT ONE.
OKAY, WHAT'S SOMETHING YOU REGRET NOT DOING?
I NEVER LEARNED GUITAR.
REALLY?
I MEAN, I CAN PLAY SOME CHORDS.
I JUST NEVER COMMITTED TO GETTING GOOD.

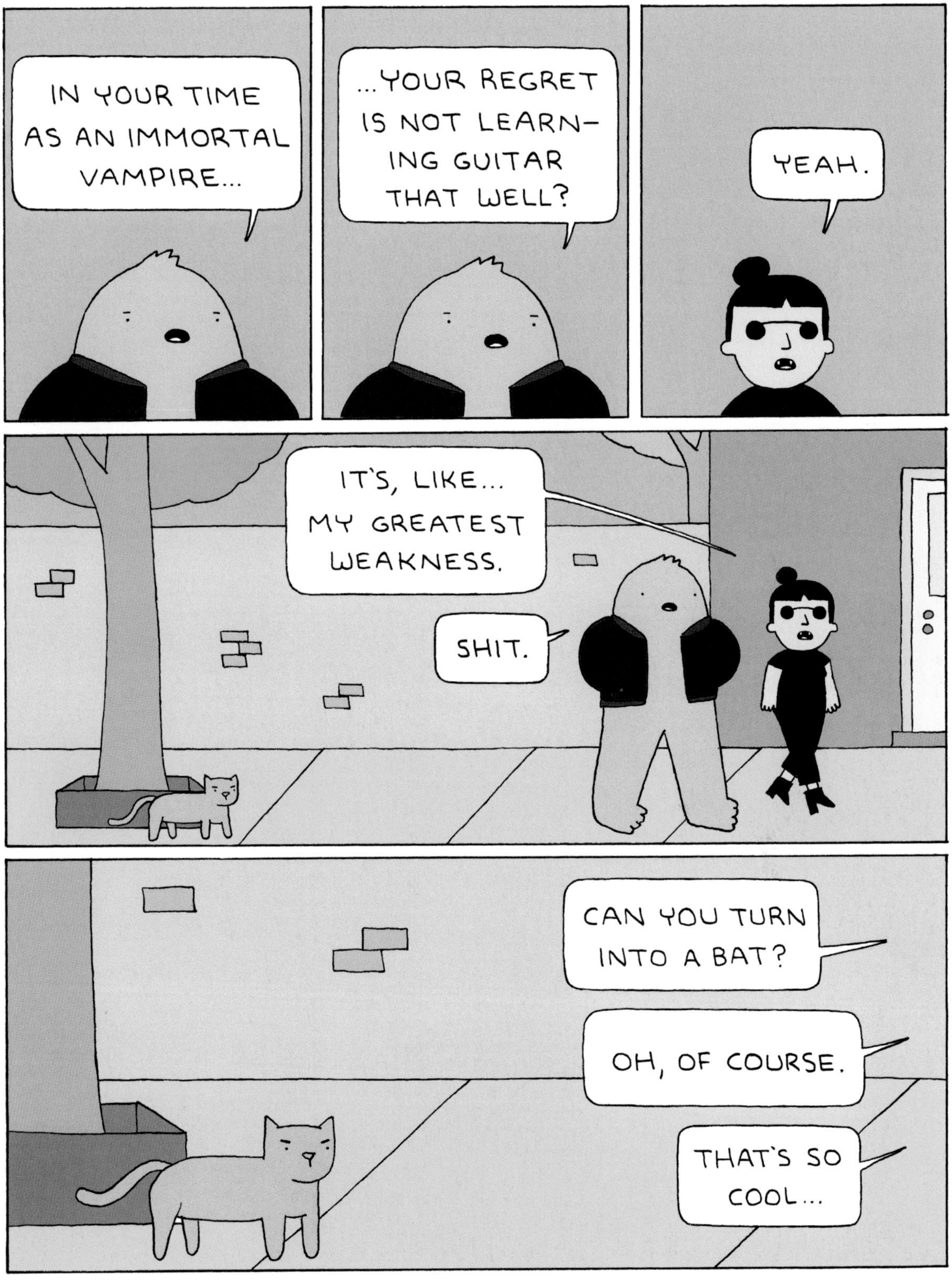
IN YOUR TIME AS AN IMMORTAL VAMPIRE...
...YOUR REGRET IS NOT LEARN-ING GUITAR THAT WELL?
YEAH.
IT'S, LIKE... MY GREATEST WEAKNESS.
SHIT.
CAN YOU TURN INTO A BAT?
OH, OF COURSE.
THAT'S SO COOL...

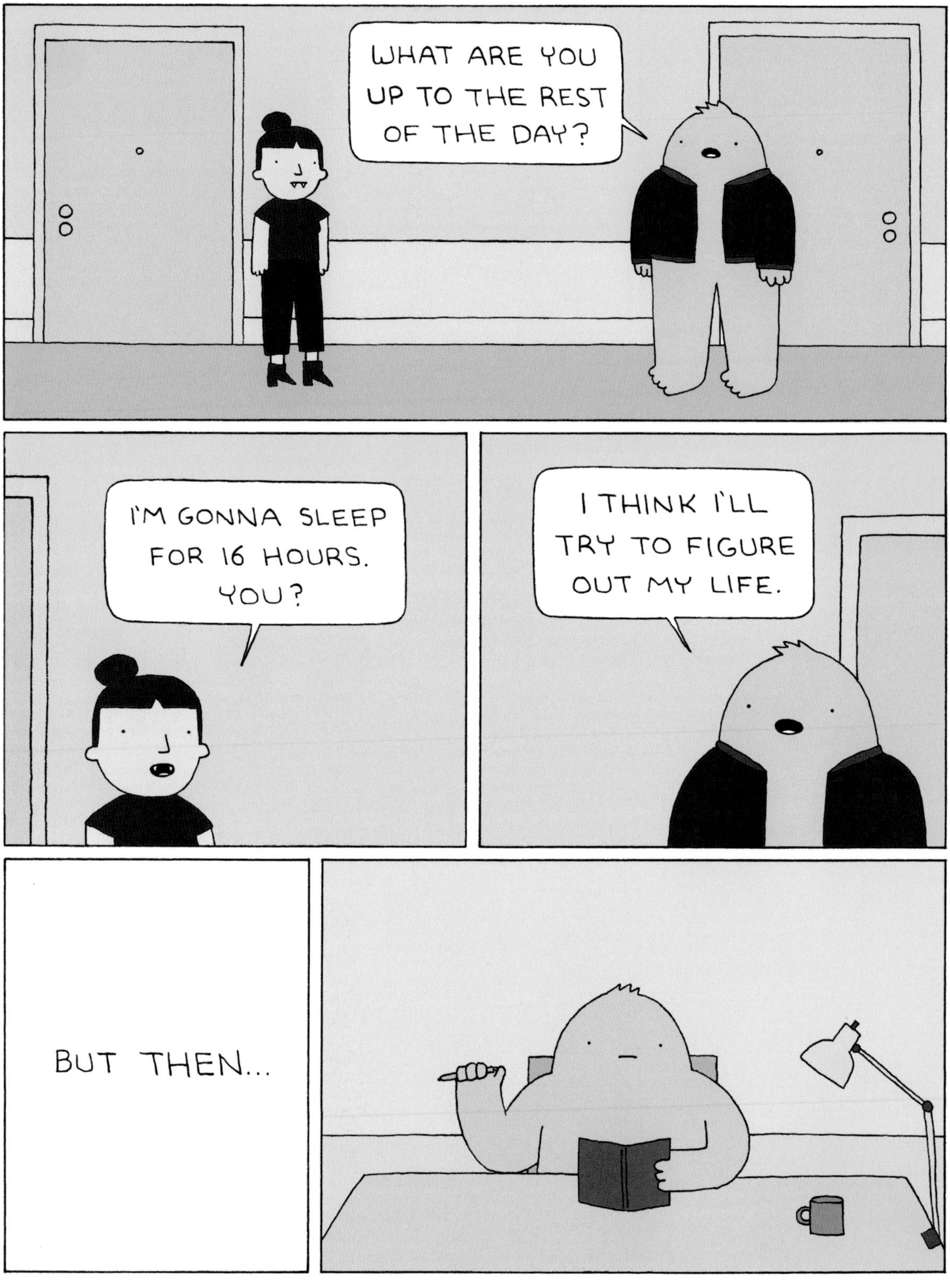
WHAT ARE YOU UP TO THE REST OF THE DAY?
I'M GONNA SLEEP FOR 16 HOURS. YOU?
I THINK I'LL TRY TO FIGURE OUT MY LIFE.
BUT THEN...

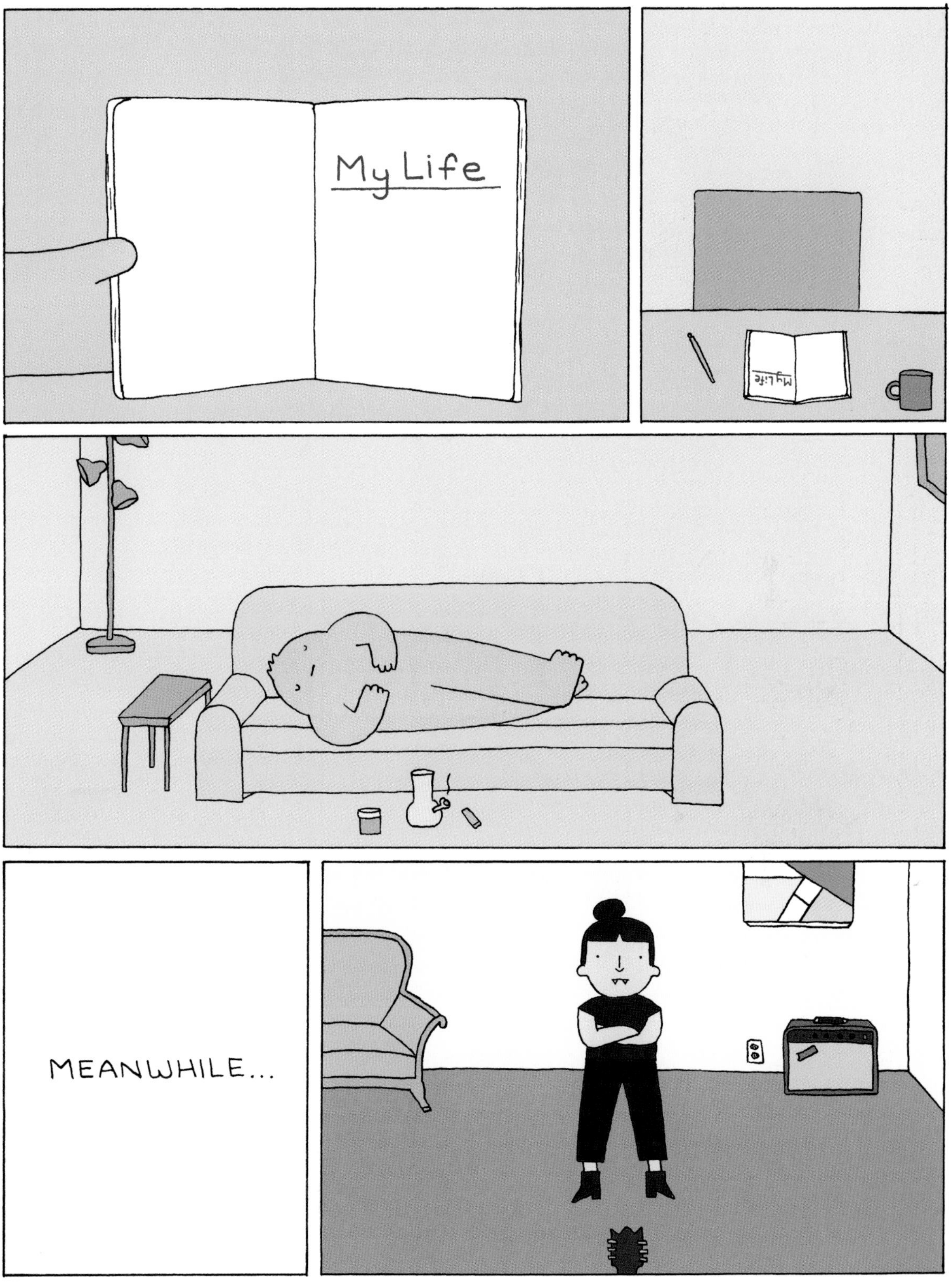
My Life
My Life
MEANWHILE...

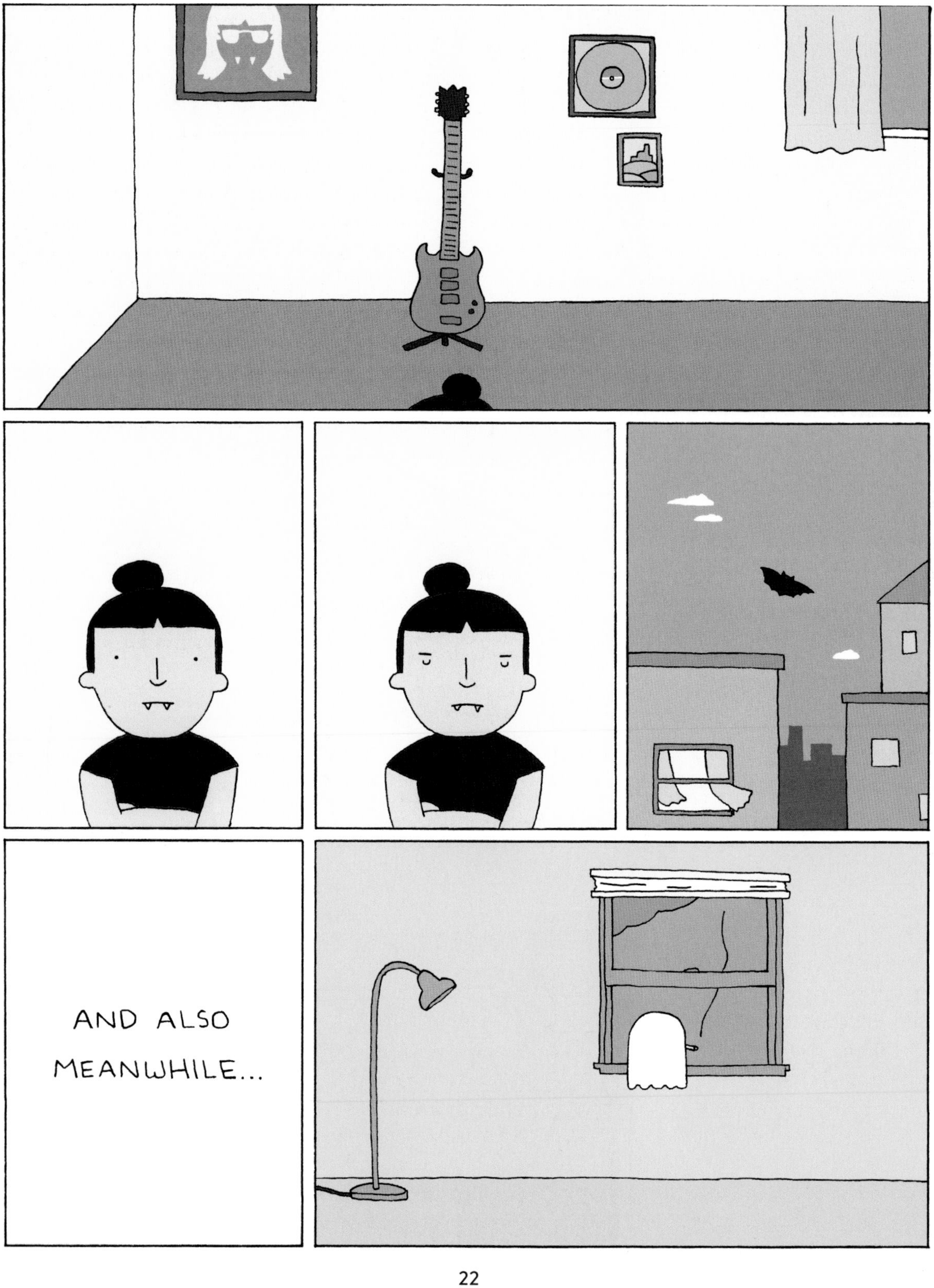
AND ALSO
MEANWHILE...

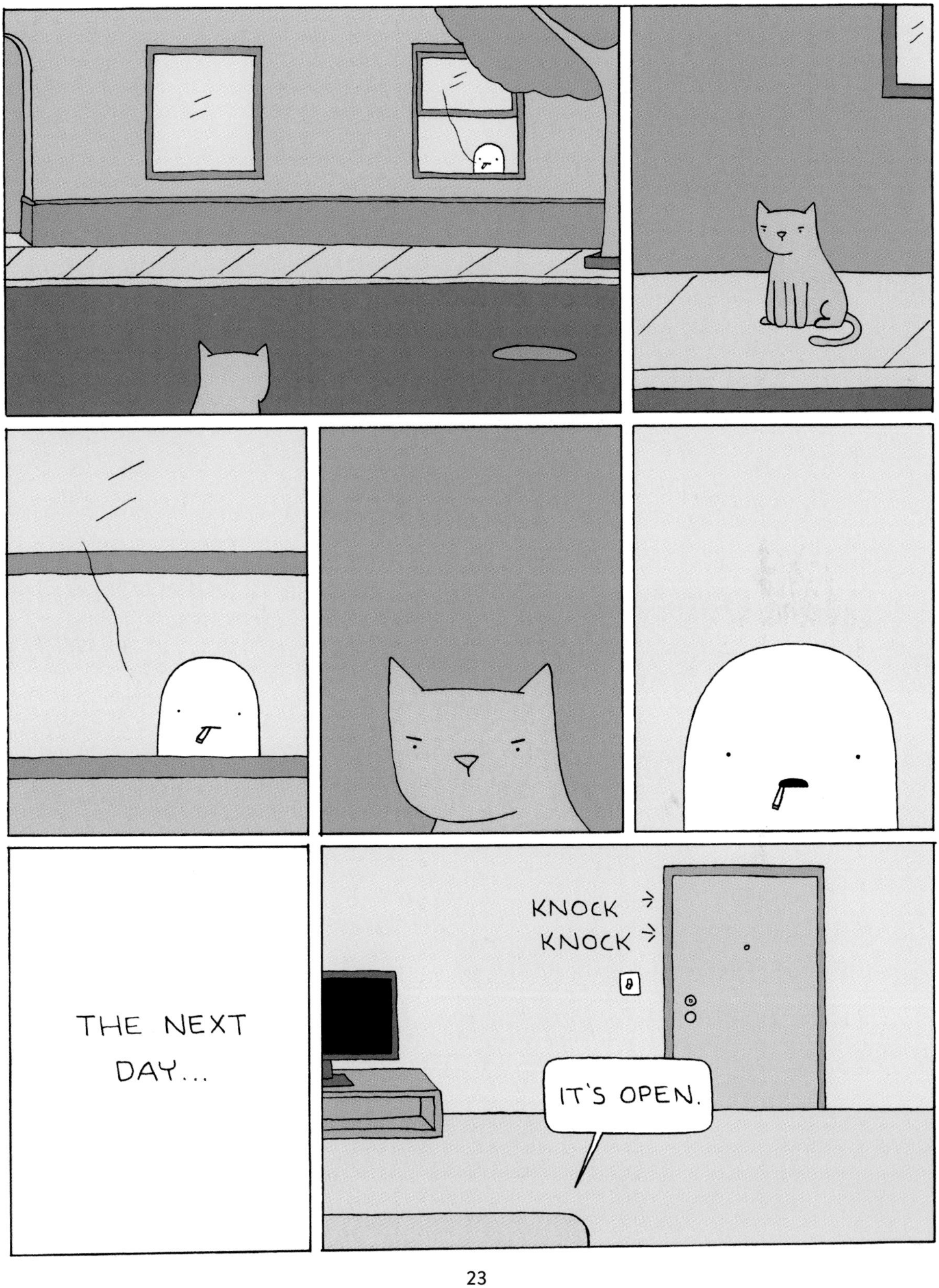
THE NEXT DAY...
KNOCK
KNOCK
IT'S OPEN.

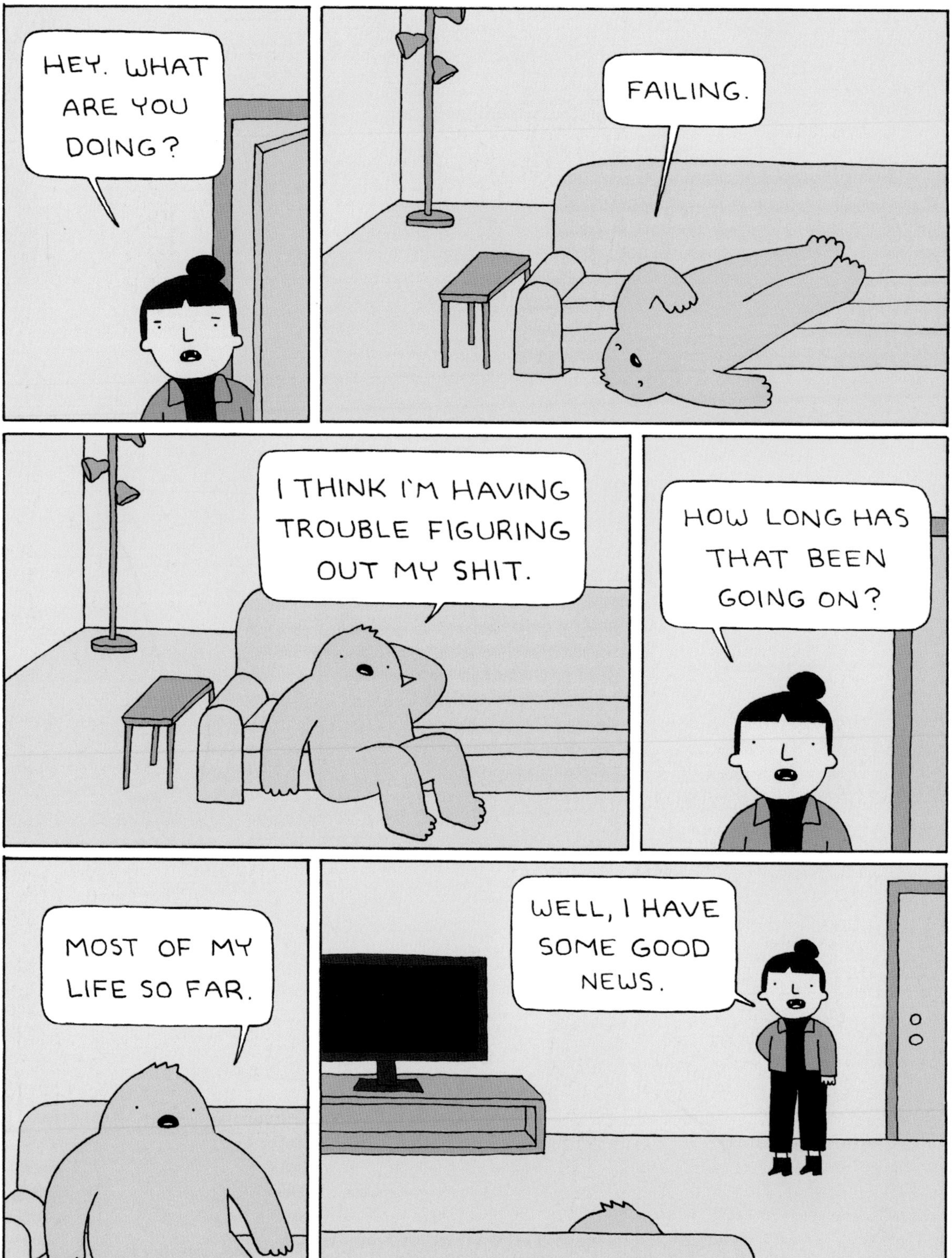
HEY. WHAT ARE YOU DOING?
FAILING.
I THINK I'M HAVING TROUBLE FIGURING OUT MY SHIT.
HOW LONG HAS THAT BEEN GOING ON?
MOST OF MY LIFE SO FAR.
WELL, I HAVE SOME GOOD NEWS.

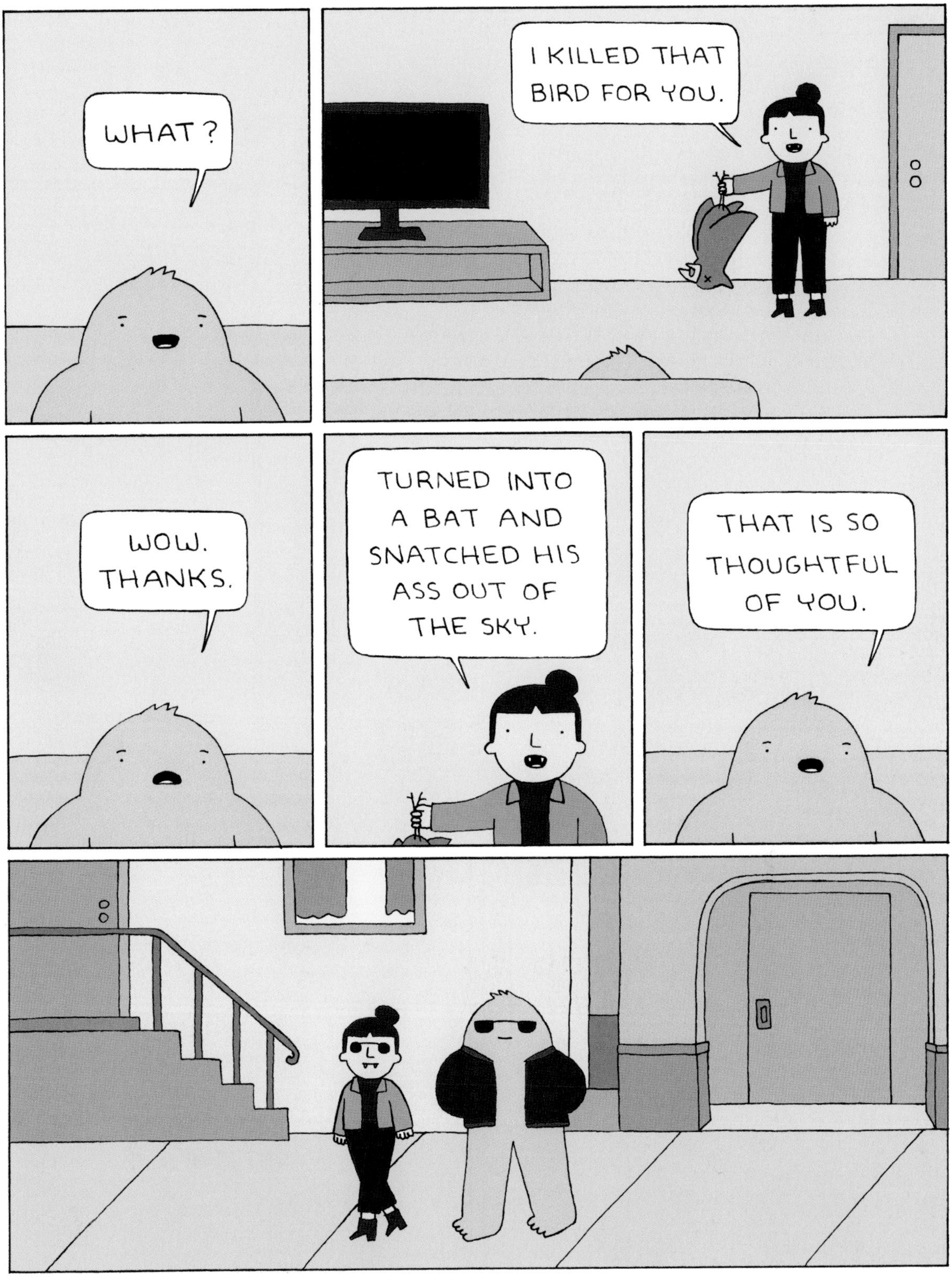
WHAT?
I KILLED THAT BIRD FOR YOU.
WOW. THANKS.
TURNED INTO A BAT AND SNATCHED HIS ASS OUT OF THE SKY.
THAT IS SO THOUGHTFUL OF YOU.

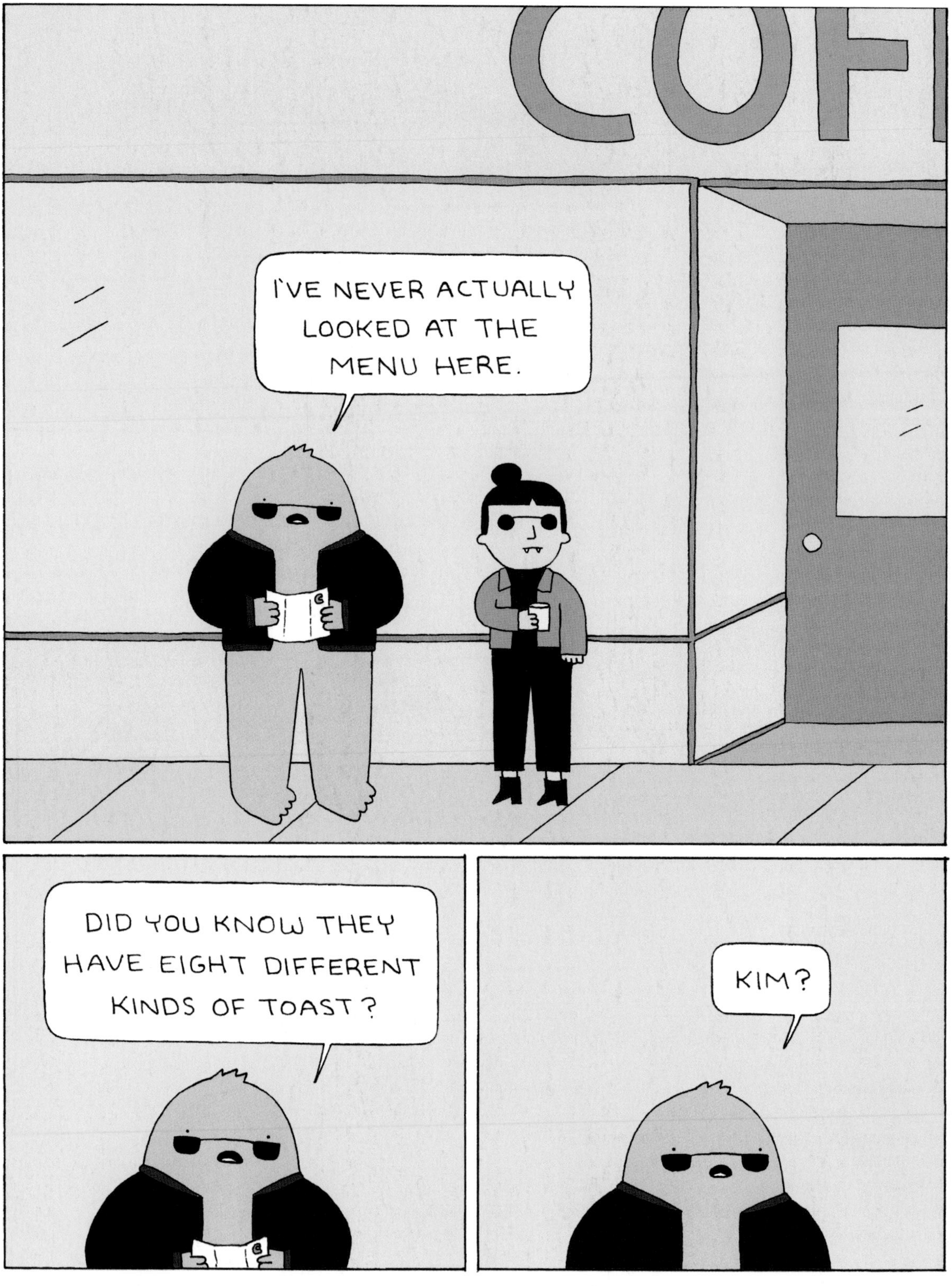
COF
I'VE NEVER ACTUALLY LOOKED AT THE MENU HERE.
DID YOU KNOW THEY HAVE EIGHT DIFFERENT KINDS OF TOAST?
KIM?

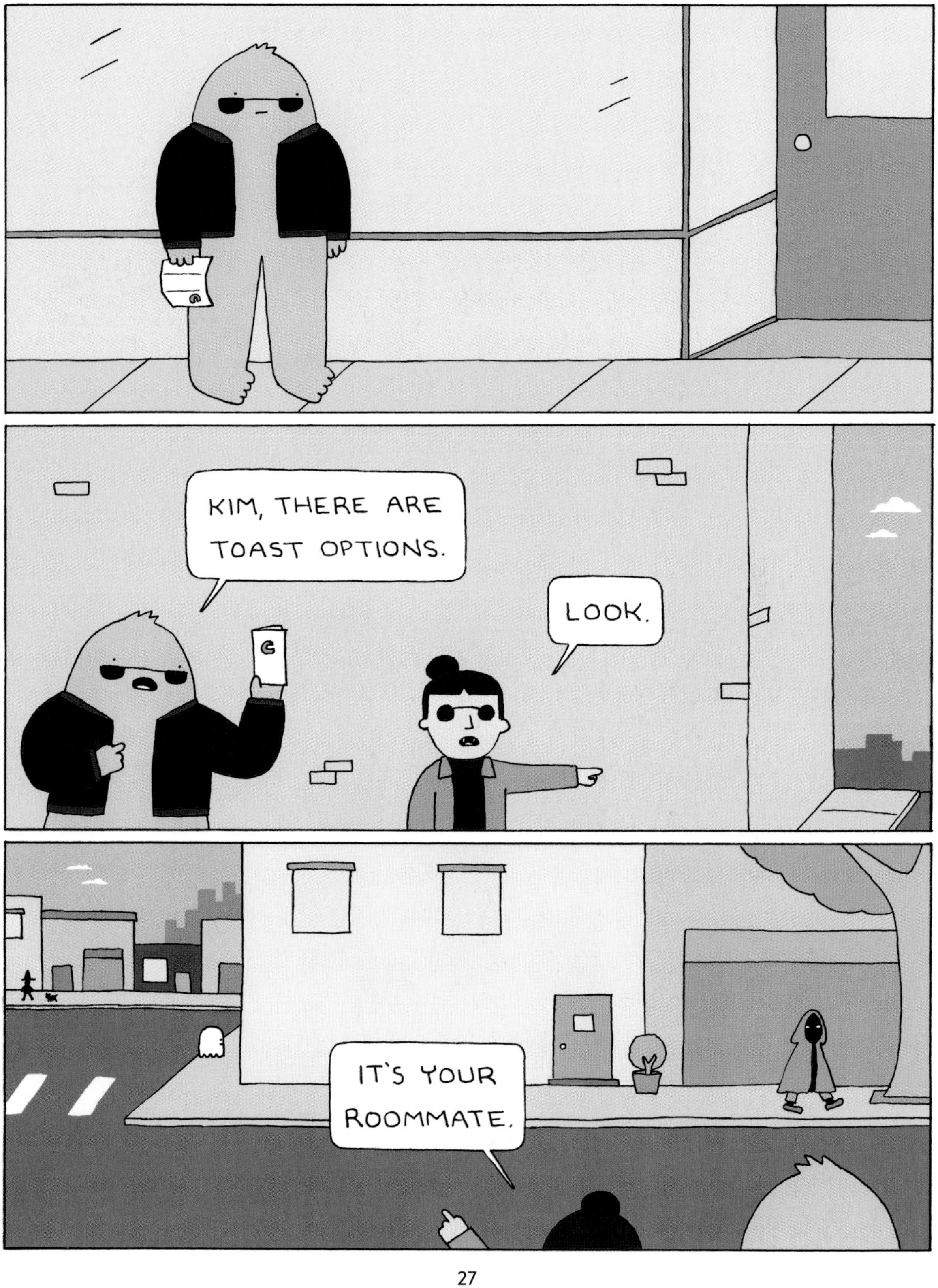
KIM, THERE ARE TOAST OPTIONS.
LOOK.
IT'S YOUR ROOMMATE.

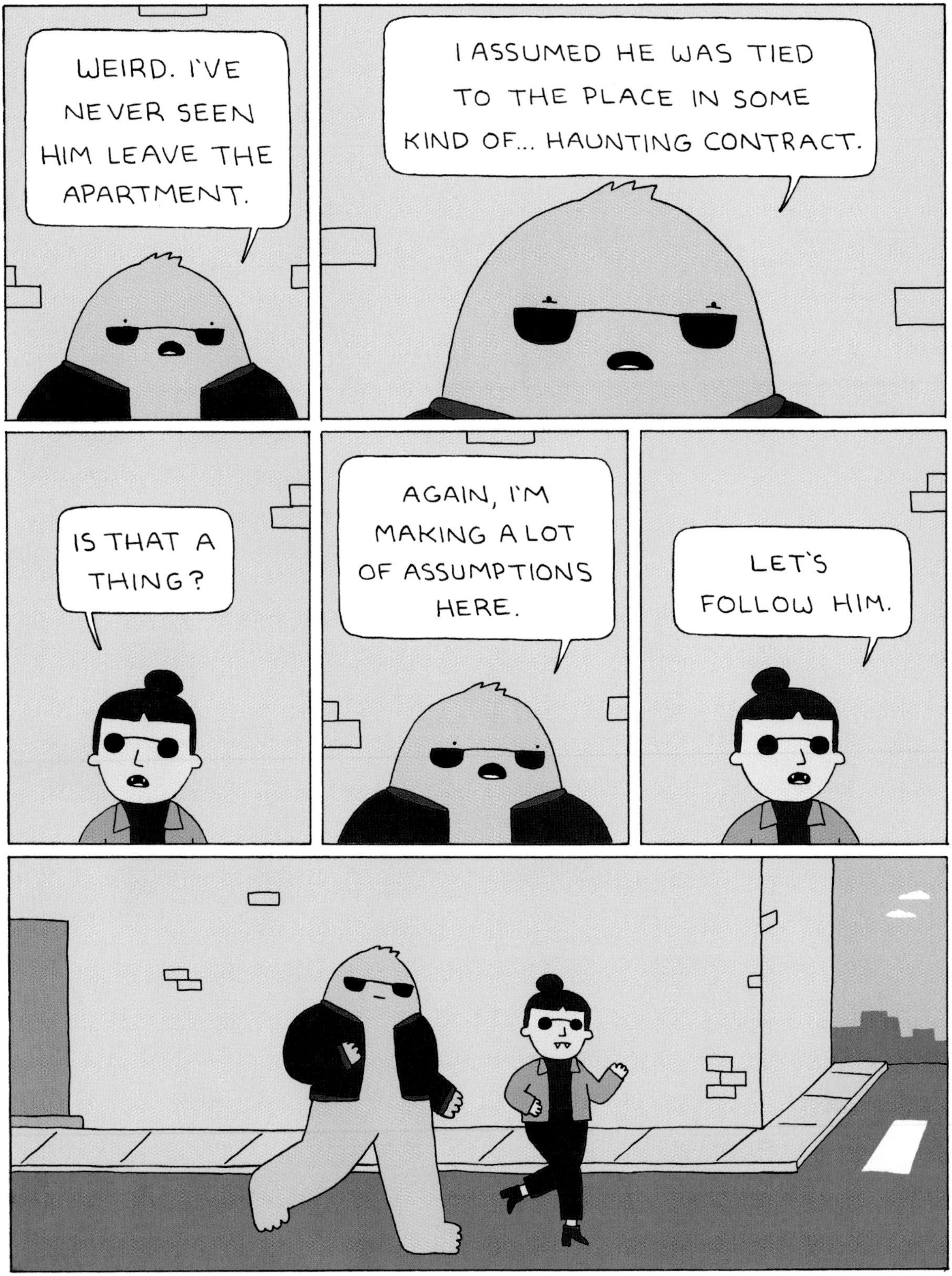
WEIRD. I'VE NEVER SEEN HIM LEAVE THE APARTMENT.
I ASSUMED HE WAS TIED TO THE PLACE IN SOME KIND OF... HAUNTING CONTRACT.
IS THAT A THING?
AGAIN, I'M MAKING A LOT OF ASSUMPTIONS HERE.
LET'S FOLLOW HIM.

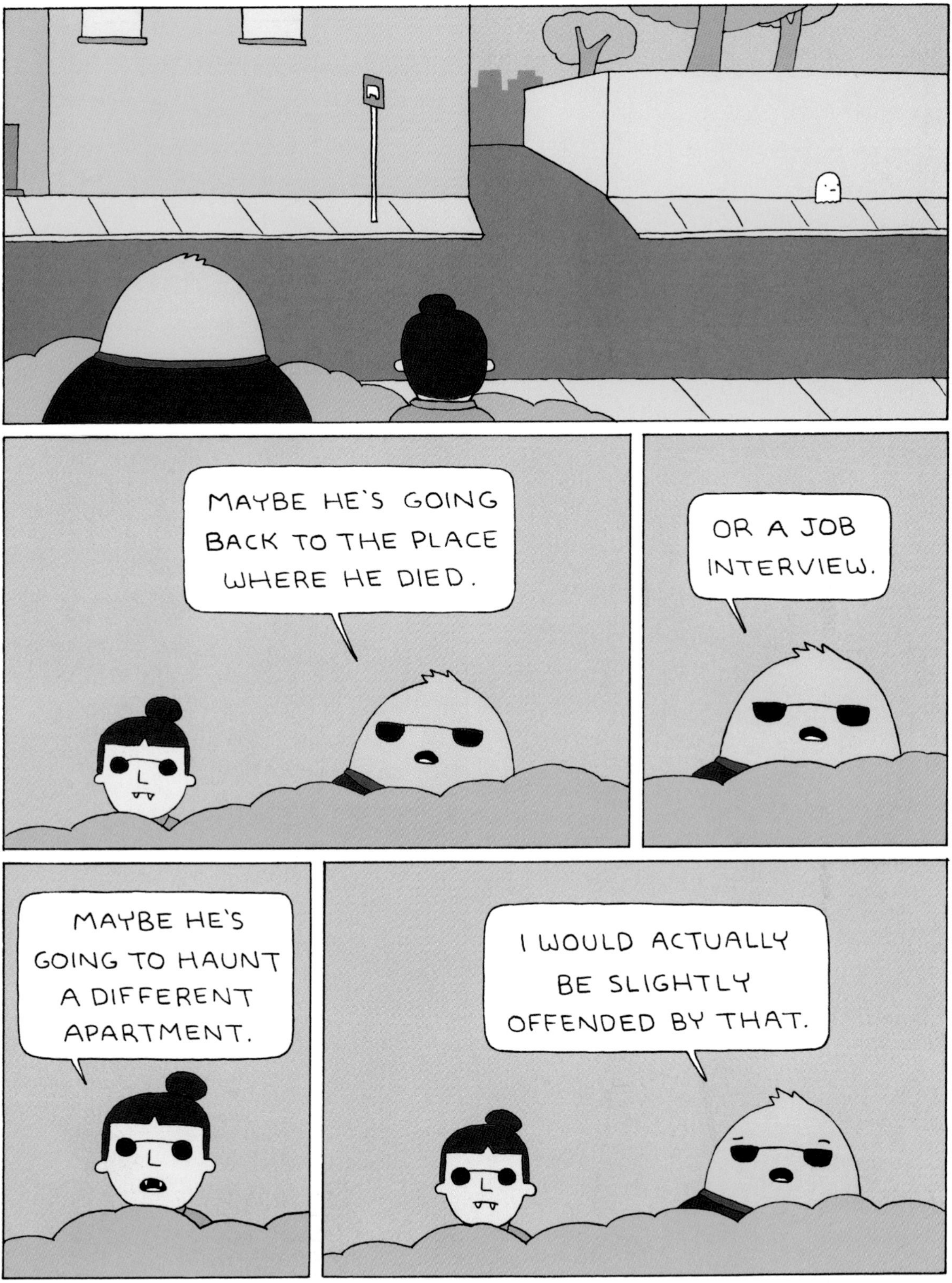
MAYBE HE'S GOING BACK TO THE PLACE WHERE HE DIED.
OR A JOB INTERVIEW.
MAYBE HE'S GOING TO HAUNT A DIFFERENT APARTMENT.
I WOULD ACTUALLY BE SLIGHTLY OFFENDED BY THAT.

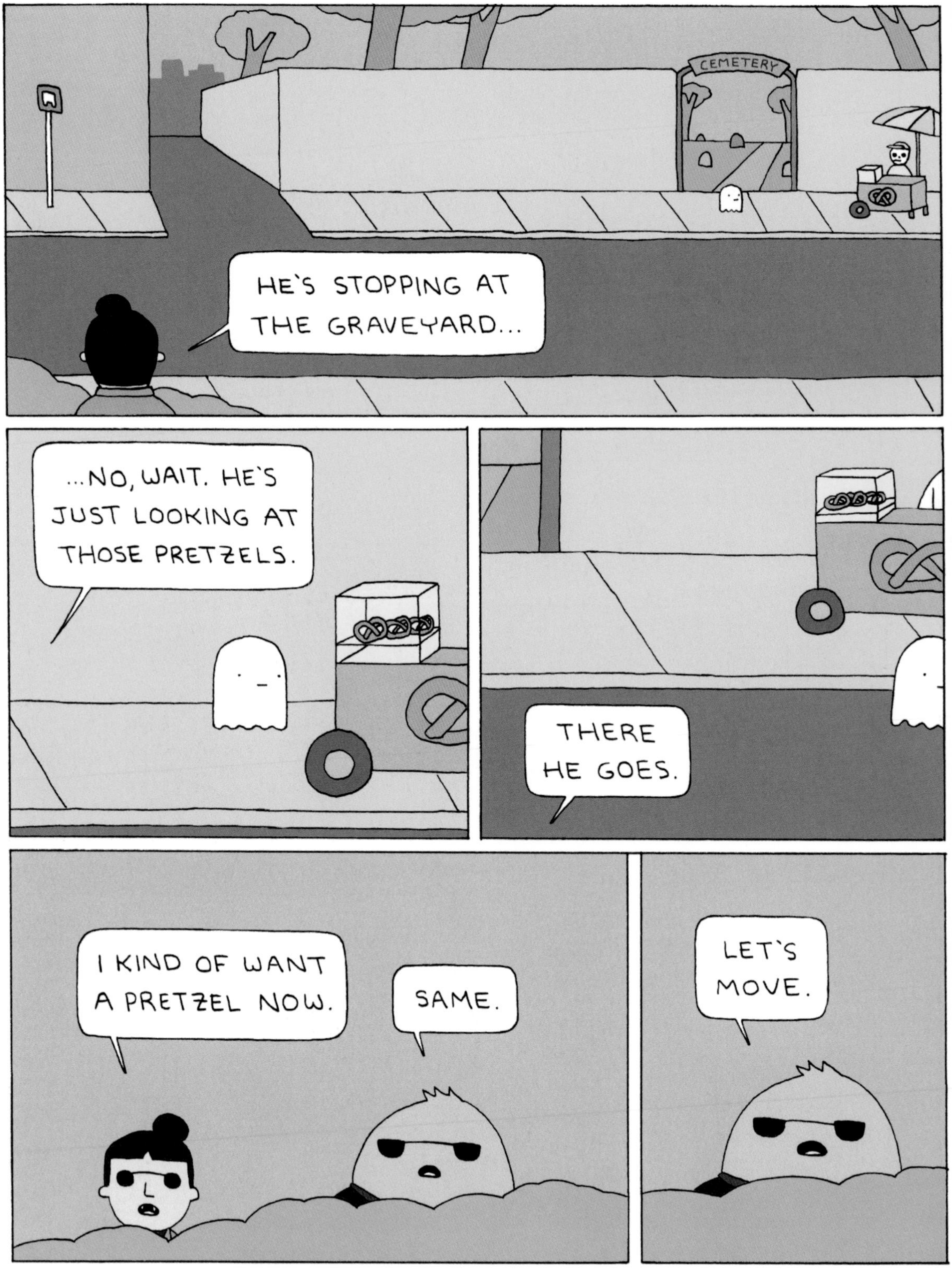
CEMETERY
HE'S STOPPING AT THE GRAVEYARD...
...NO, WAIT. HE'S JUST LOOKING AT THOSE PRETZELS.
THERE HE GOES.
I KIND OF WANT A PRETZEL NOW.
SAME.
LET'S MOVE.

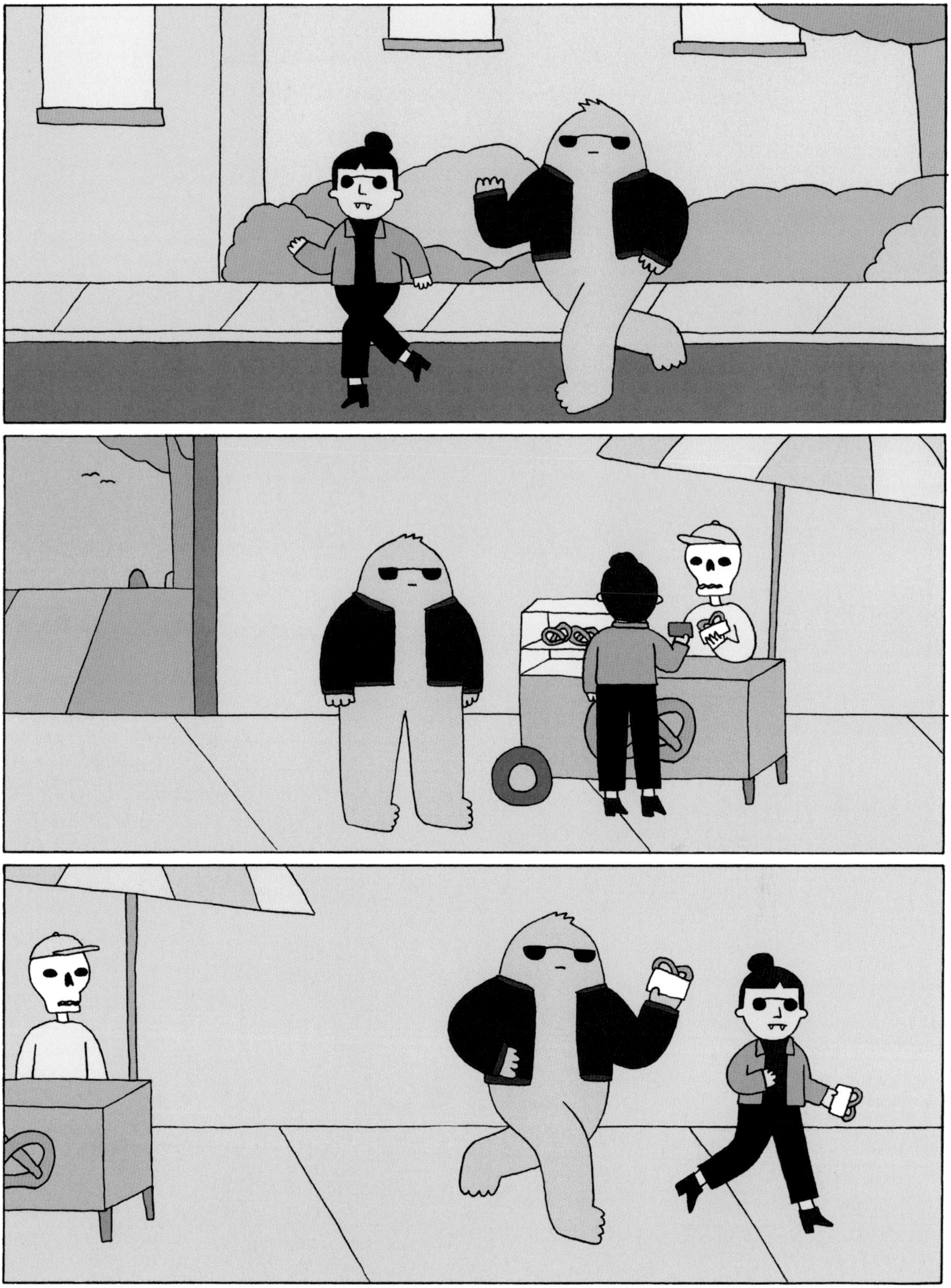

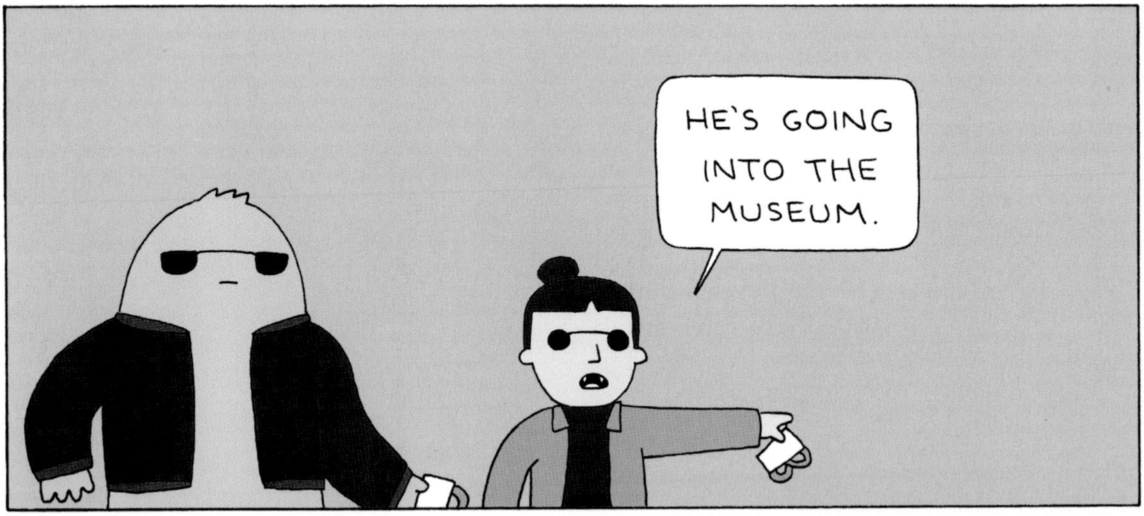
HE'S GOING INTO THE MUSEUM.

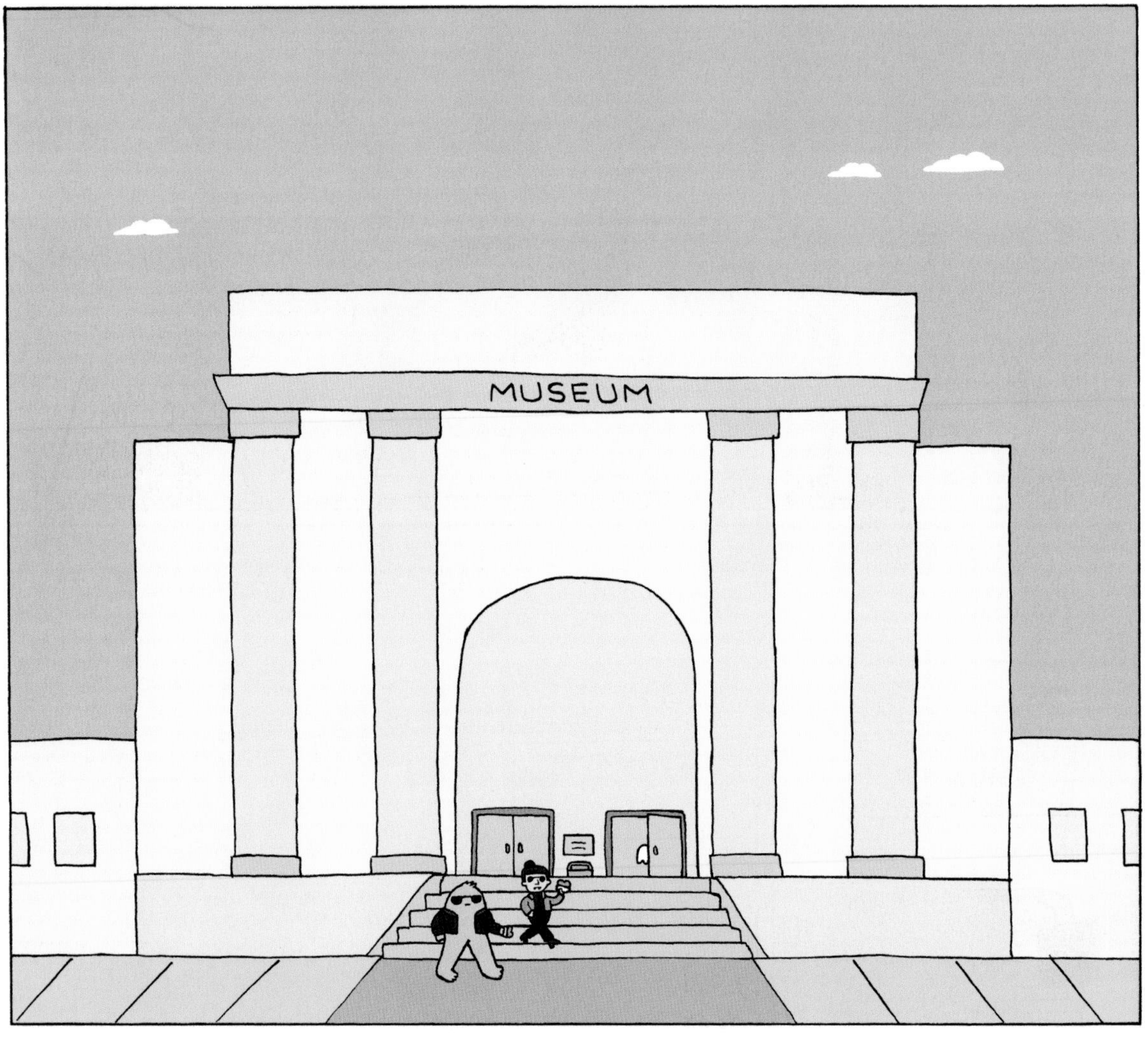
MUSEUM

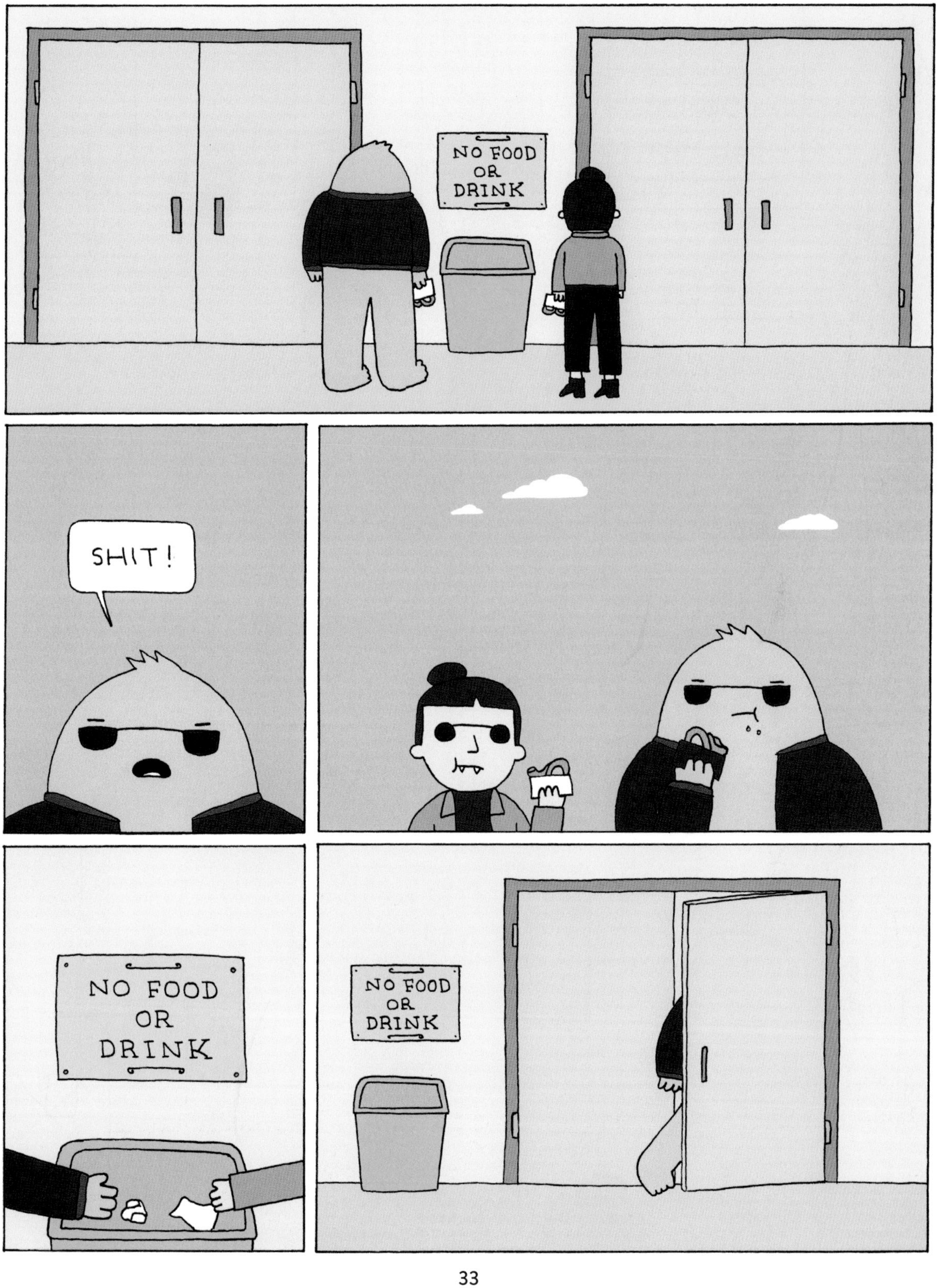
NO FOOD OR DRINK
SHIT!
NO FOOD OR DRINK
NO FOOD OR DRINK

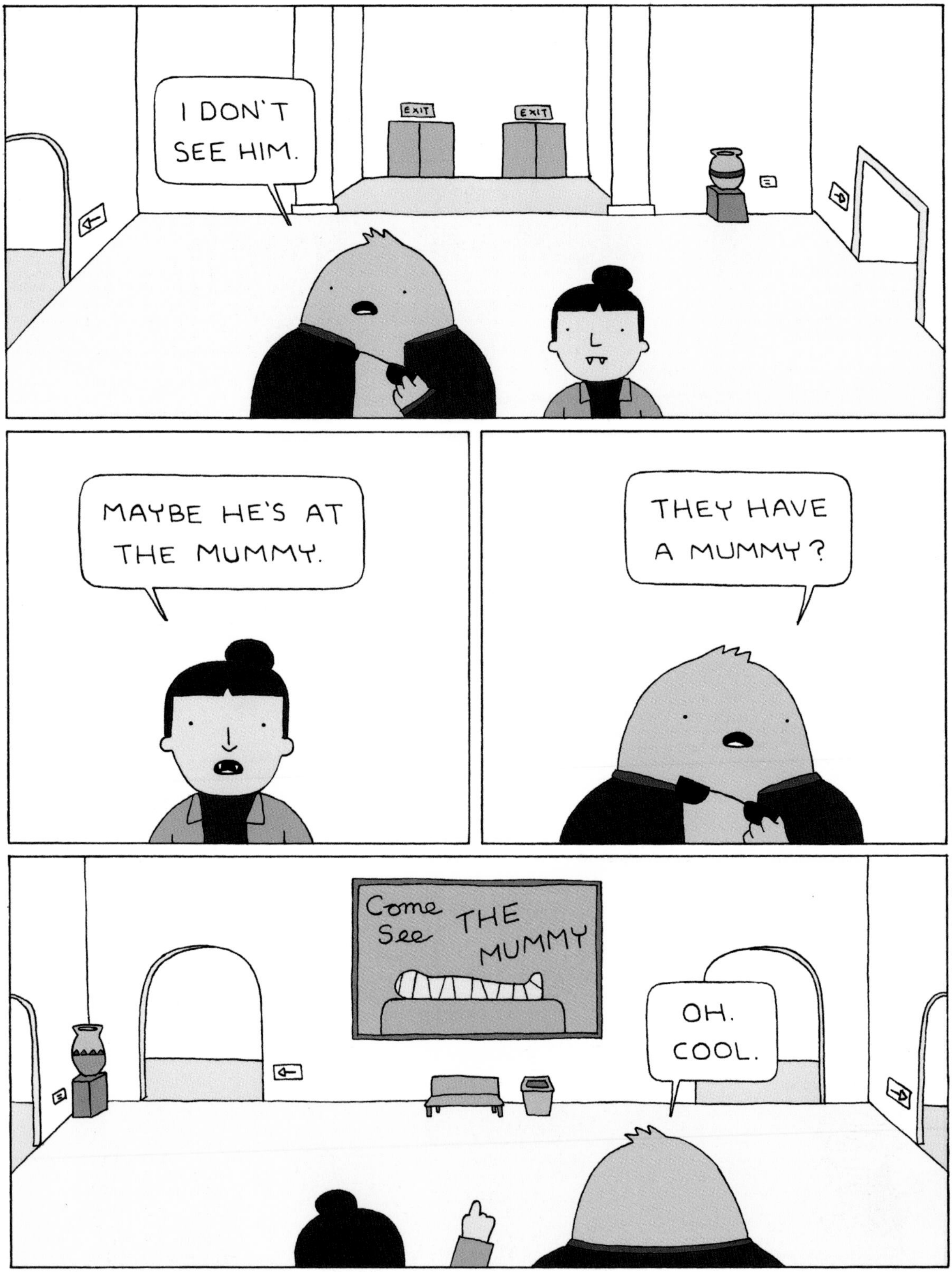
I DON'T SEE HIM.
EXIT
EXIT
MAYBE HE'S AT THE MUMMY.
THEY HAVE A MUMMY?
Come See THE MUMMY
OH. COOL.

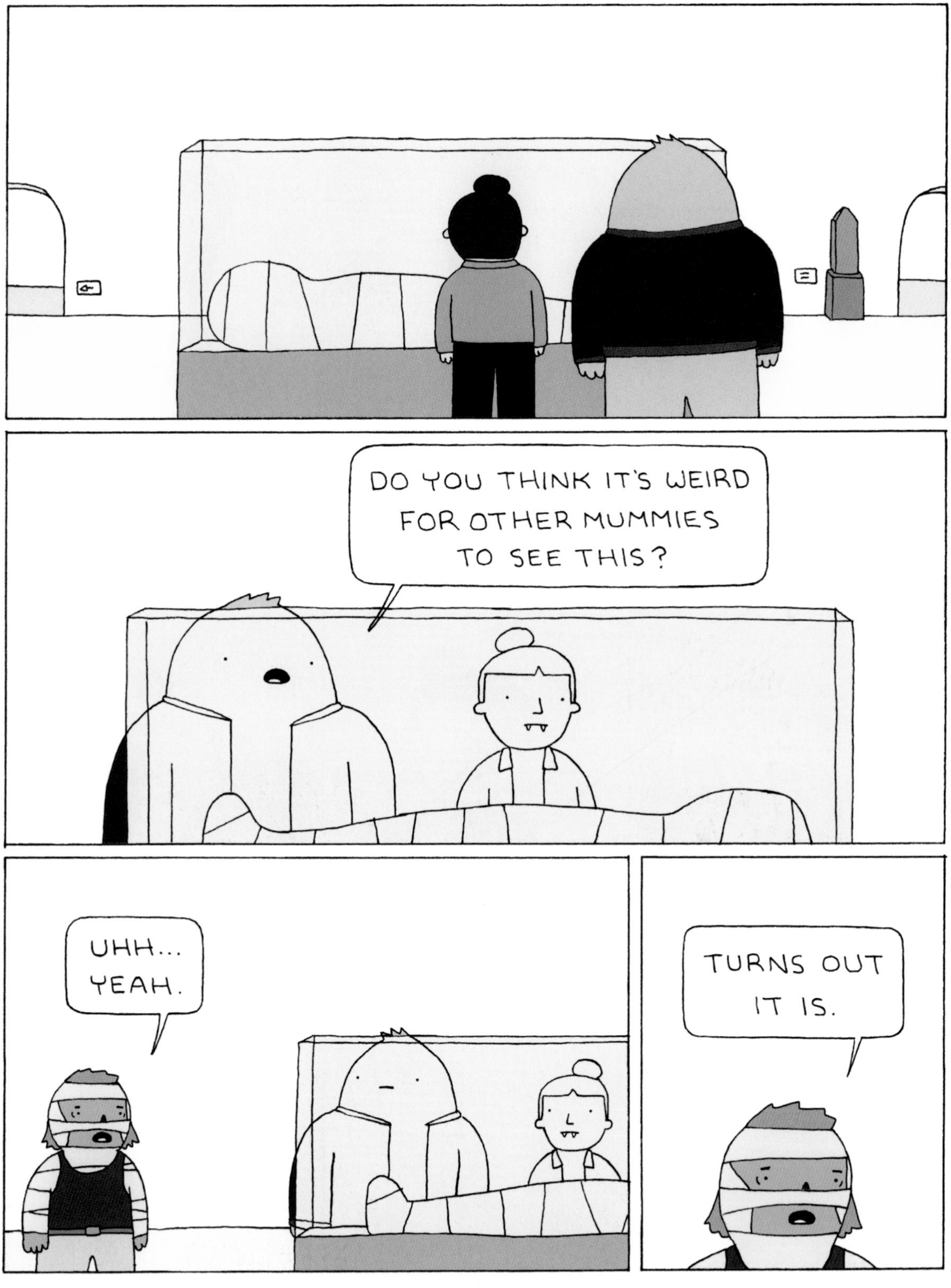
DO YOU THINK IT'S WEIRD FOR OTHER MUMMIES TO SEE THIS?
UHH... YEAH.
TURNS OUT IT IS.

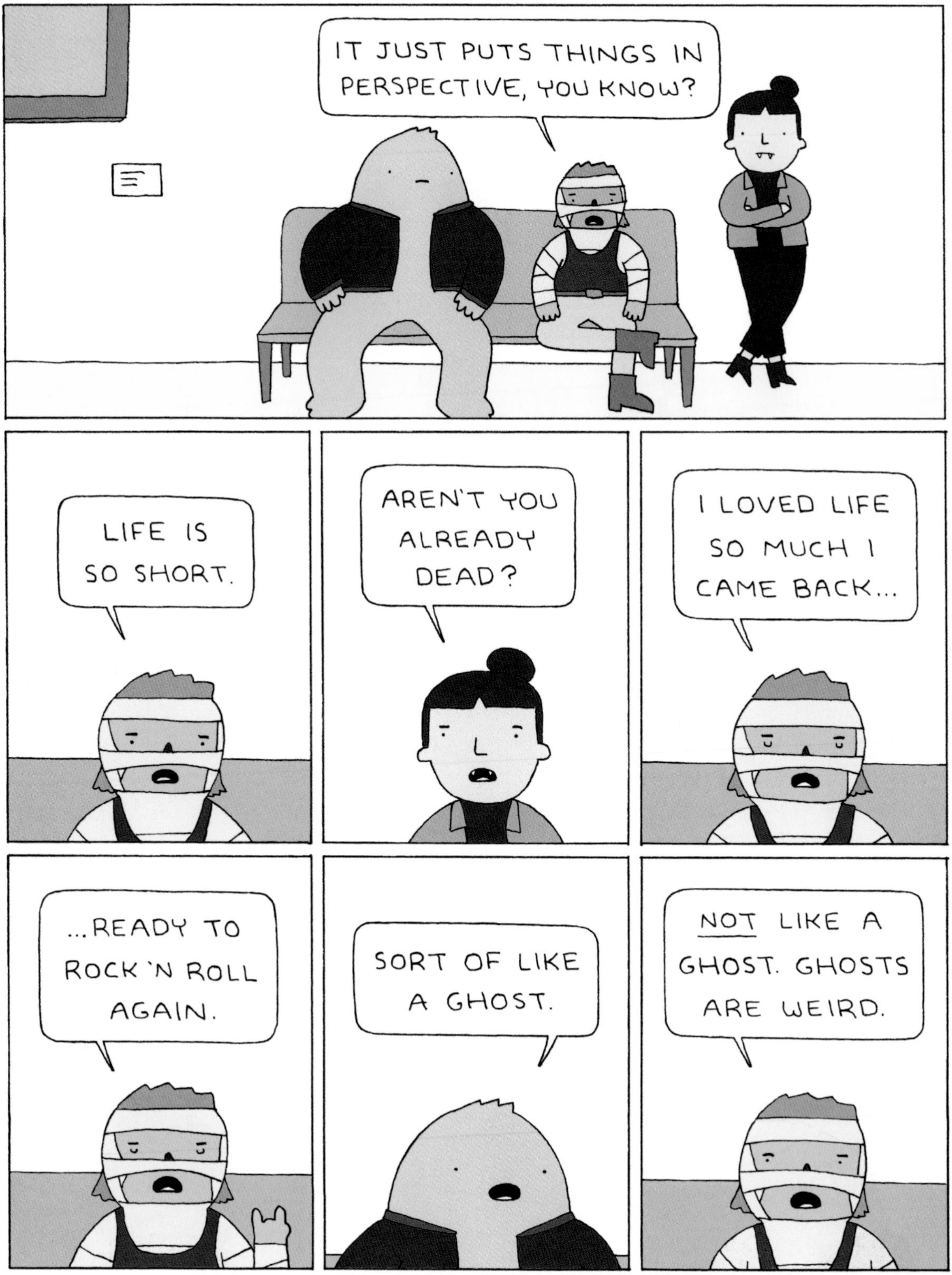
IT JUST PUTS THINGS IN PERSPECTIVE, YOU KNOW?
LIFE IS SO SHORT.
AREN'T YOU ALREADY DEAD?
I LOVED LIFE SO MUCH I CAME BACK...
...READY TO ROCK 'N ROLL AGAIN.
SORT OF LIKE A GHOST.
NOT LIKE A GHOST. GHOSTS ARE WEIRD.

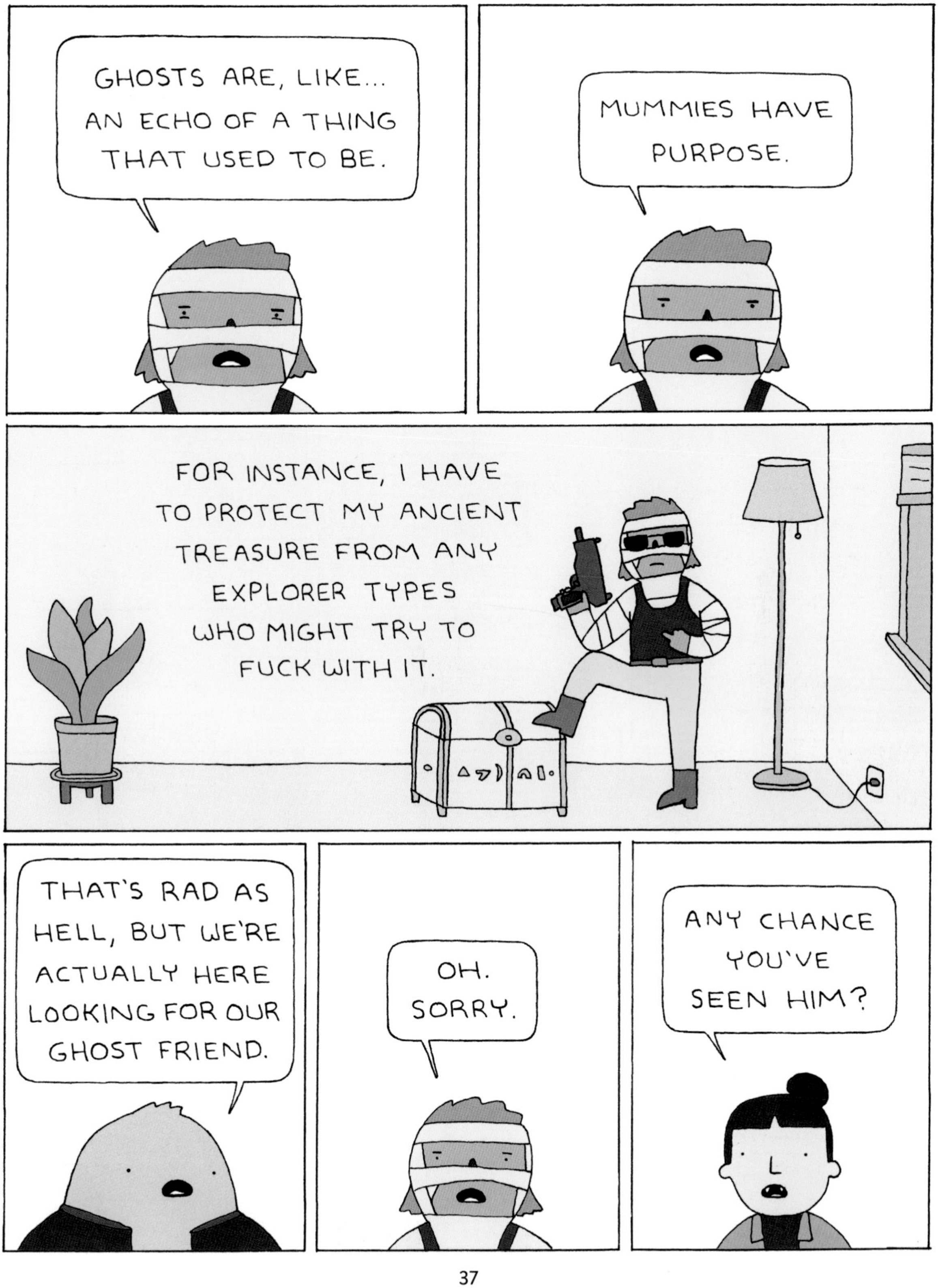
GHOSTS ARE, LIKE... AN ECHO OF A THING THAT USED TO BE.
MUMMIES HAVE PURPOSE.
FOR INSTANCE, I HAVE TO PROTECT MY ANCIENT TREASURE FROM ANY EXPLORER TYPES WHO MIGHT TRY TO FUCK WITH IT.
THAT'S RAD AS HELL, BUT WE'RE ACTUALLY HERE LOOKING FOR OUR GHOST FRIEND.
OH. SORRY.
ANY CHANCE YOU'VE SEEN HIM?

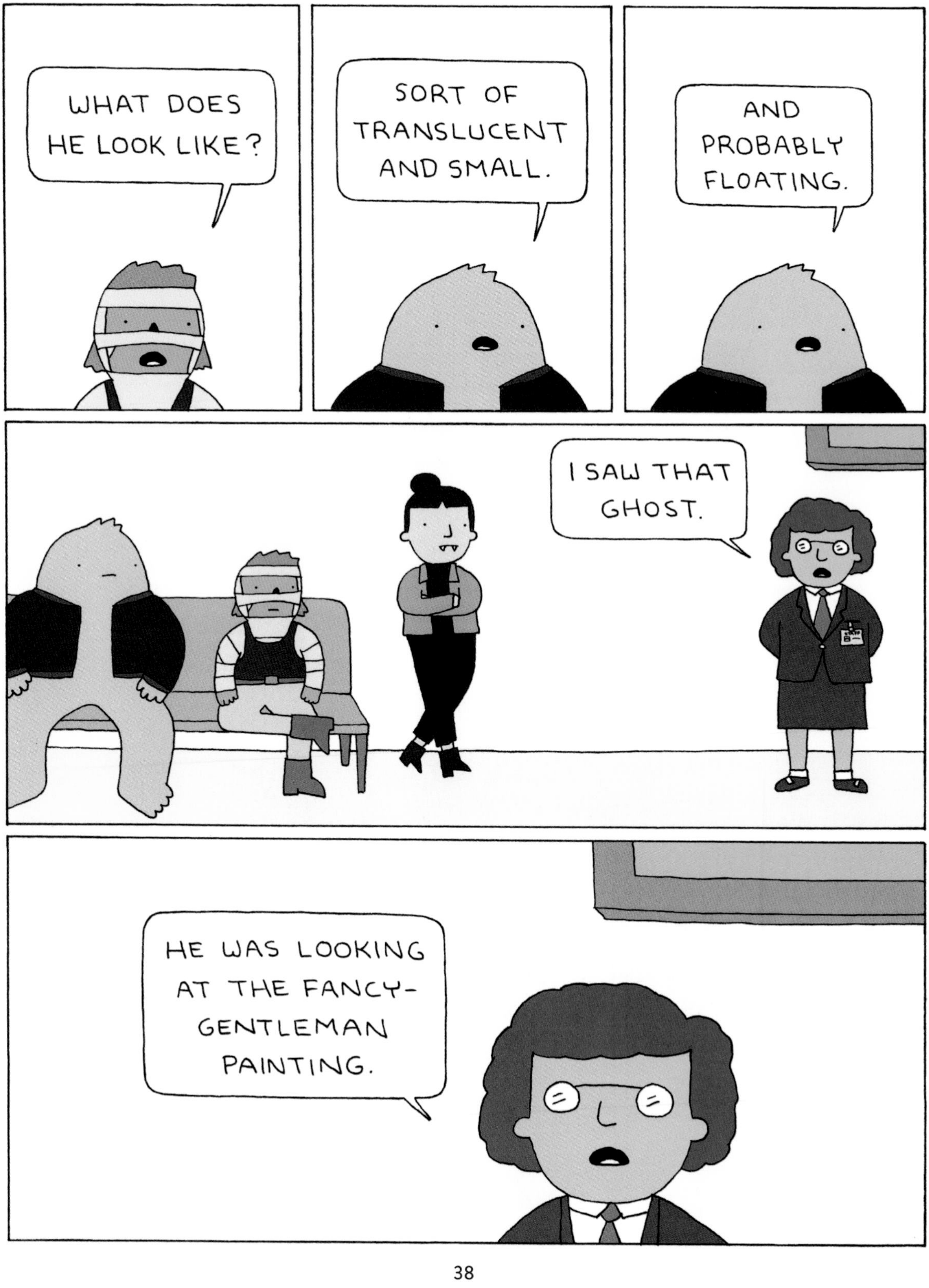
WHAT DOES HE LOOK LIKE?
SORT OF TRANSLUCENT AND SMALL.
AND PROBABLY FLOATING.
I SAW THAT GHOST.
HE WAS LOOKING AT THE FANCY-GENTLEMAN PAINTING.

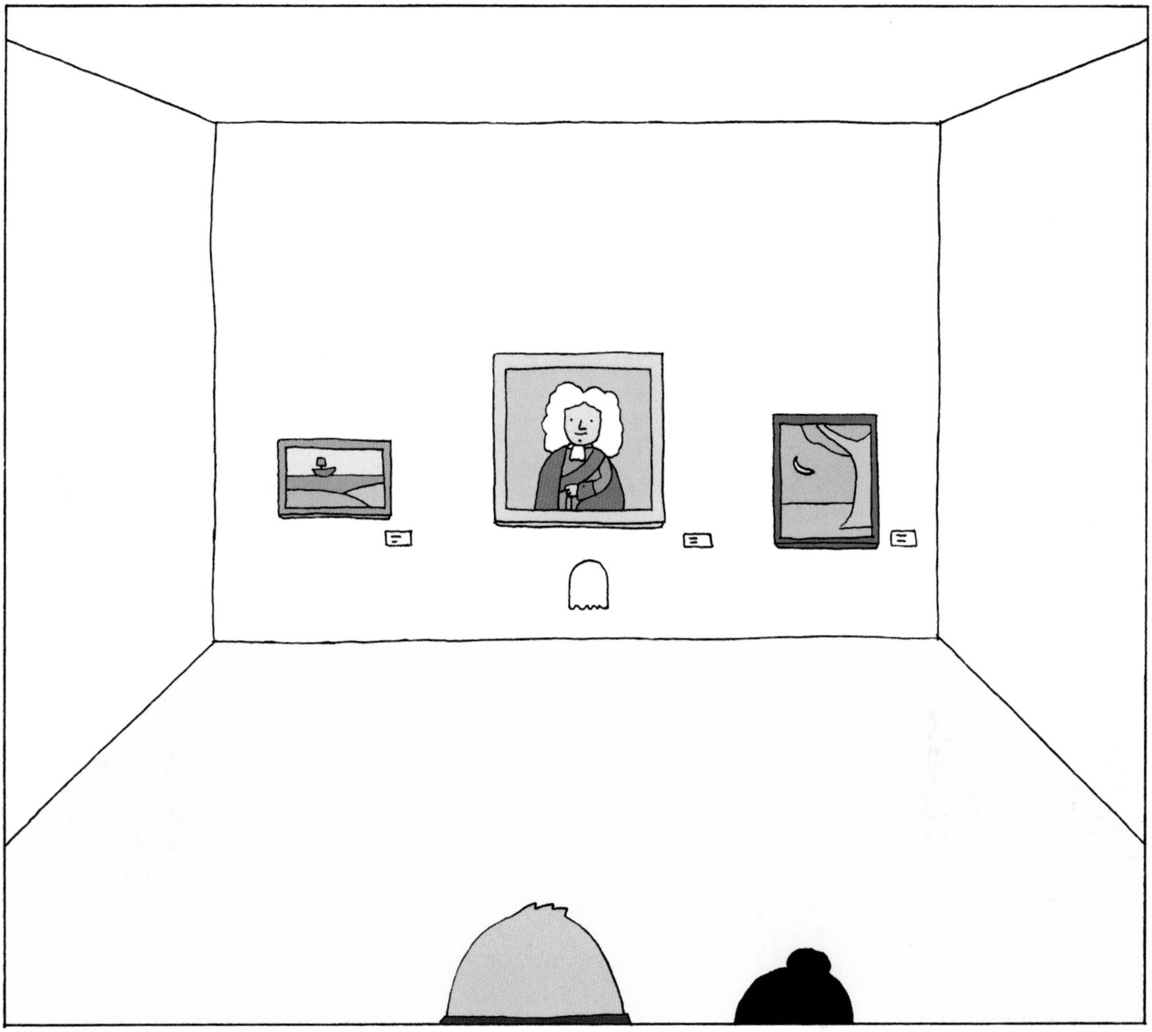

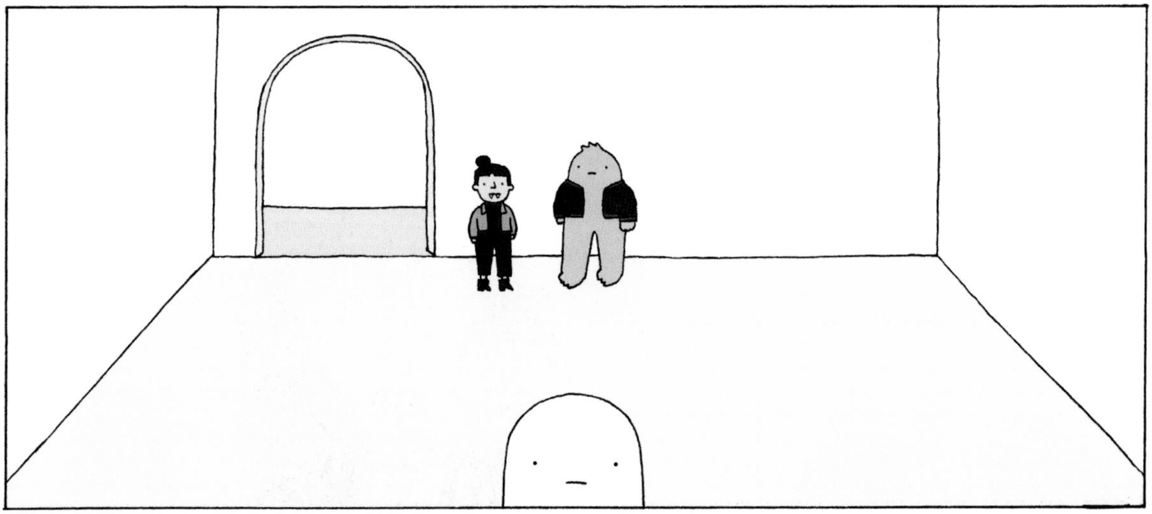

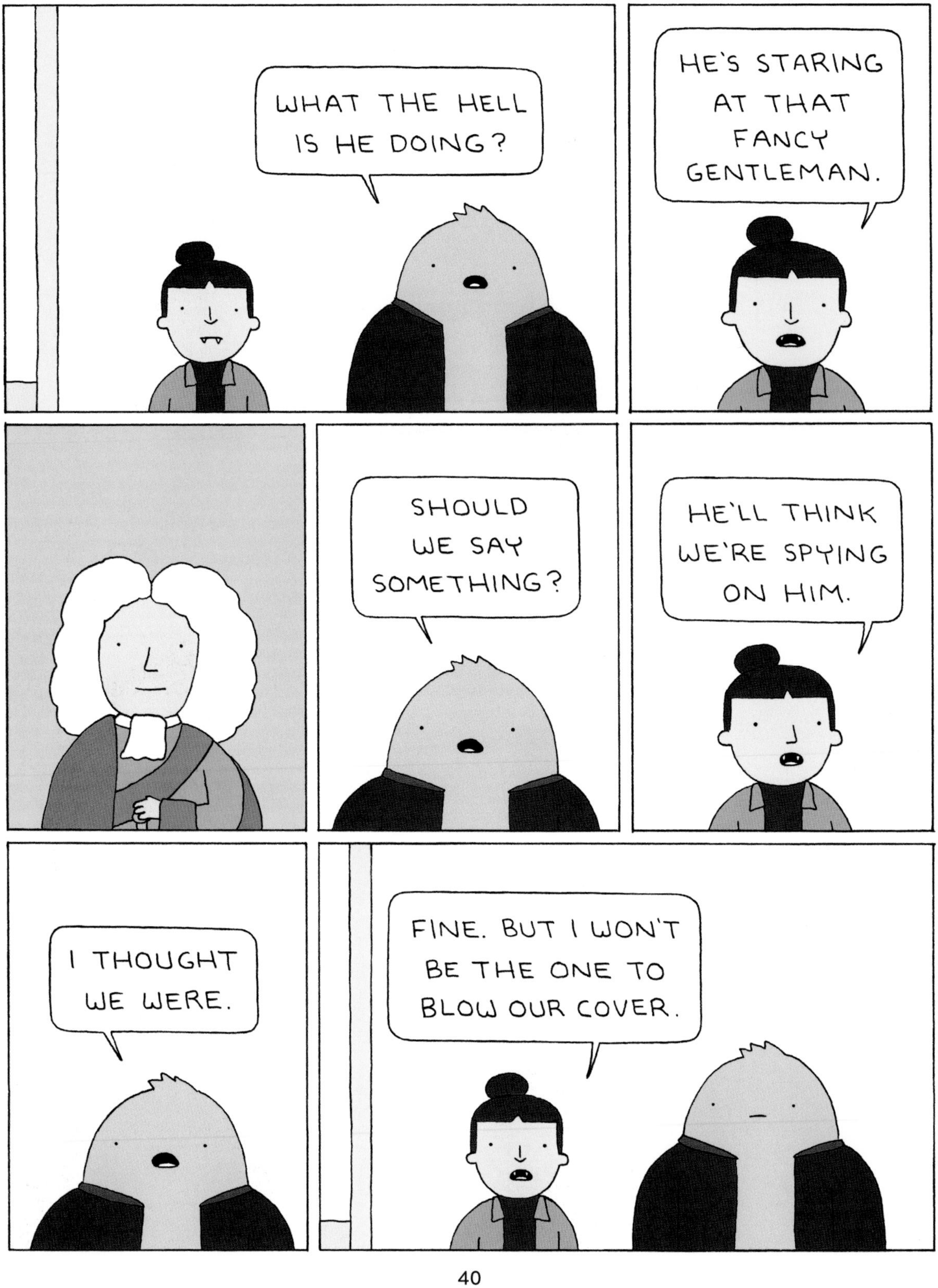
WHAT THE HELL IS HE DOING?
HE'S STARING AT THAT FANCY GENTLEMAN.
SHOULD WE SAY SOMETHING?
HE'LL THINK WE'RE SPYING ON HIM.
I THOUGHT WE WERE.
FINE. BUT I WON'T BE THE ONE TO BLOW OUR COVER.

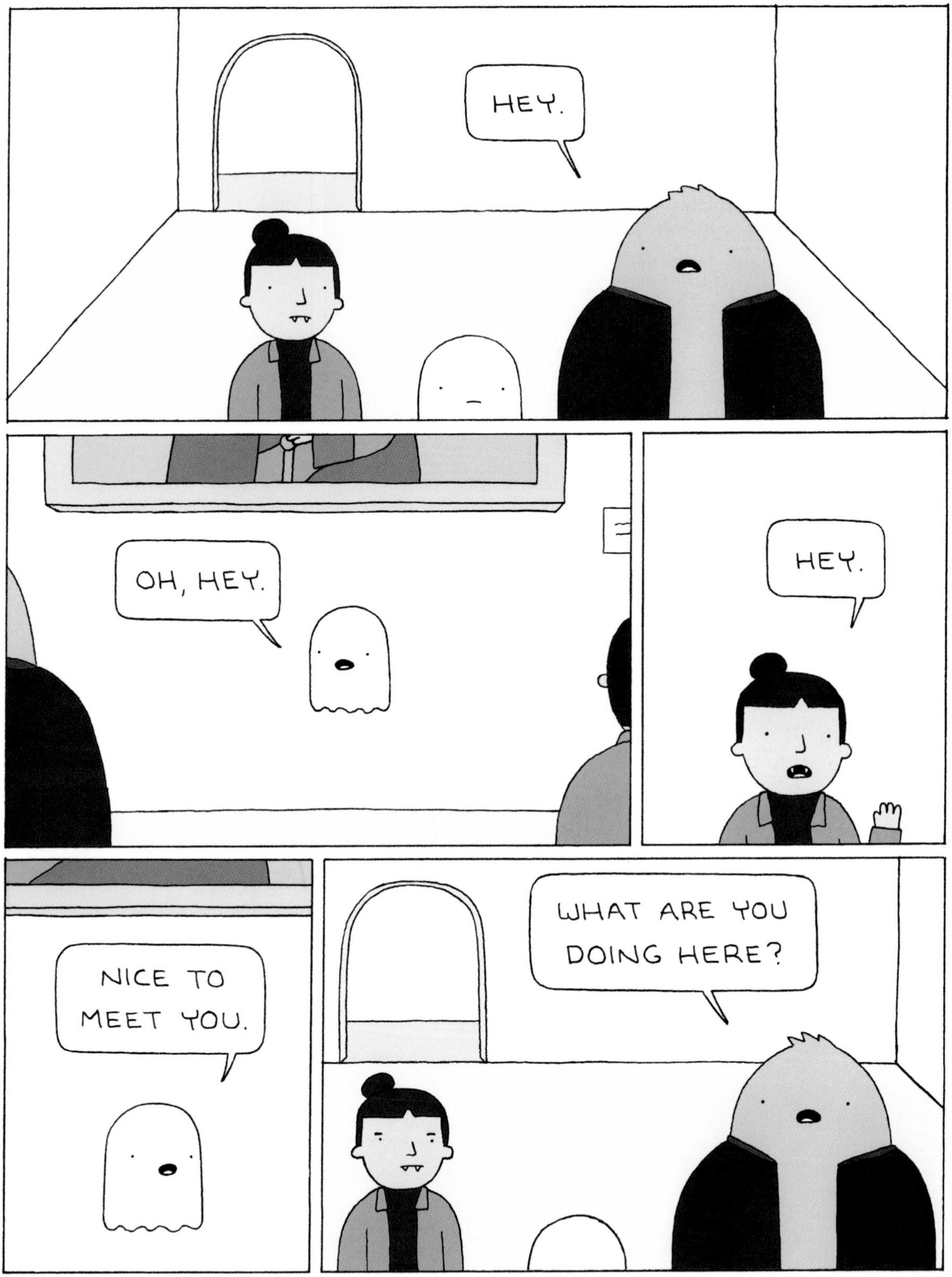
HEY.
OH, HEY.
HEY.
NICE TO MEET YOU.
WHAT ARE YOU DOING HERE?

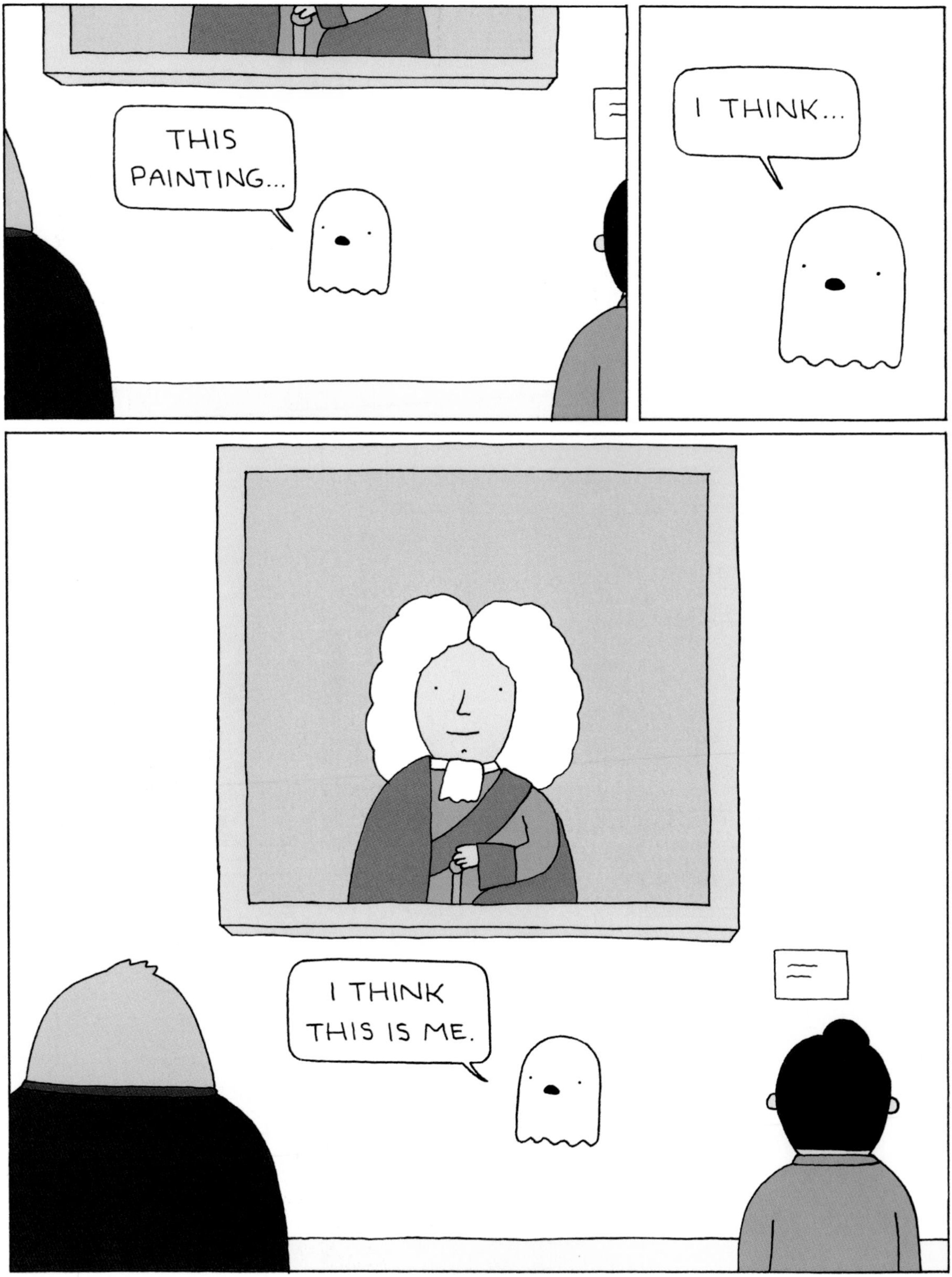
THIS PAINTING...
I THINK...
I THINK THIS IS ME.

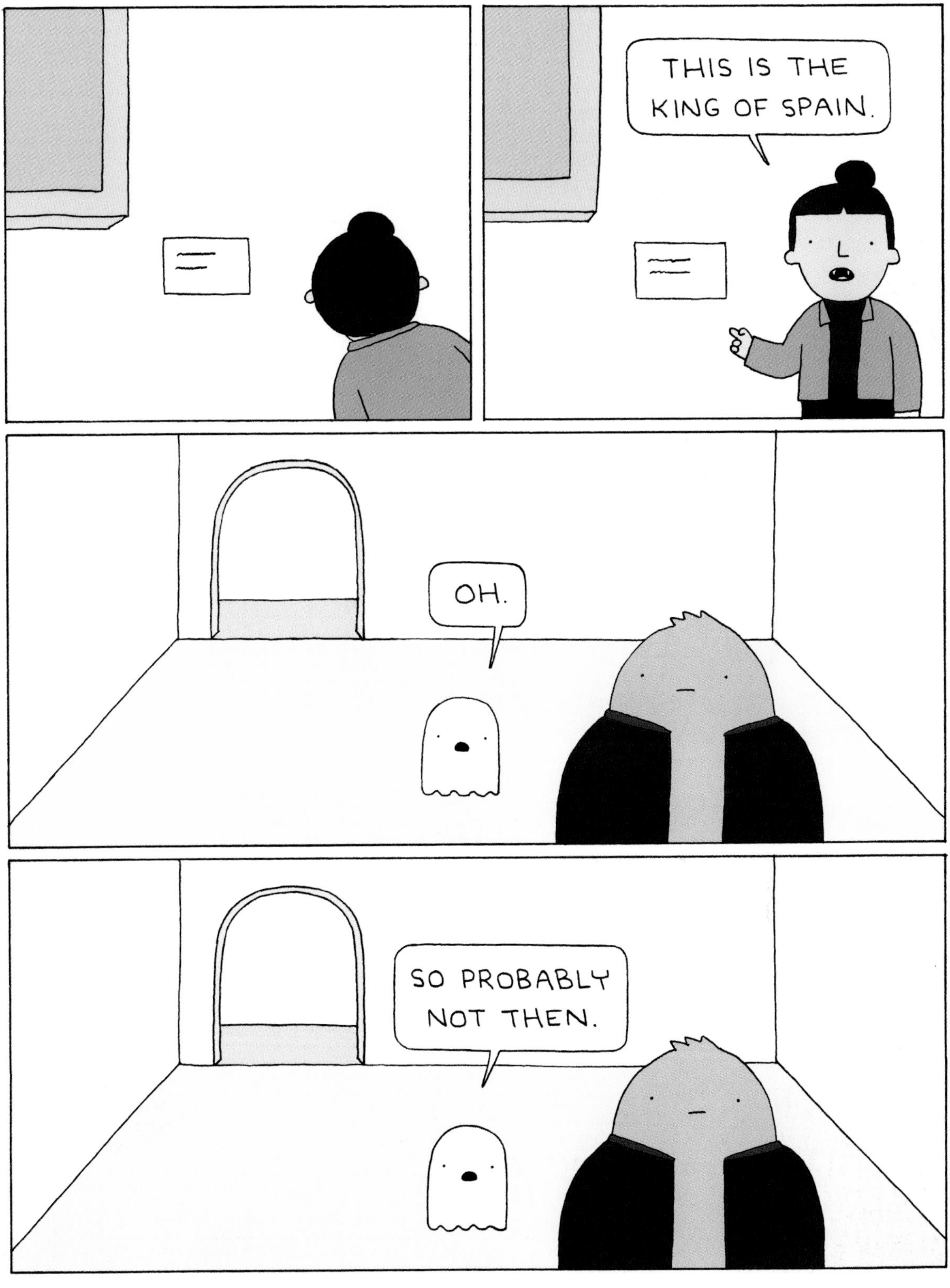
THIS IS THE KING OF SPAIN.
OH.
SO PROBABLY NOT THEN.

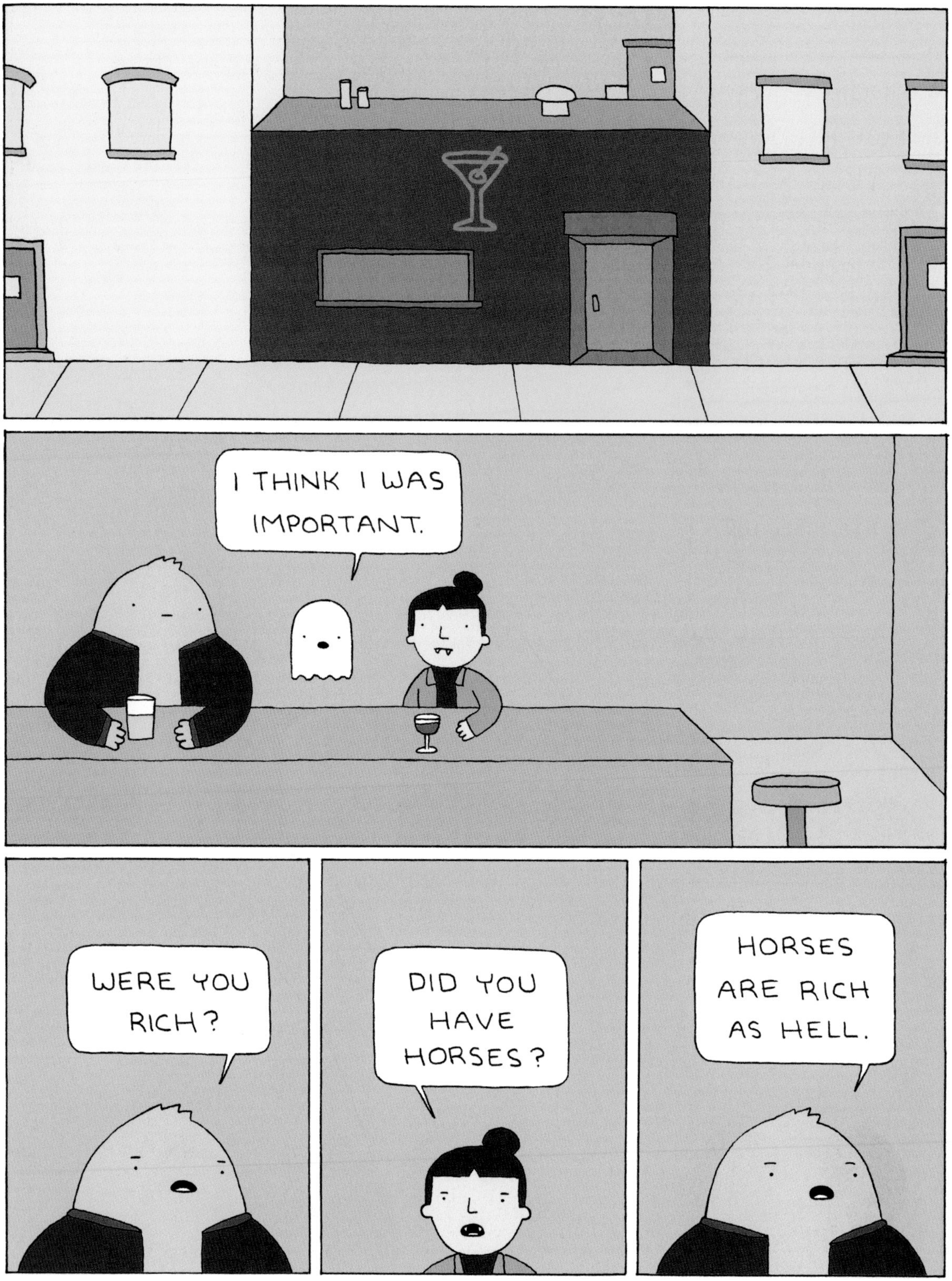
I THINK I WAS IMPORTANT.
WERE YOU RICH?
DID YOU HAVE HORSES?
HORSES ARE RICH AS HELL.

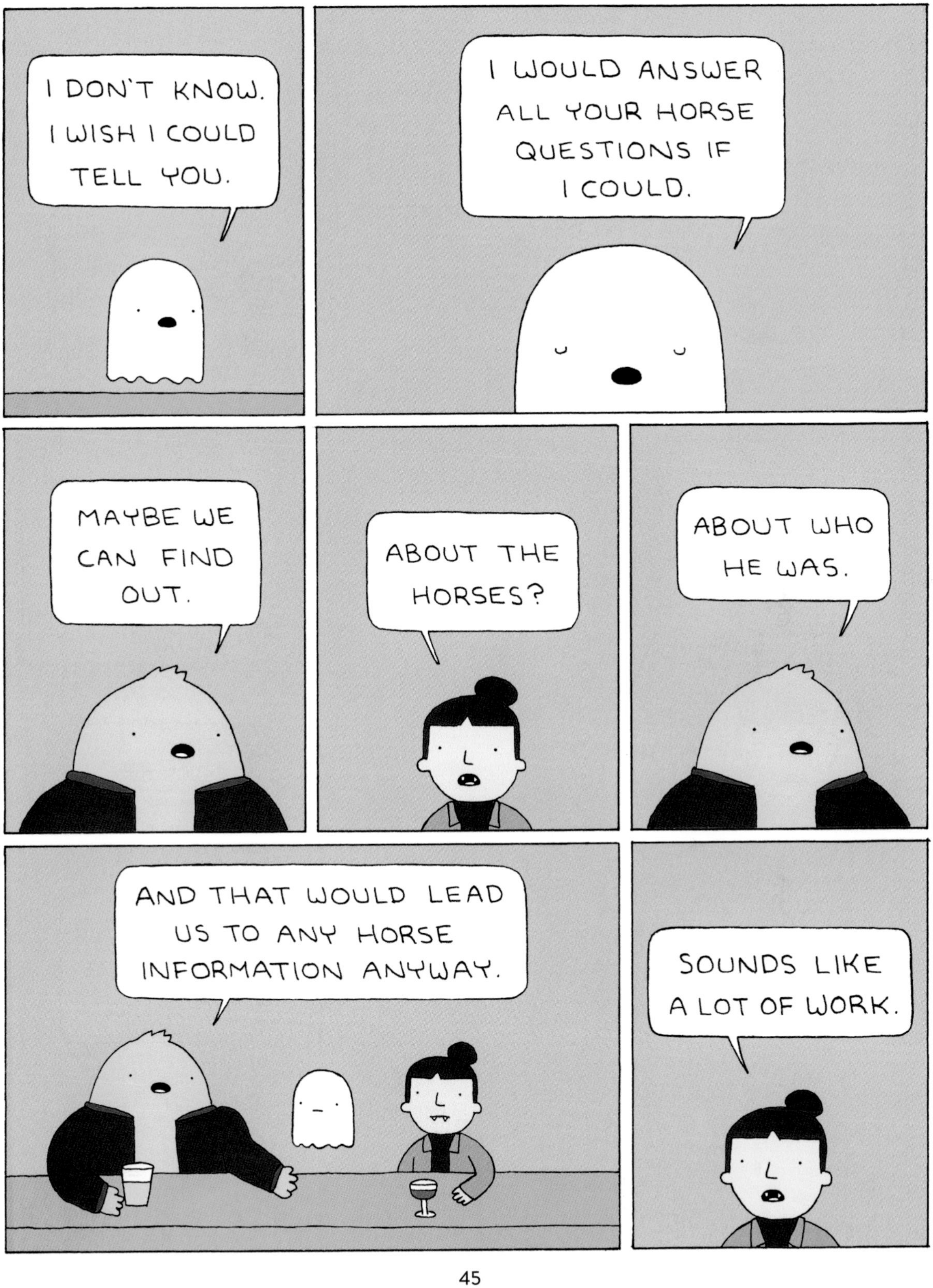
I DON'T KNOW. I WISH I COULD TELL YOU.
I WOULD ANSWER ALL YOUR HORSE QUESTIONS IF I COULD.
MAYBE WE CAN FIND OUT.
ABOUT THE HORSES?
ABOUT WHO HE WAS.
AND THAT WOULD LEAD US TO ANY HORSE INFORMATION ANYWAY.
SOUNDS LIKE A LOT OF WORK.

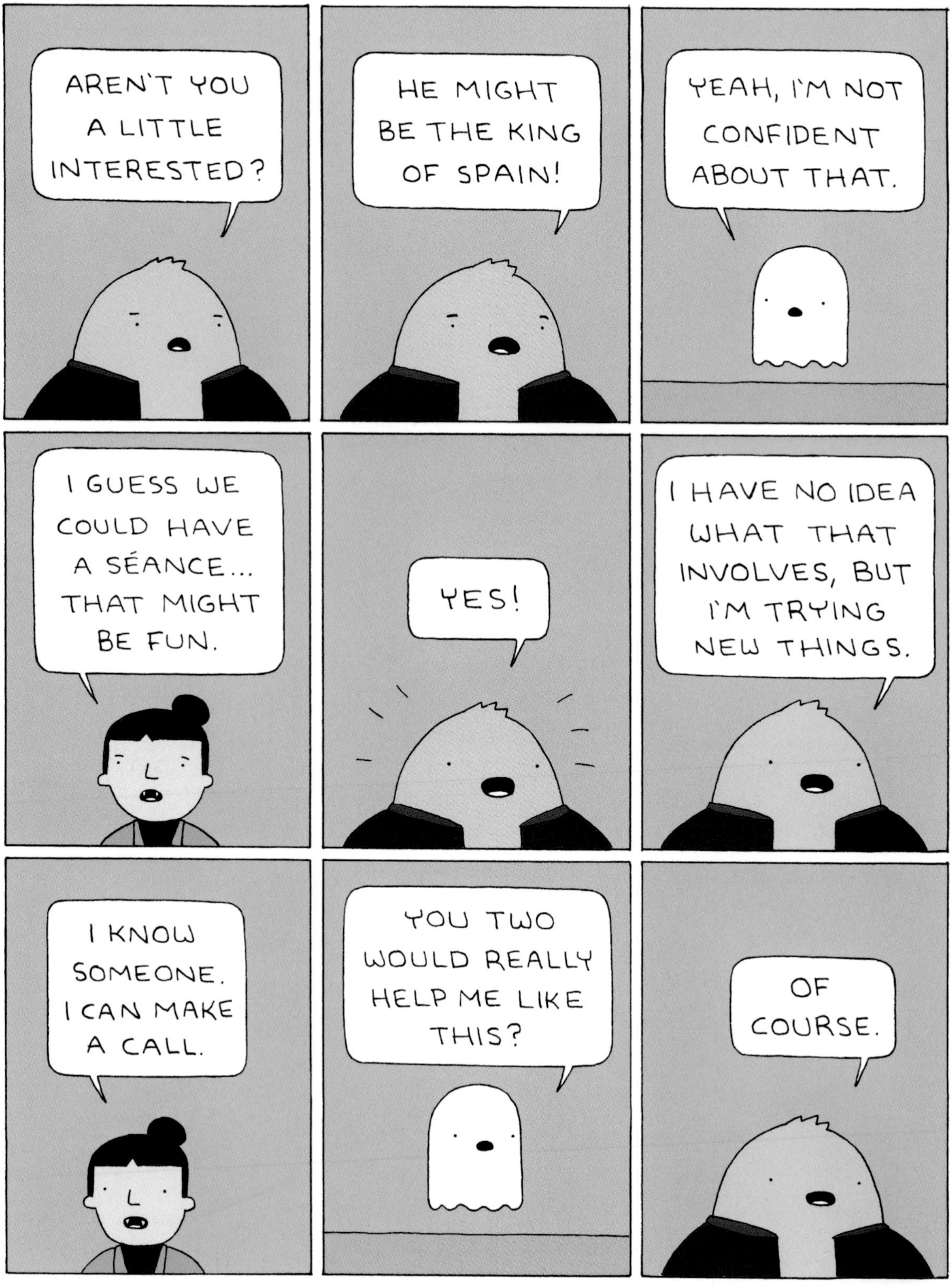
AREN'T YOU A LITTLE INTERESTED?
HE MIGHT BE THE KING OF SPAIN!
YEAH, I'M NOT CONFIDENT ABOUT THAT.
I GUESS WE COULD HAVE A SÉANCE... THAT MIGHT BE FUN.
YES!
I HAVE NO IDEA WHAT THAT INVOLVES, BUT I'M TRYING NEW THINGS.
I KNOW SOMEONE. I CAN MAKE A CALL.
YOU TWO WOULD REALLY HELP ME LIKE THIS?
OF COURSE.

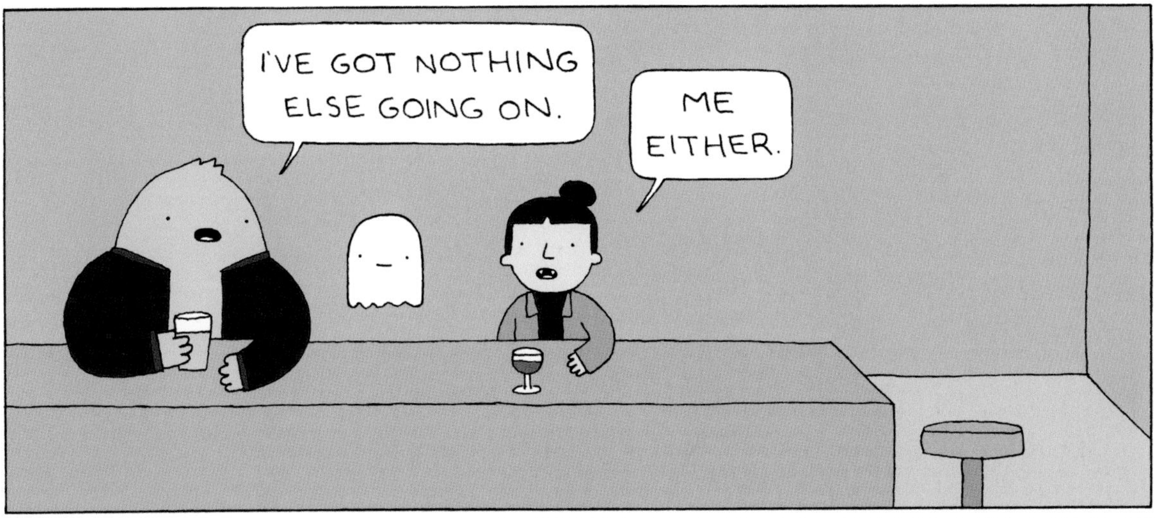
I'VE GOT NOTHING ELSE GOING ON.
ME EITHER.

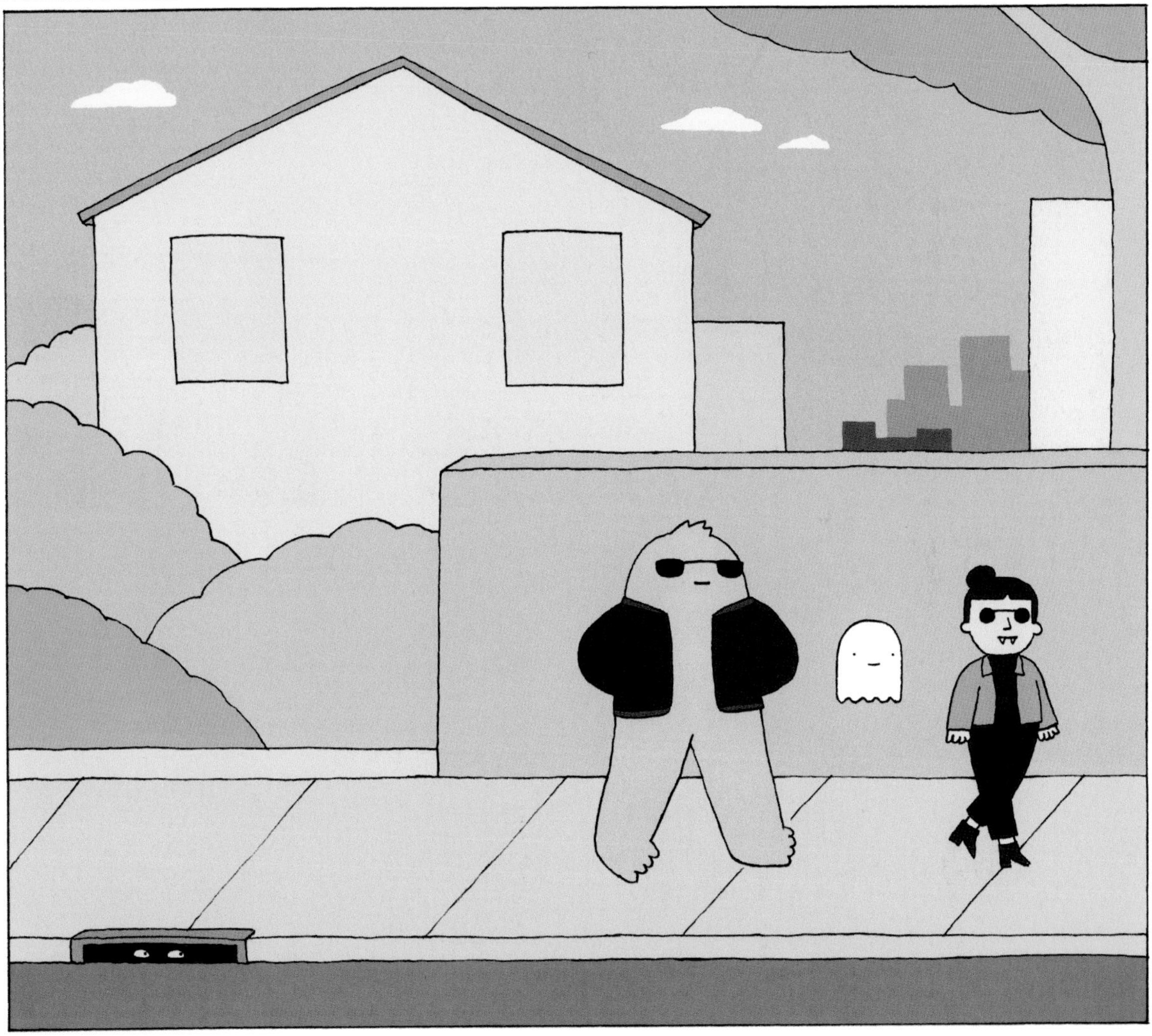

THE SÉANCE

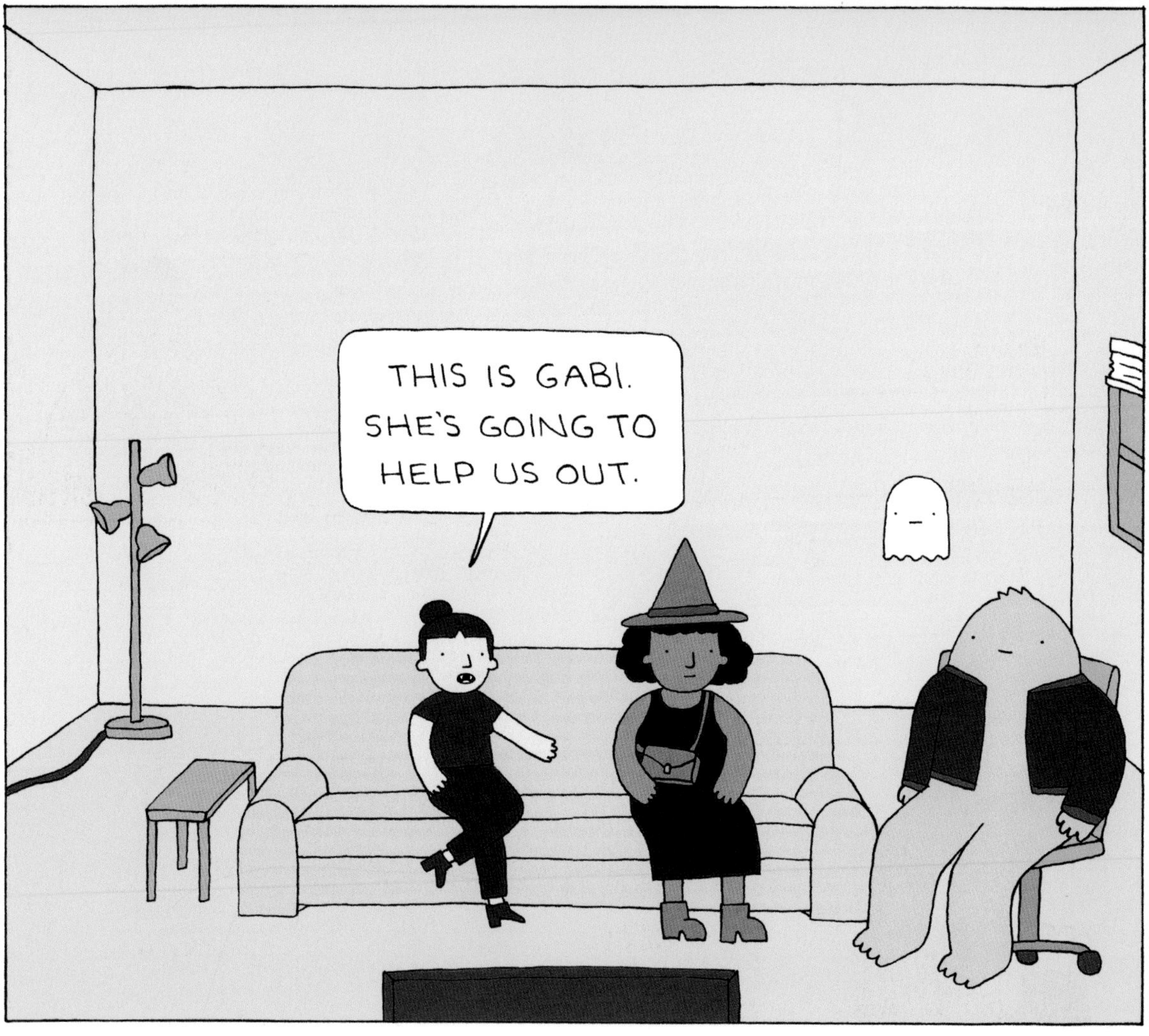
THIS IS GABI. SHE'S GOING TO HELP US OUT.

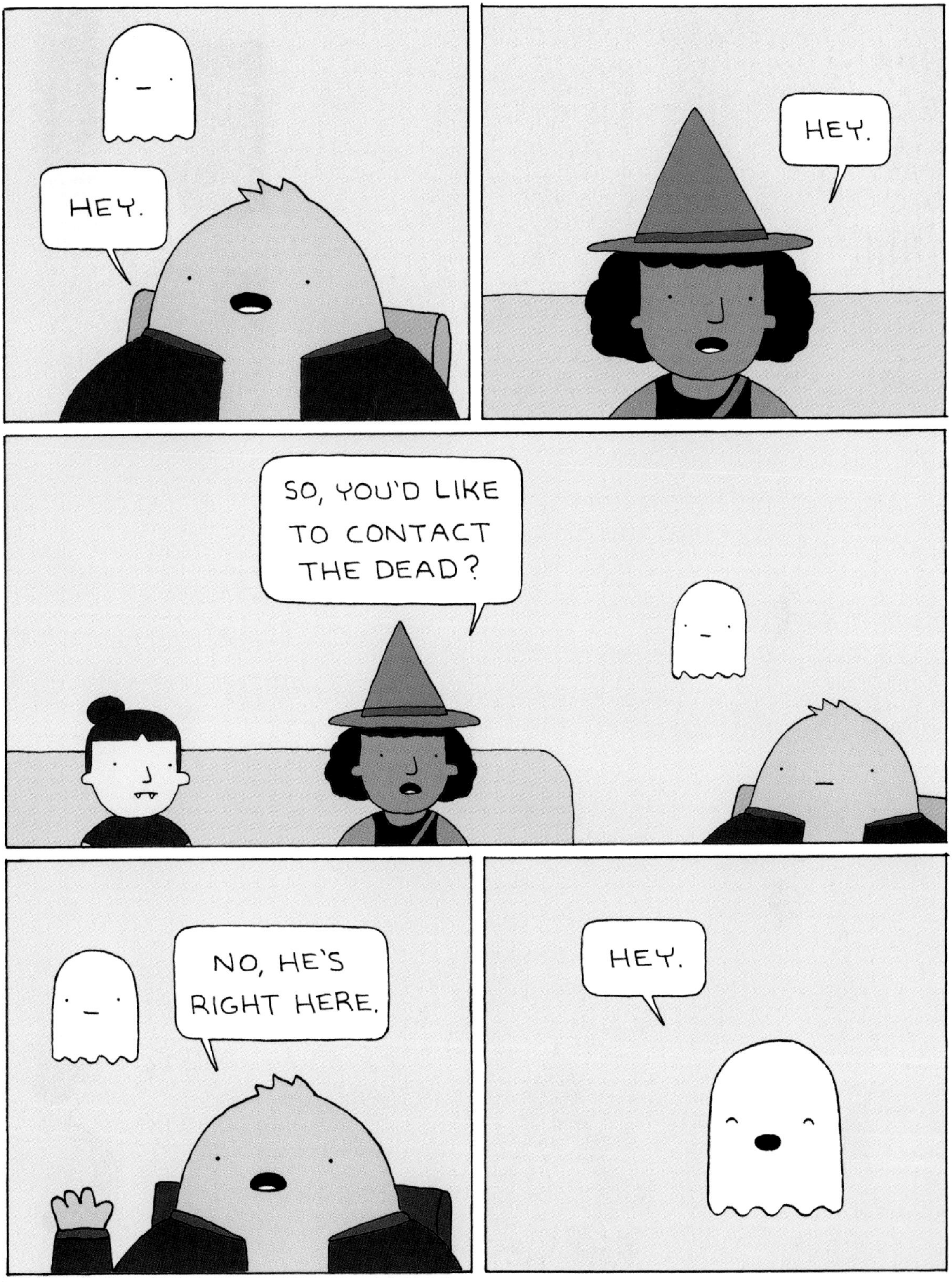
HEY.
HEY.
SO, YOU'D LIKE TO CONTACT THE DEAD?
NO, HE'S RIGHT HERE.
HEY.

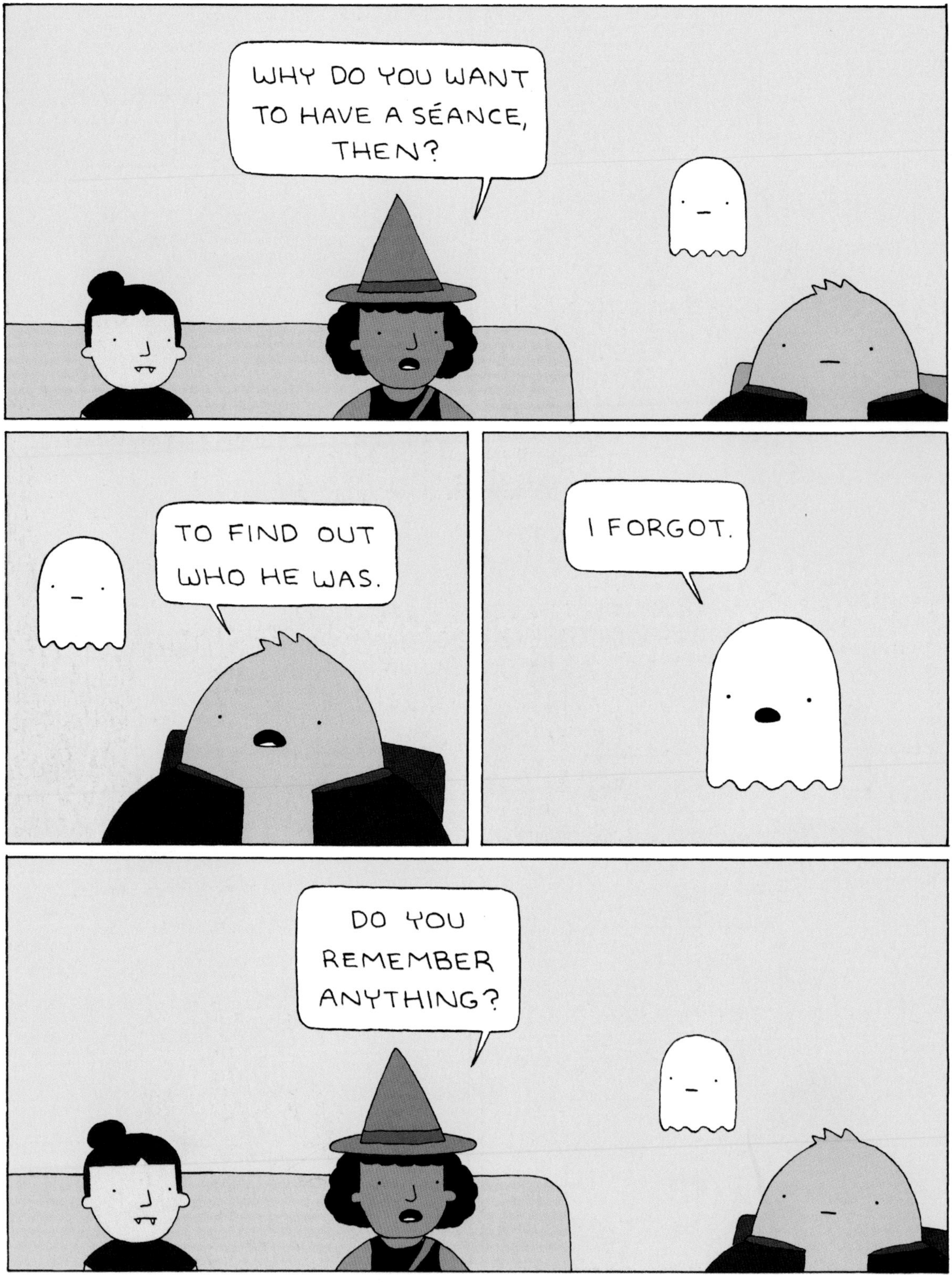
WHY DO YOU WANT TO HAVE A SÉANCE, THEN?
TO FIND OUT WHO HE WAS.
I FORGOT.
DO YOU REMEMBER ANYTHING?

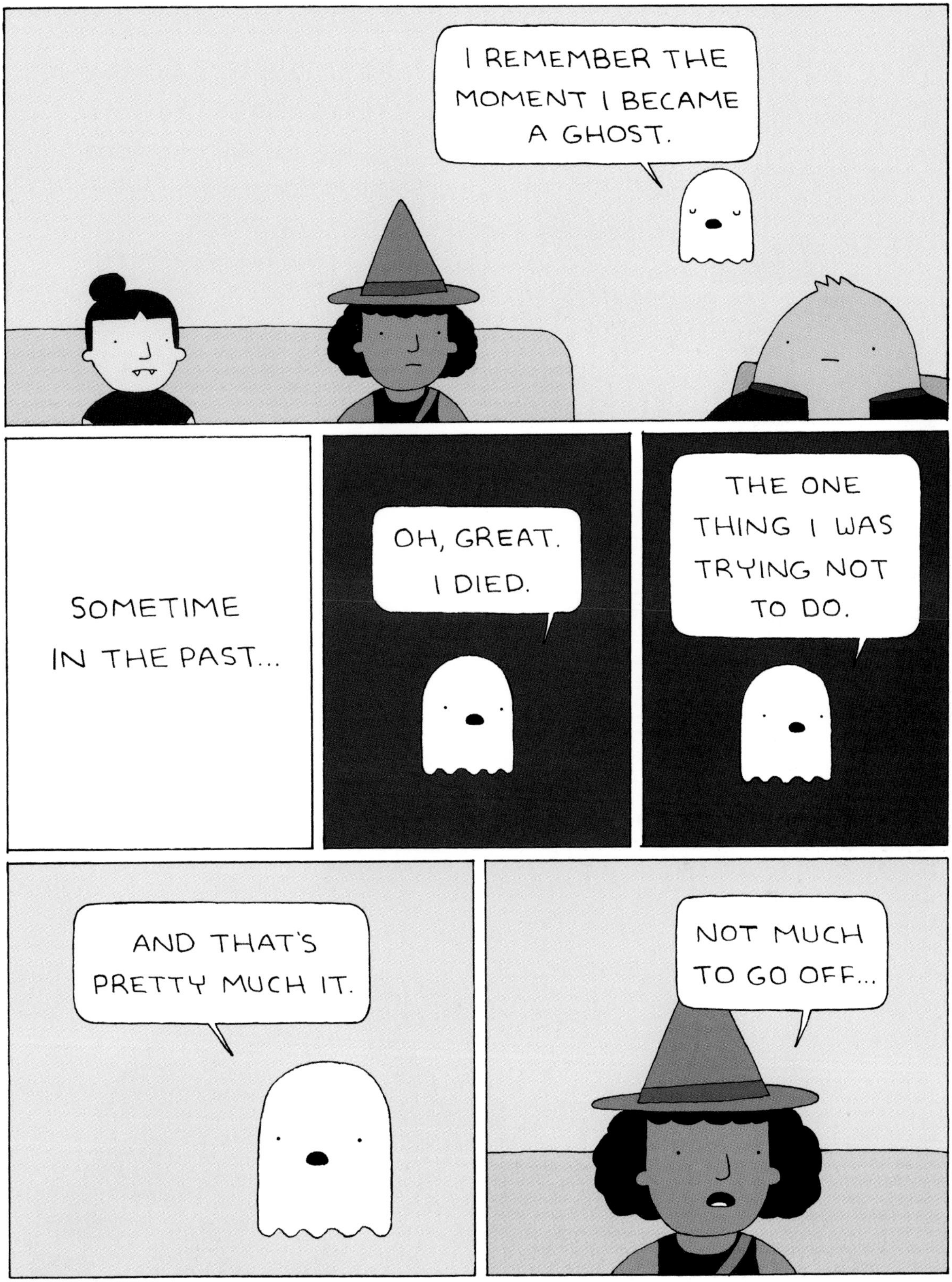

I REMEMBER THE MOMENT I BECAME A GHOST.
SOMETIME IN THE PAST...
OH, GREAT. I DIED.
THE ONE THING I WAS TRYING NOT TO DO.
AND THAT'S PRETTY MUCH IT.
NOT MUCH TO GO OFF...

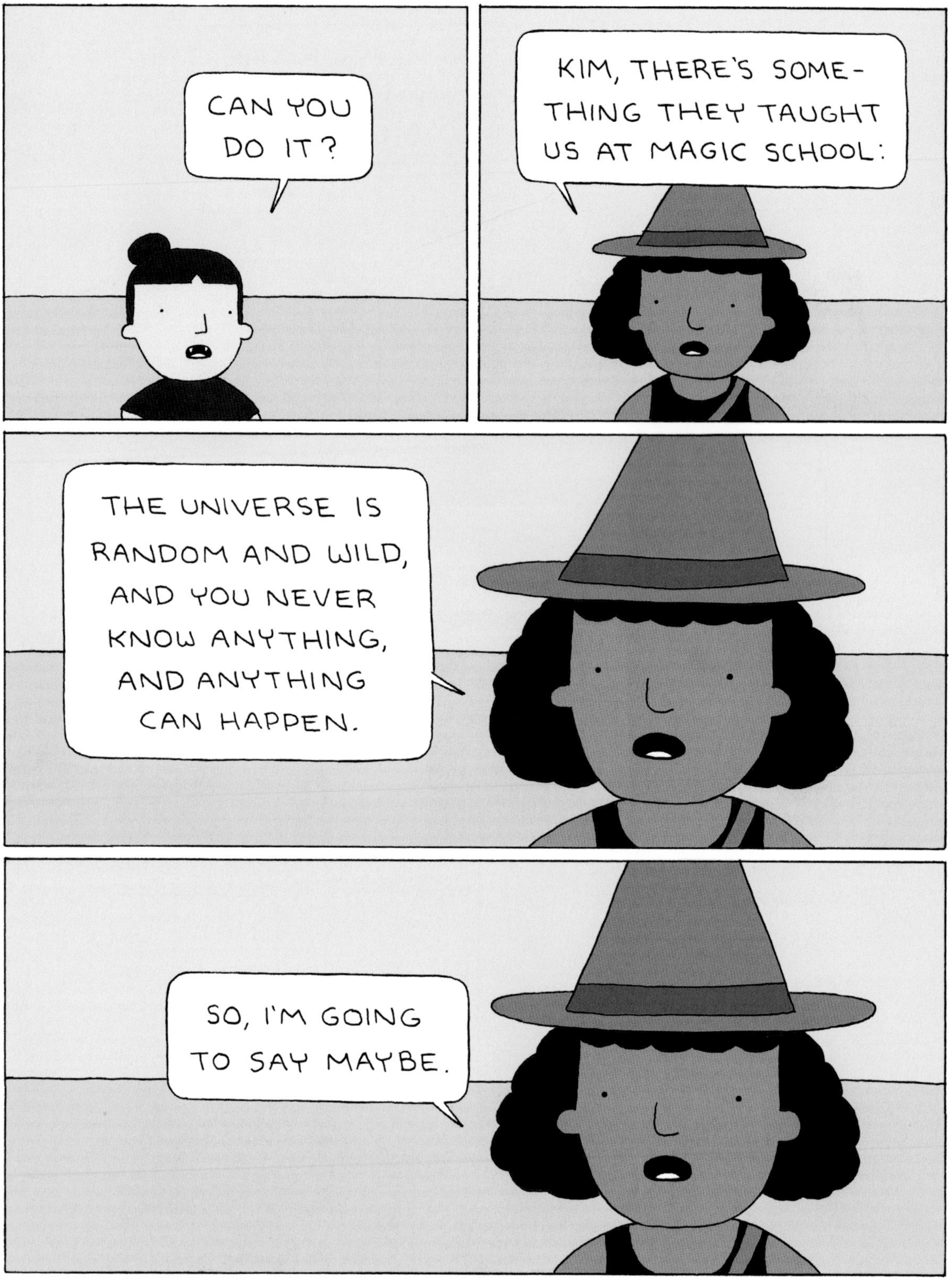
CAN YOU DO IT?
KIM, THERE'S SOME-THING THEY TAUGHT US AT MAGIC SCHOOL:
THE UNIVERSE IS RANDOM AND WILD, AND YOU NEVER KNOW ANYTHING, AND ANYTHING CAN HAPPEN.
SO, I'M GOING TO SAY MAYBE.

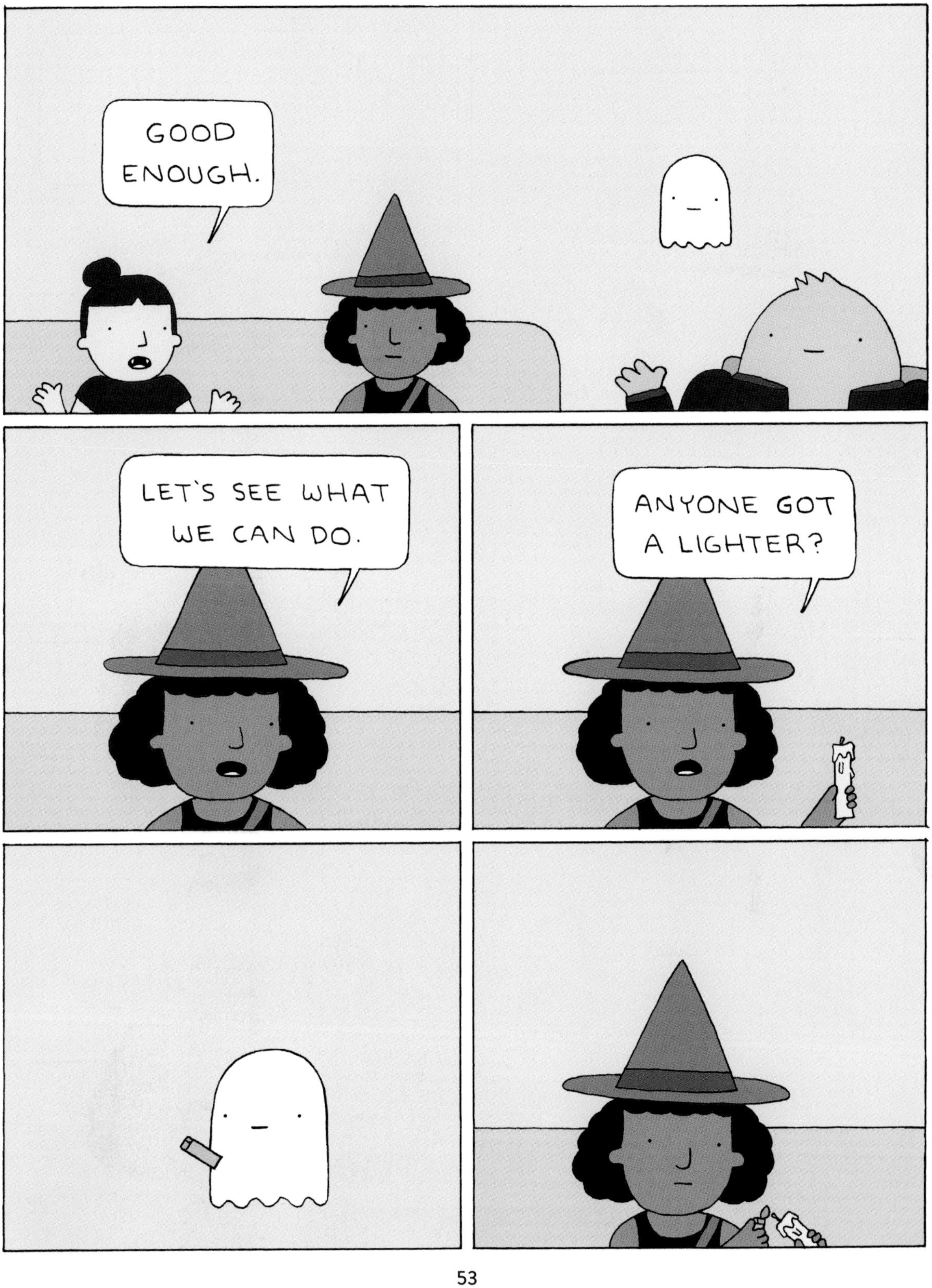
GOOD ENOUGH.
LET'S SEE WHAT WE CAN DO.
ANYONE GOT A LIGHTER?

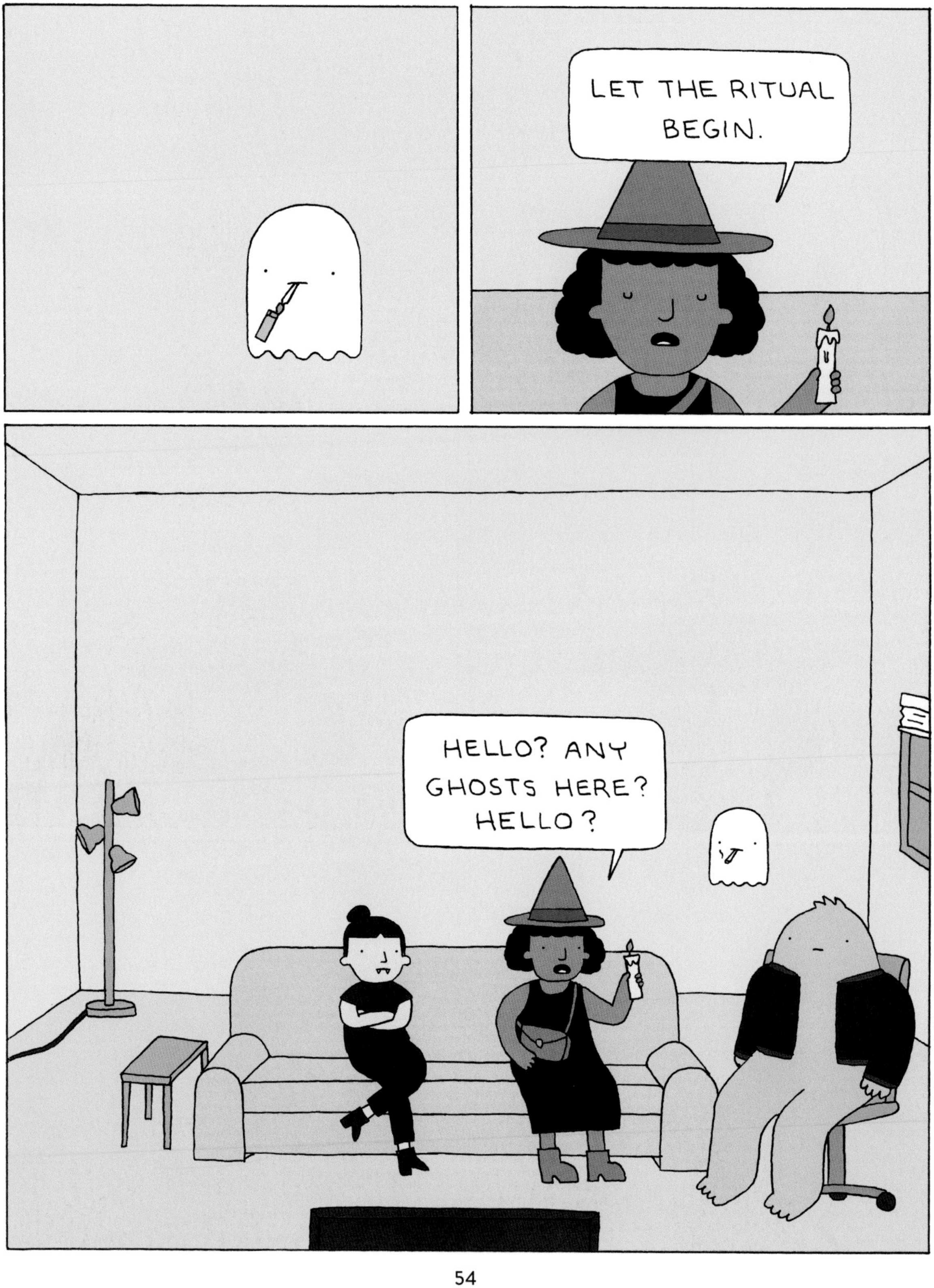
LET THE RITUAL BEGIN.
HELLO? ANY GHOSTS HERE? HELLO?

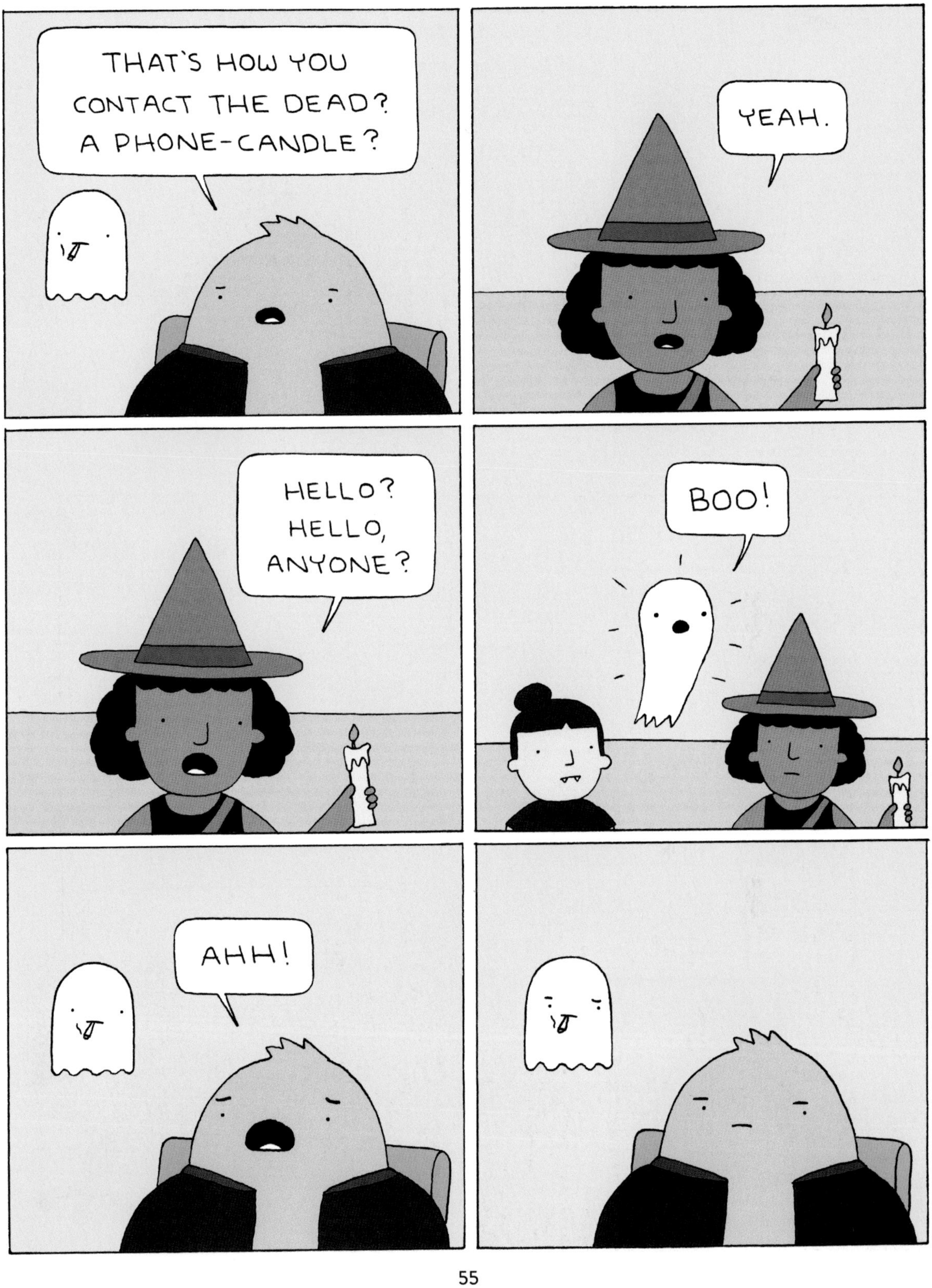
THAT'S HOW YOU CONTACT THE DEAD? A PHONE-CANDLE?
YEAH.
HELLO? HELLO, ANYONE?
BOO!
AHH!

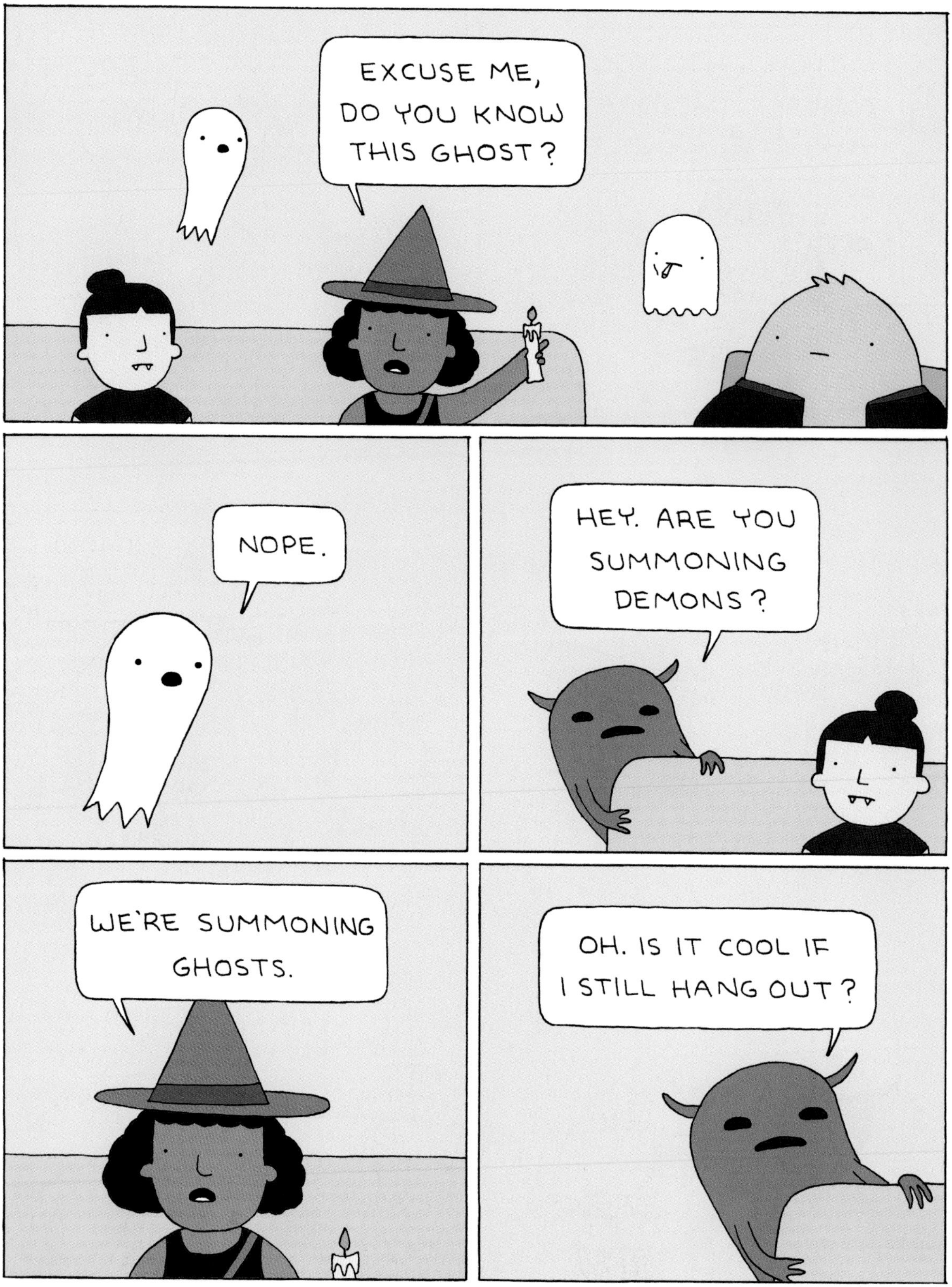
EXCUSE ME, DO YOU KNOW THIS GHOST?
NOPE.
HEY. ARE YOU SUMMONING DEMONS?
WE'RE SUMMONING GHOSTS.
OH. IS IT COOL IF I STILL HANG OUT?

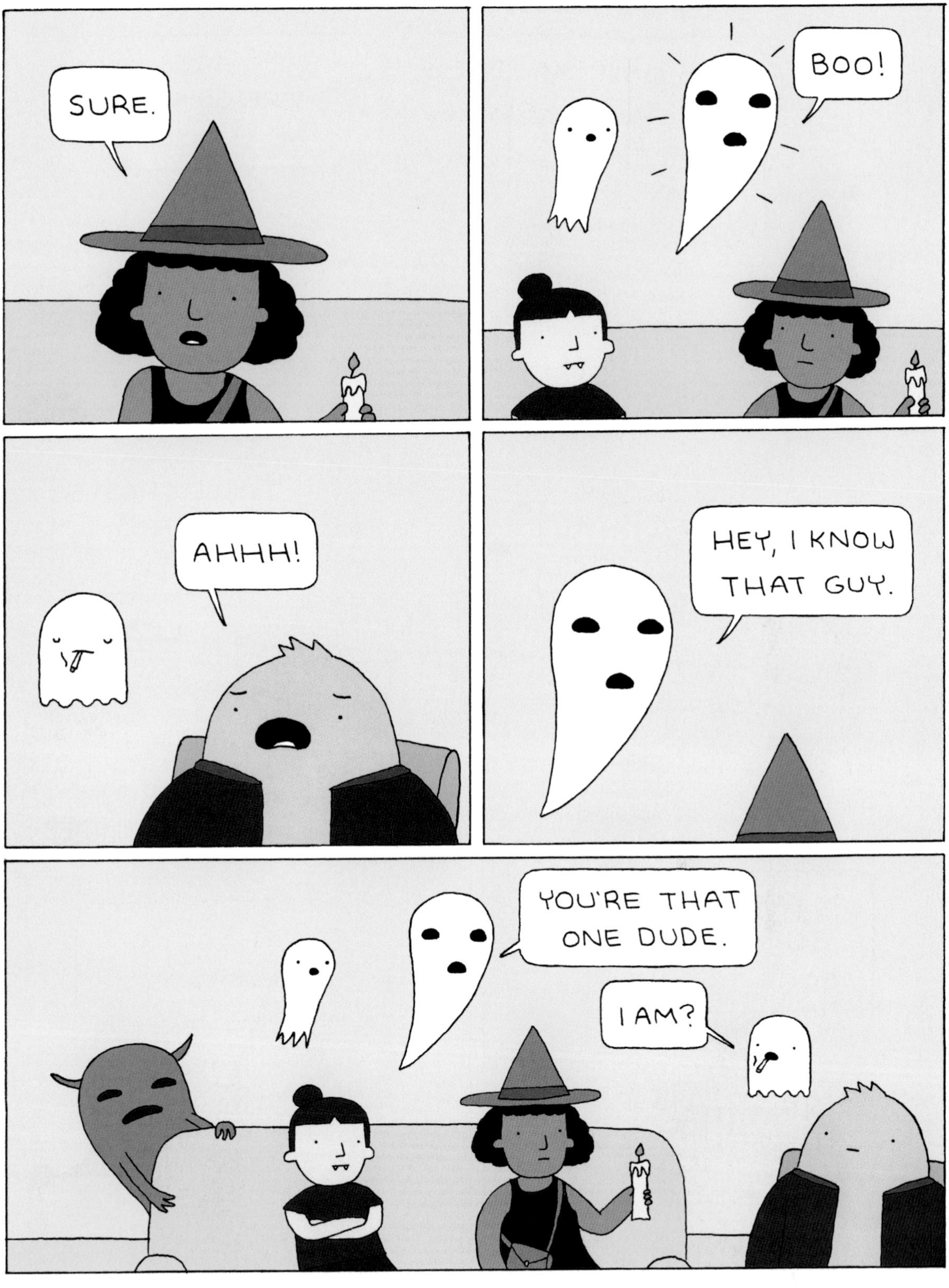
SURE.
BOO!
AHHH!
HEY, I KNOW THAT GUY.
YOU'RE THAT ONE DUDE.
I AM?

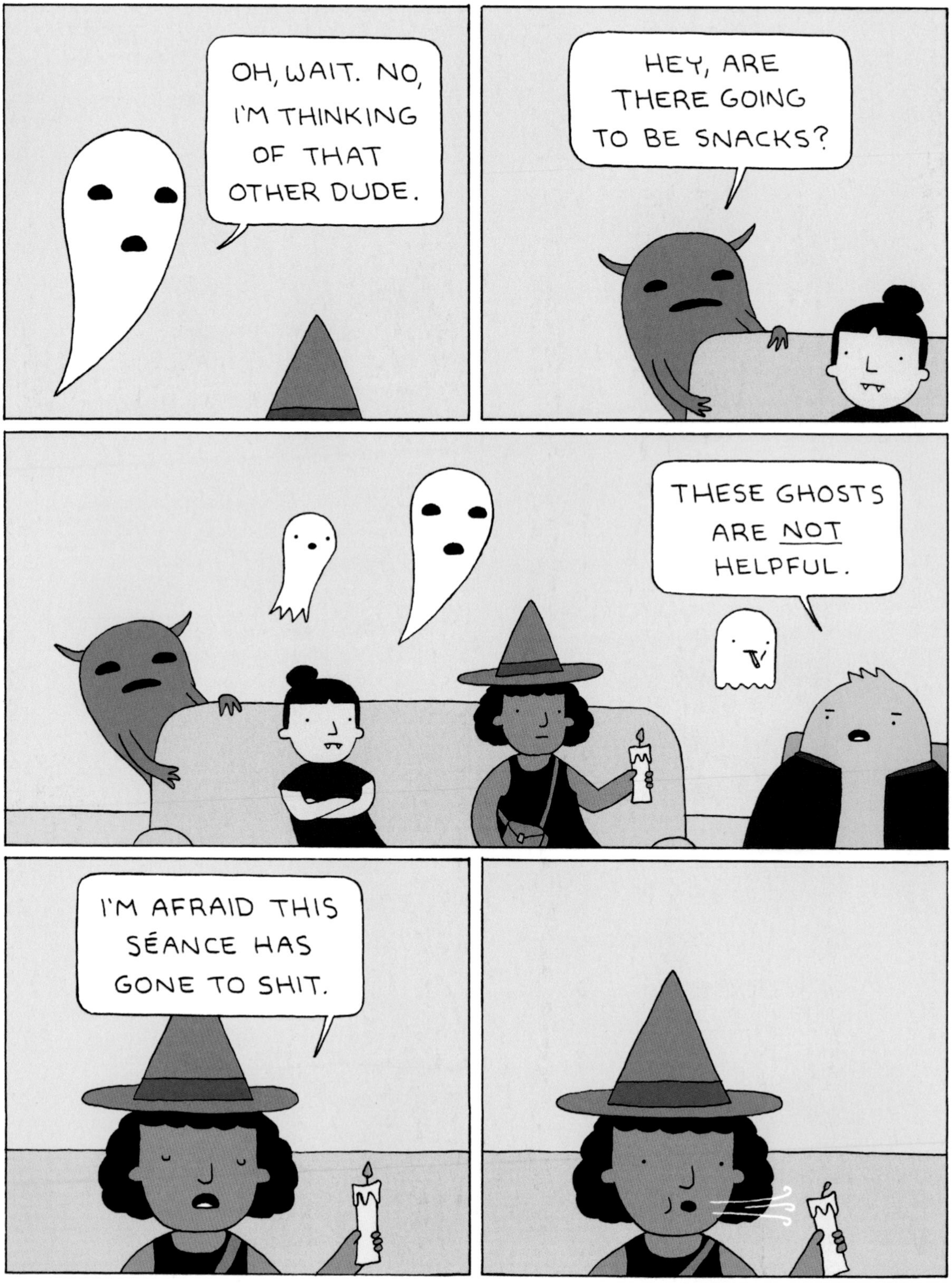

OH, WAIT. NO, I'M THINKING OF THAT OTHER DUDE.
HEY, ARE THERE GOING TO BE SNACKS?
THESE GHOSTS ARE NOT HELPFUL.
I'M AFRAID THIS SÉANCE HAS GONE TO SHIT.

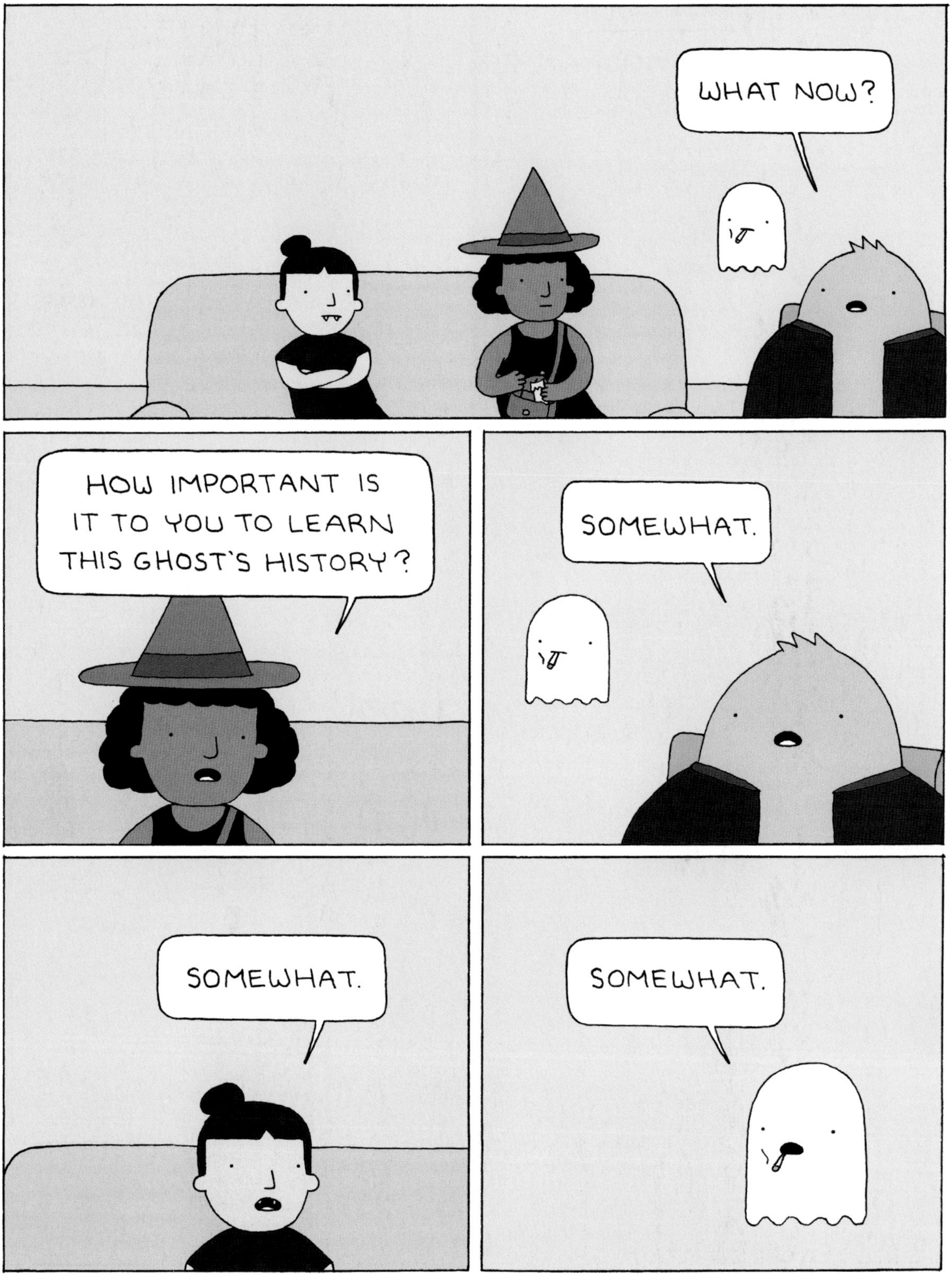
WHAT NOW?
HOW IMPORTANT IS IT TO YOU TO LEARN THIS GHOST'S HISTORY?
SOMEWHAT.
SOMEWHAT.
SOMEWHAT.

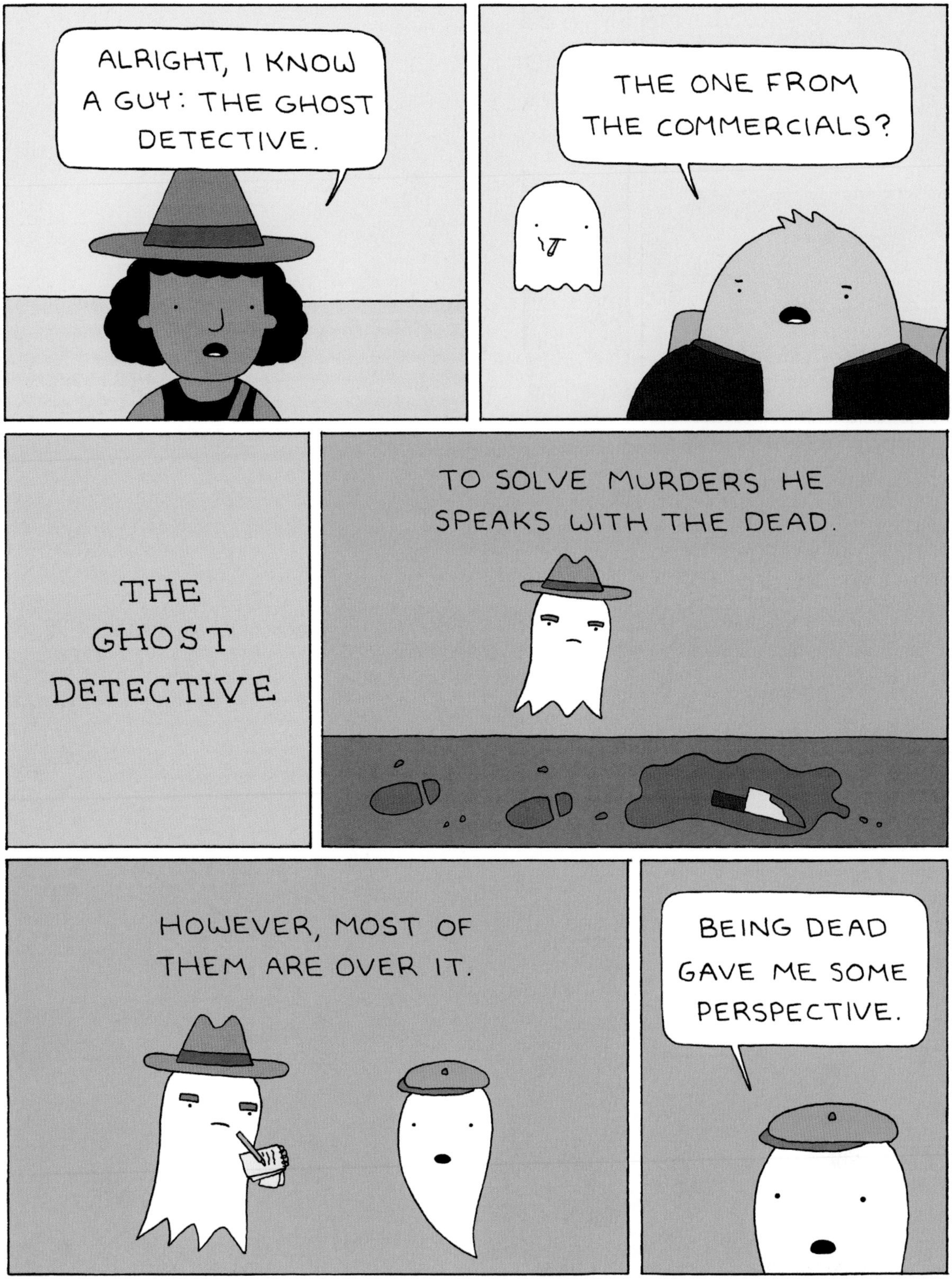
ALRIGHT, I KNOW A GUY: THE GHOST DETECTIVE.
THE ONE FROM THE COMMERCIALS?
THE GHOST DETECTIVE
TO SOLVE MURDERS HE SPEAKS WITH THE DEAD.
HOWEVER, MOST OF THEM ARE OVER IT.
BEING DEAD GAVE ME SOME PERSPECTIVE.

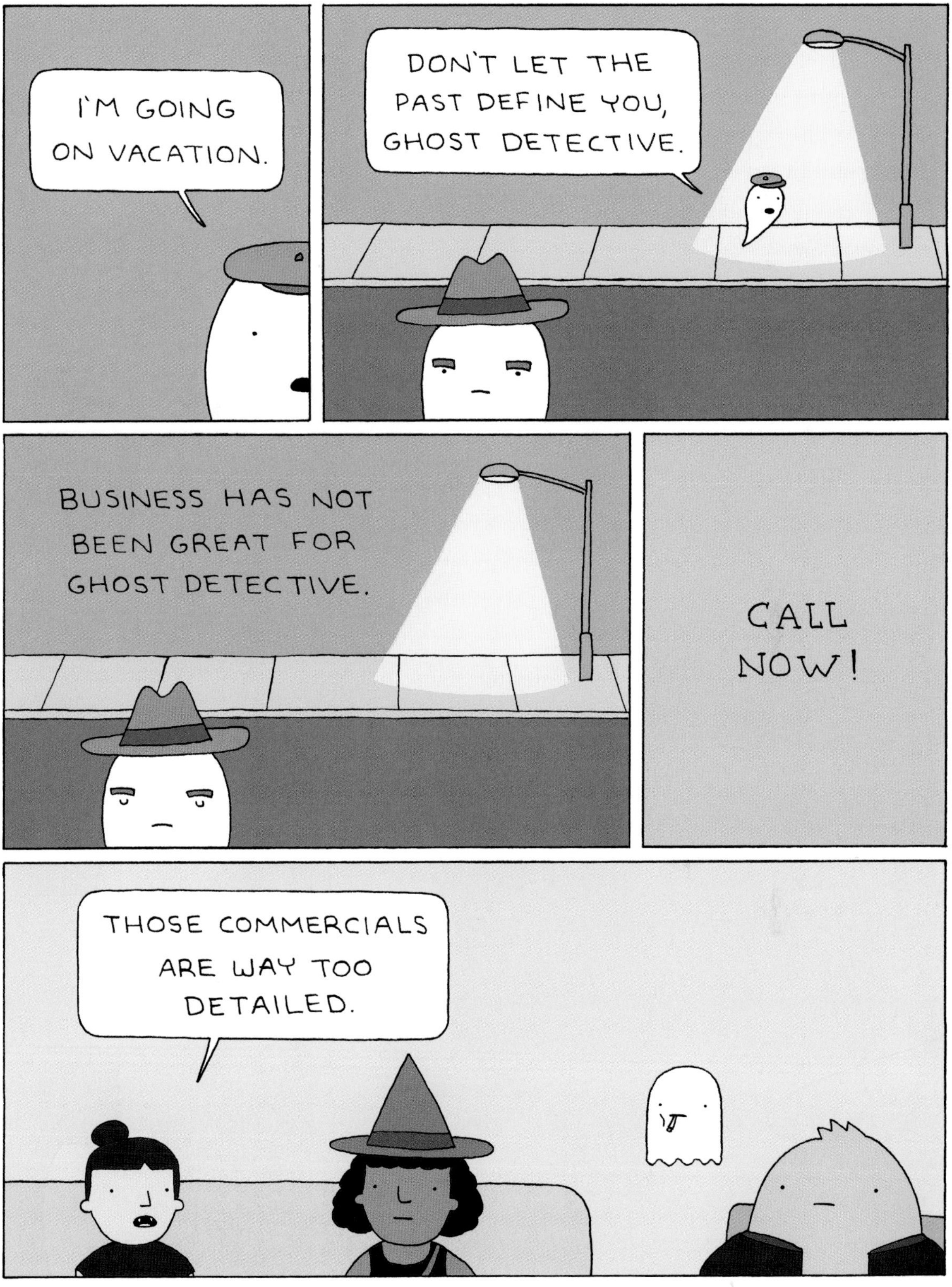
I'M GOING ON VACATION.
DON'T LET THE PAST DEFINE YOU, GHOST DETECTIVE.
BUSINESS HAS NOT BEEN GREAT FOR GHOST DETECTIVE.
CALL NOW!
THOSE COMMERCIALS ARE WAY TOO DETAILED.

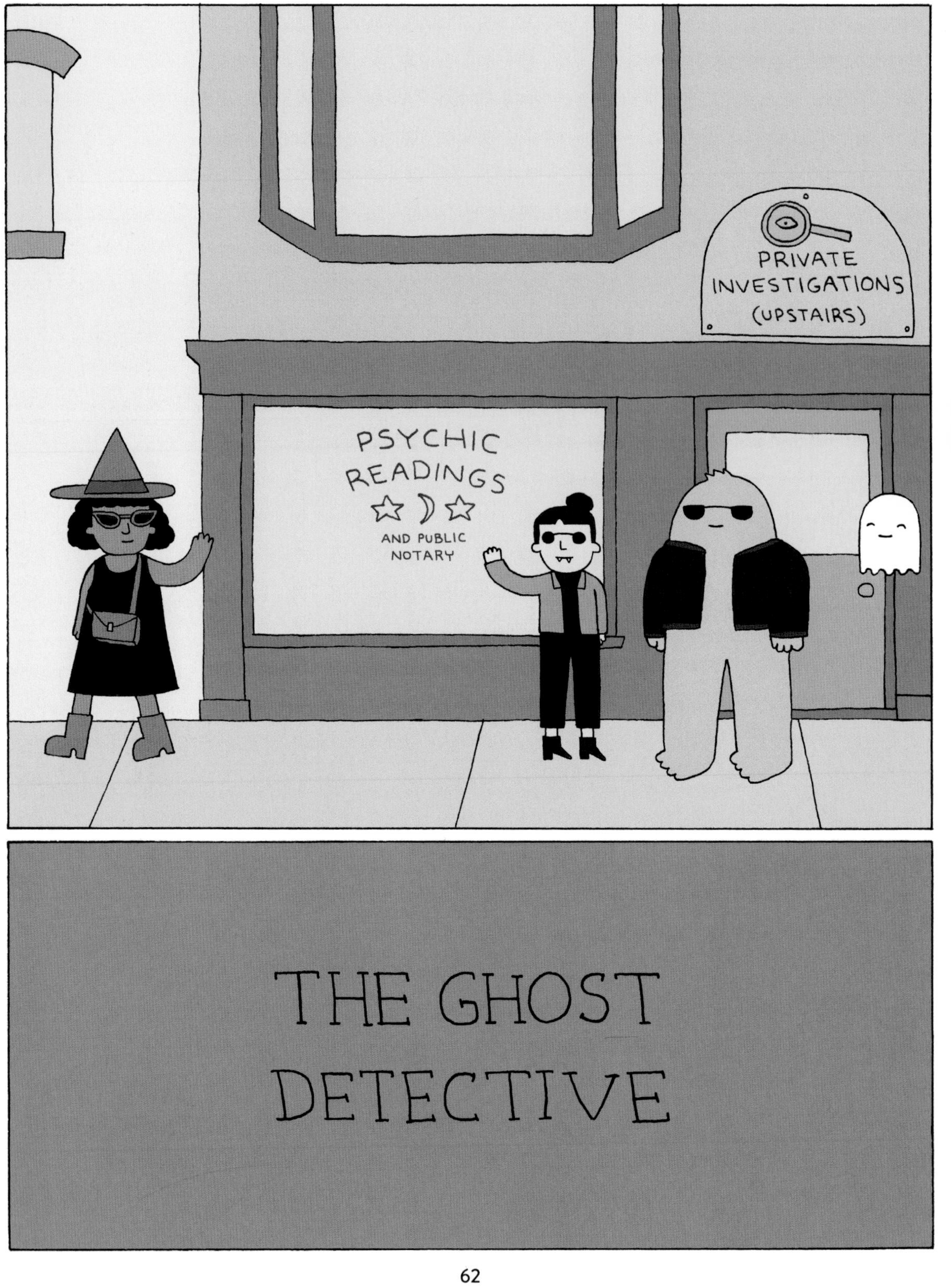
PRIVATE
INVESTIGATIONS
(UPSTAIRS)
PSYCHIC
READINGS
AND PUBLIC
NOTARY

THE GHOST DETECTIVE

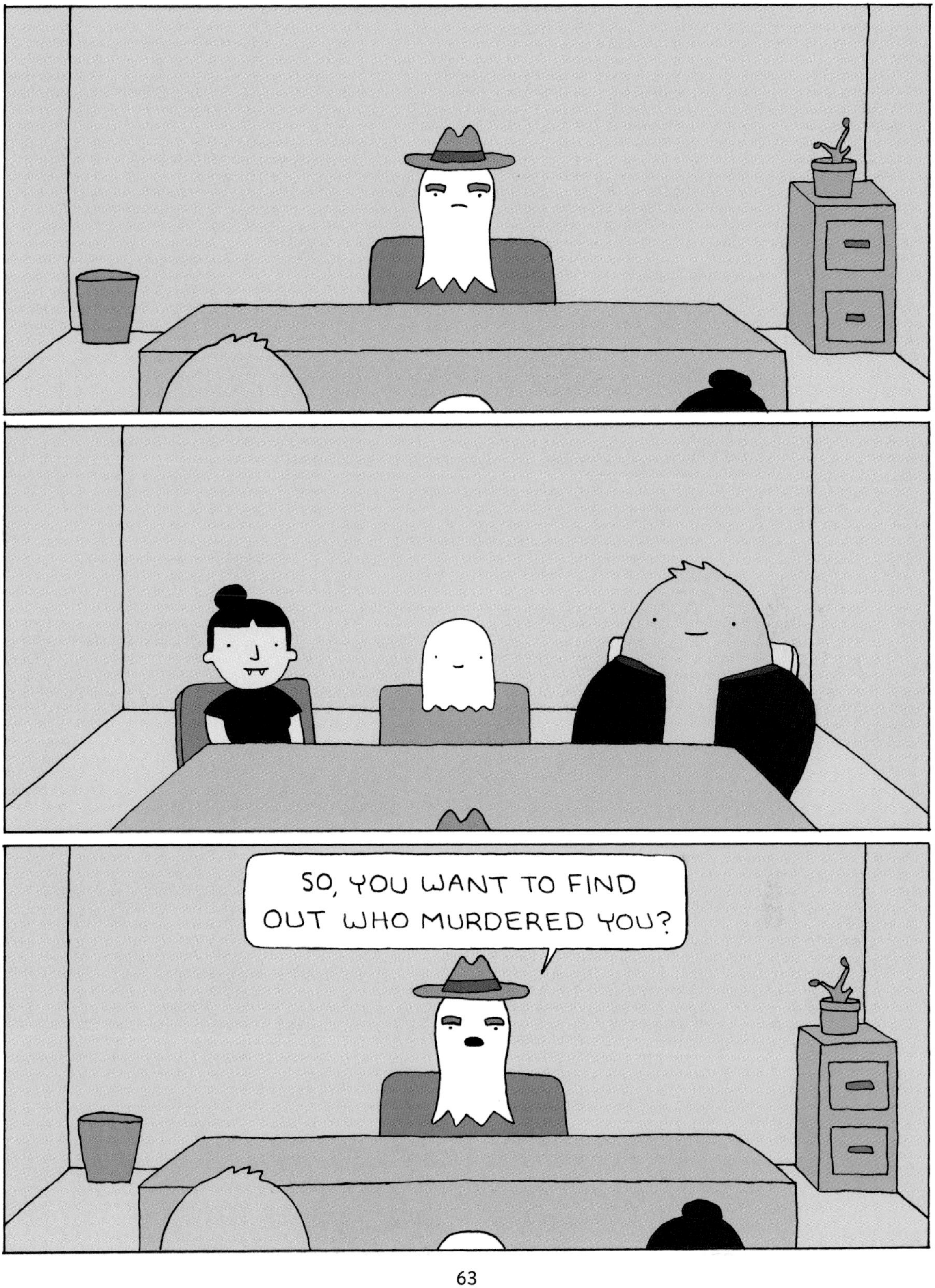
SO, YOU WANT TO FIND OUT WHO MURDERED YOU?

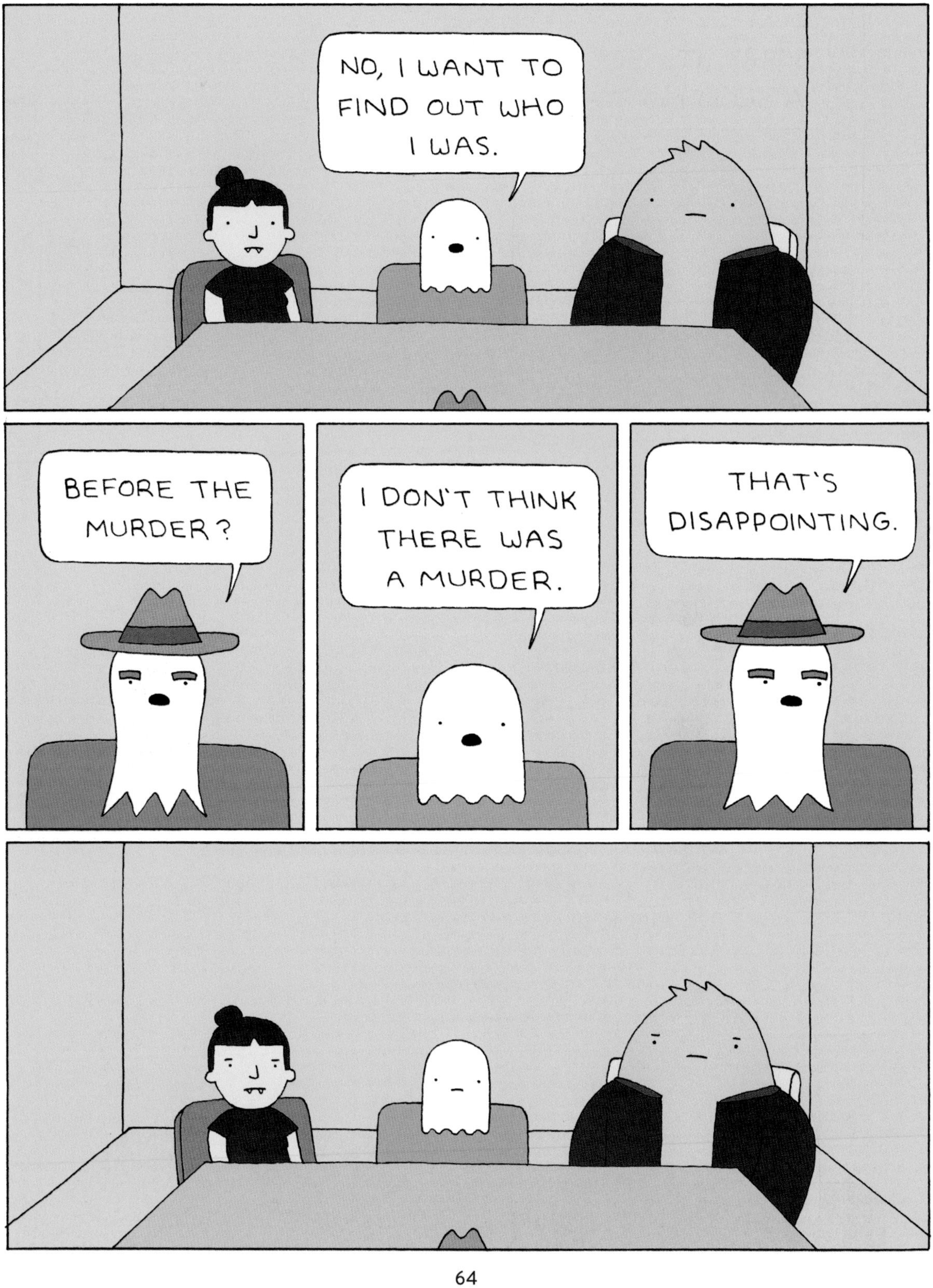
NO, I WANT TO FIND OUT WHO I WAS.
BEFORE THE MURDER?
I DON'T THINK THERE WAS A MURDER.
THAT'S DISAPPOINTING.

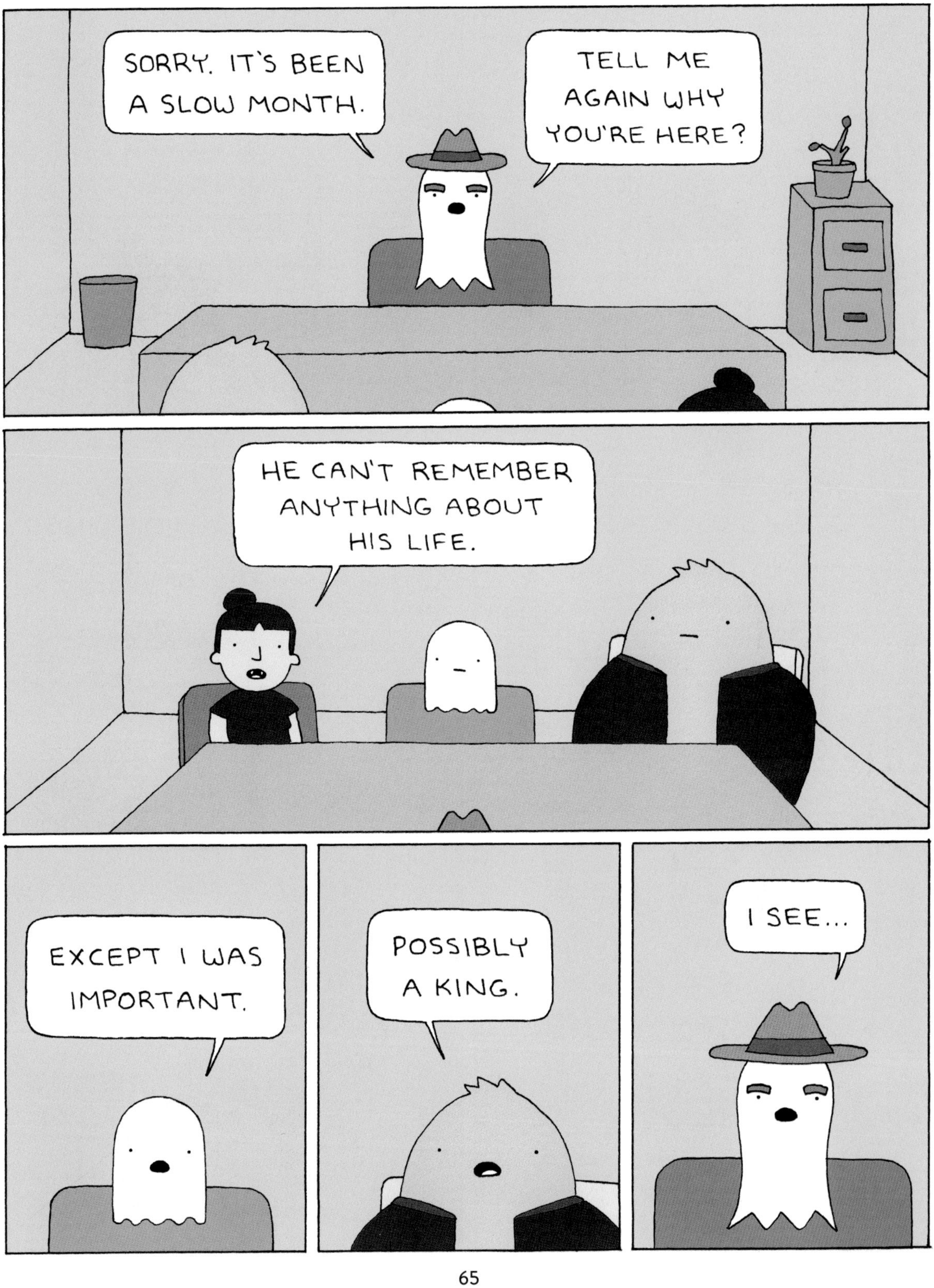

SORRY. IT'S BEEN A SLOW MONTH.
TELL ME AGAIN WHY YOU'RE HERE?
HE CAN'T REMEMBER ANYTHING ABOUT HIS LIFE.
EXCEPT I WAS IMPORTANT.
POSSIBLY A KING.
I SEE...

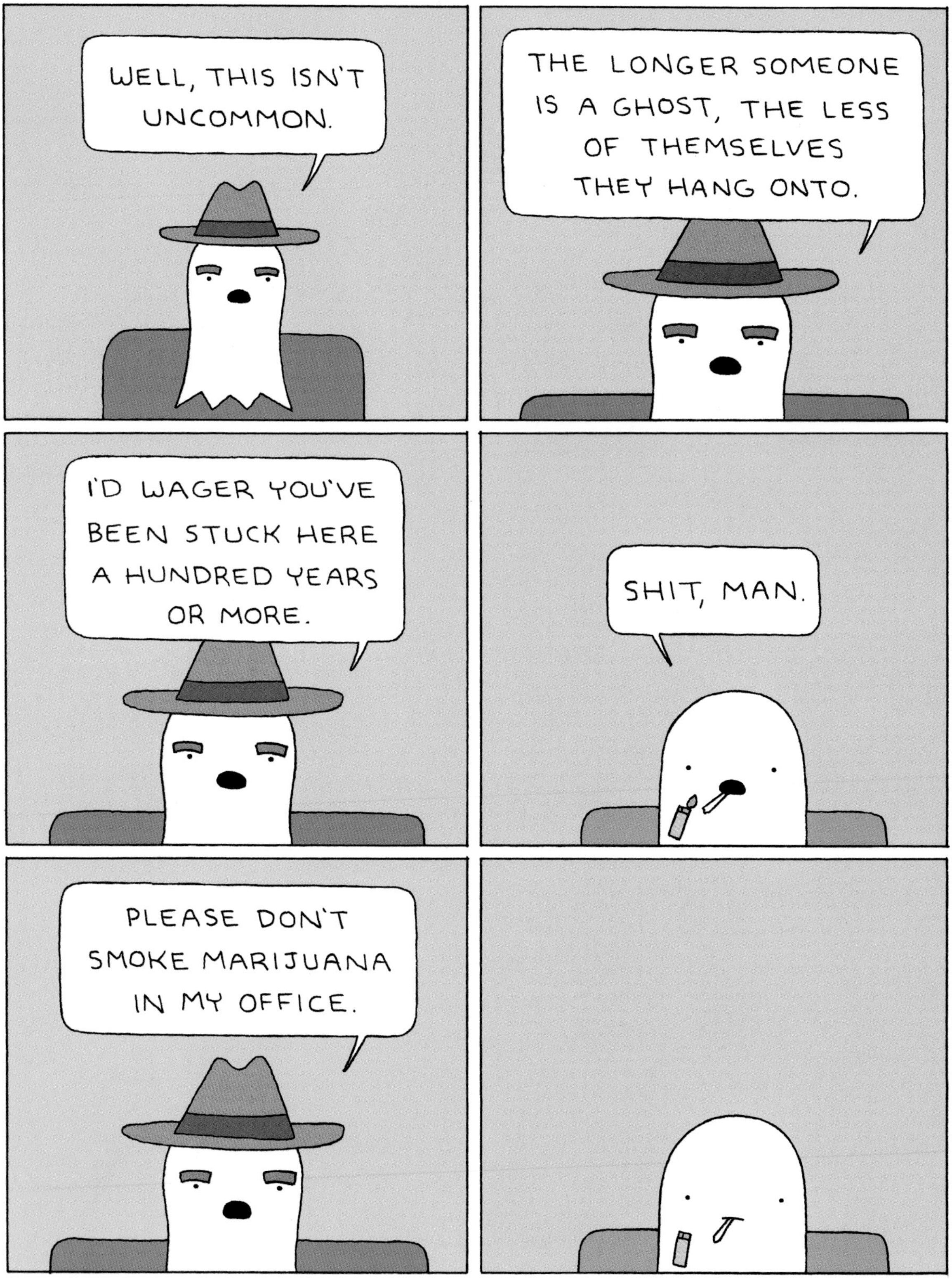
WELL, THIS ISN'T UNCOMMON.
THE LONGER SOMEONE IS A GHOST, THE LESS OF THEMSELVES THEY HANG ONTO.
I'D WAGER YOU'VE BEEN STUCK HERE A HUNDRED YEARS OR MORE.
SHIT, MAN.
PLEASE DON'T SMOKE MARIJUANA IN MY OFFICE.

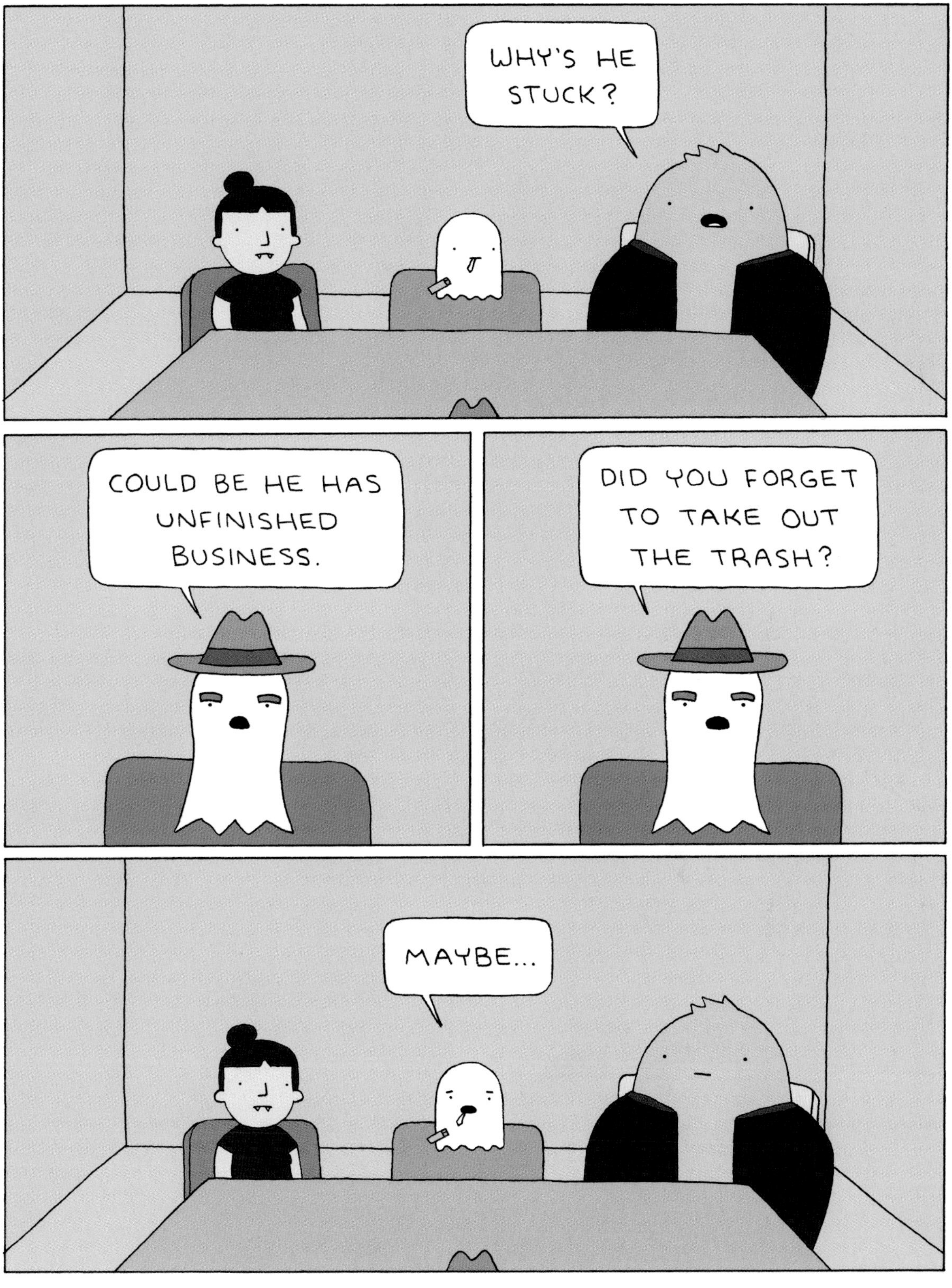
WHY'S HE STUCK?
COULD BE HE HAS UNFINISHED BUSINESS.
DID YOU FORGET TO TAKE OUT THE TRASH?
MAYBE...

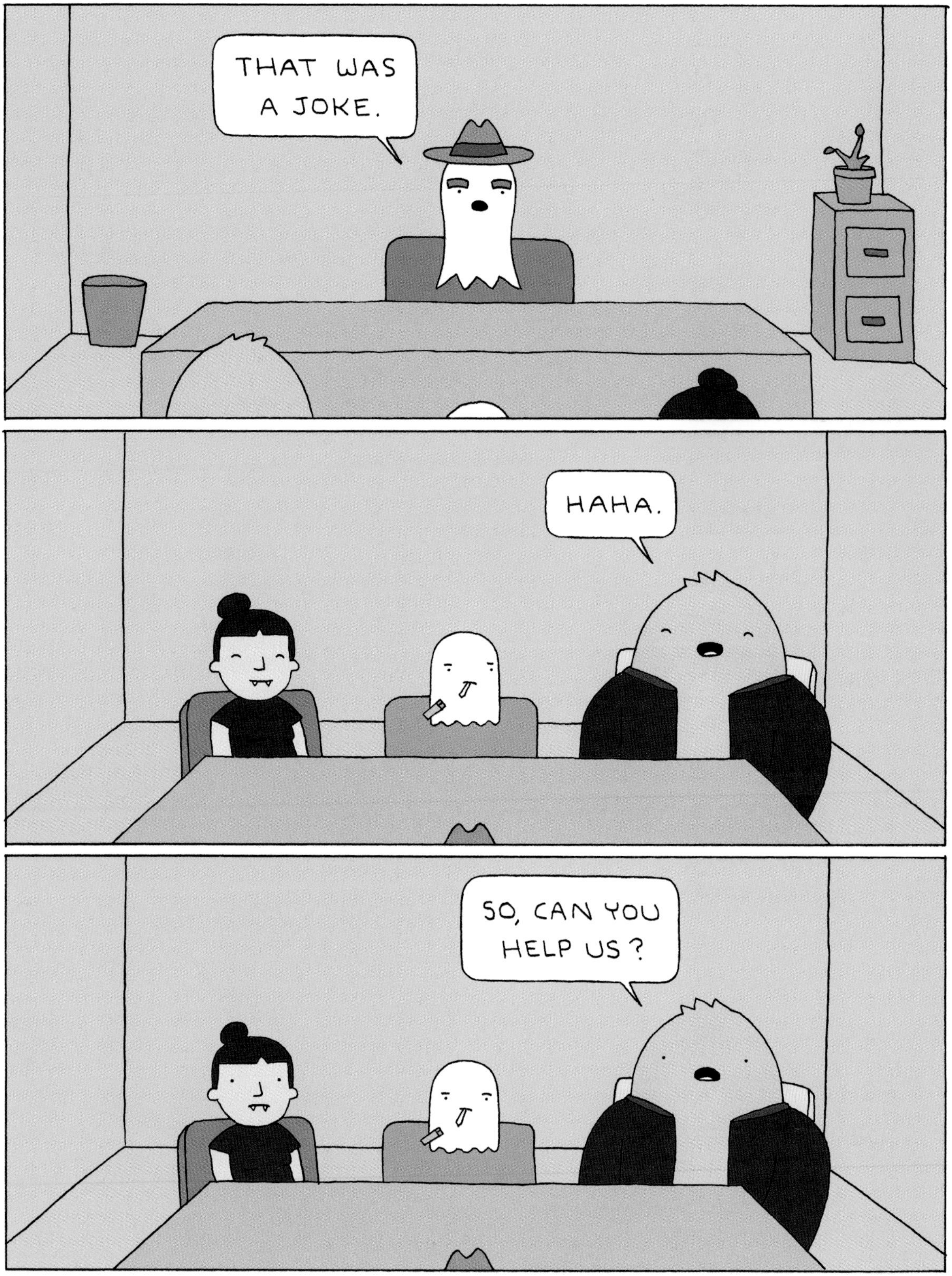
THAT WAS A JOKE.
HAHA.
SO, CAN YOU HELP US?

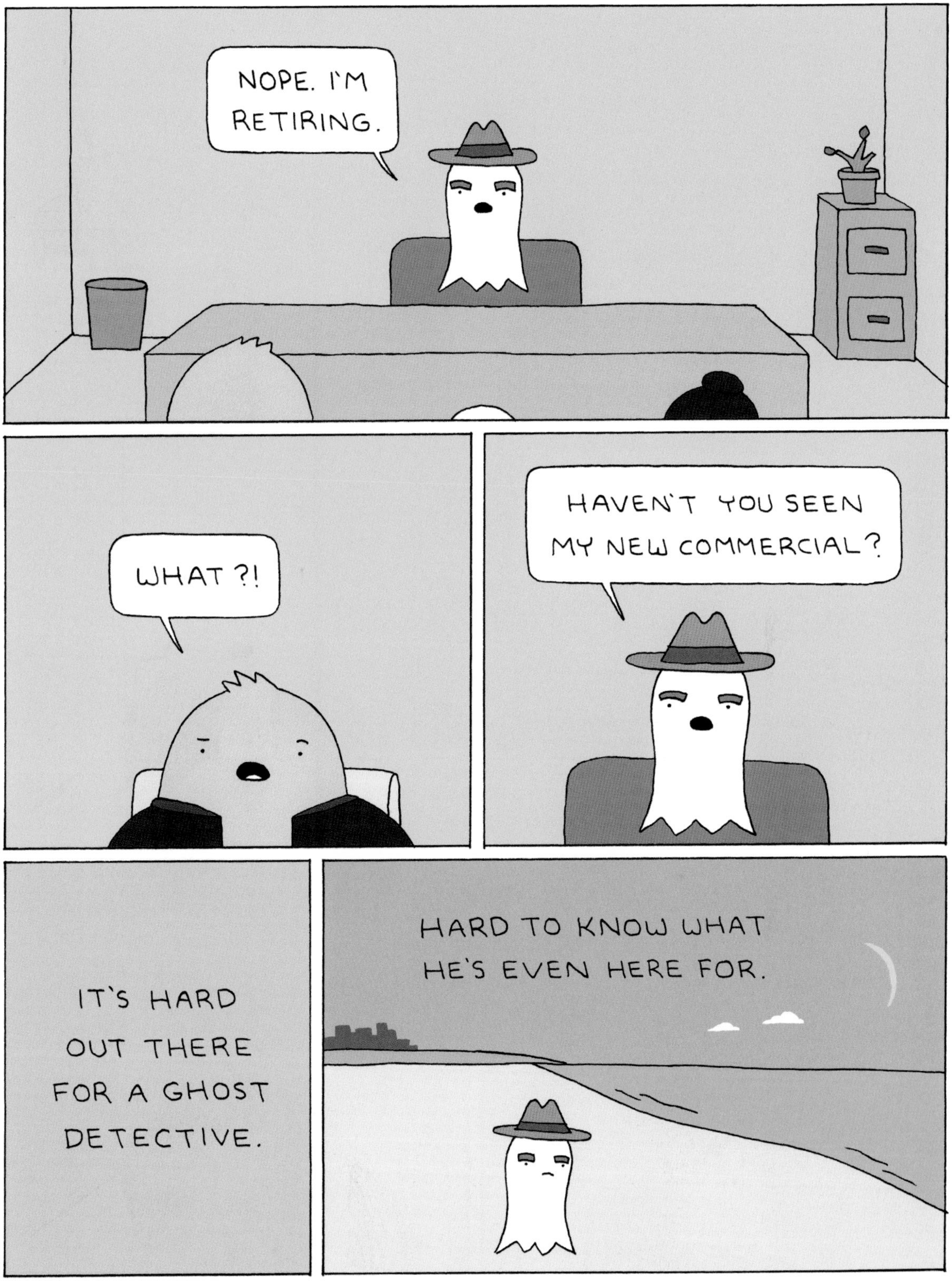
NOPE. I'M RETIRING.
WHAT?!
HAVEN'T YOU SEEN MY NEW COMMERCIAL?
IT'S HARD OUT THERE FOR A GHOST DETECTIVE.
HARD TO KNOW WHAT HE'S EVEN HERE FOR.

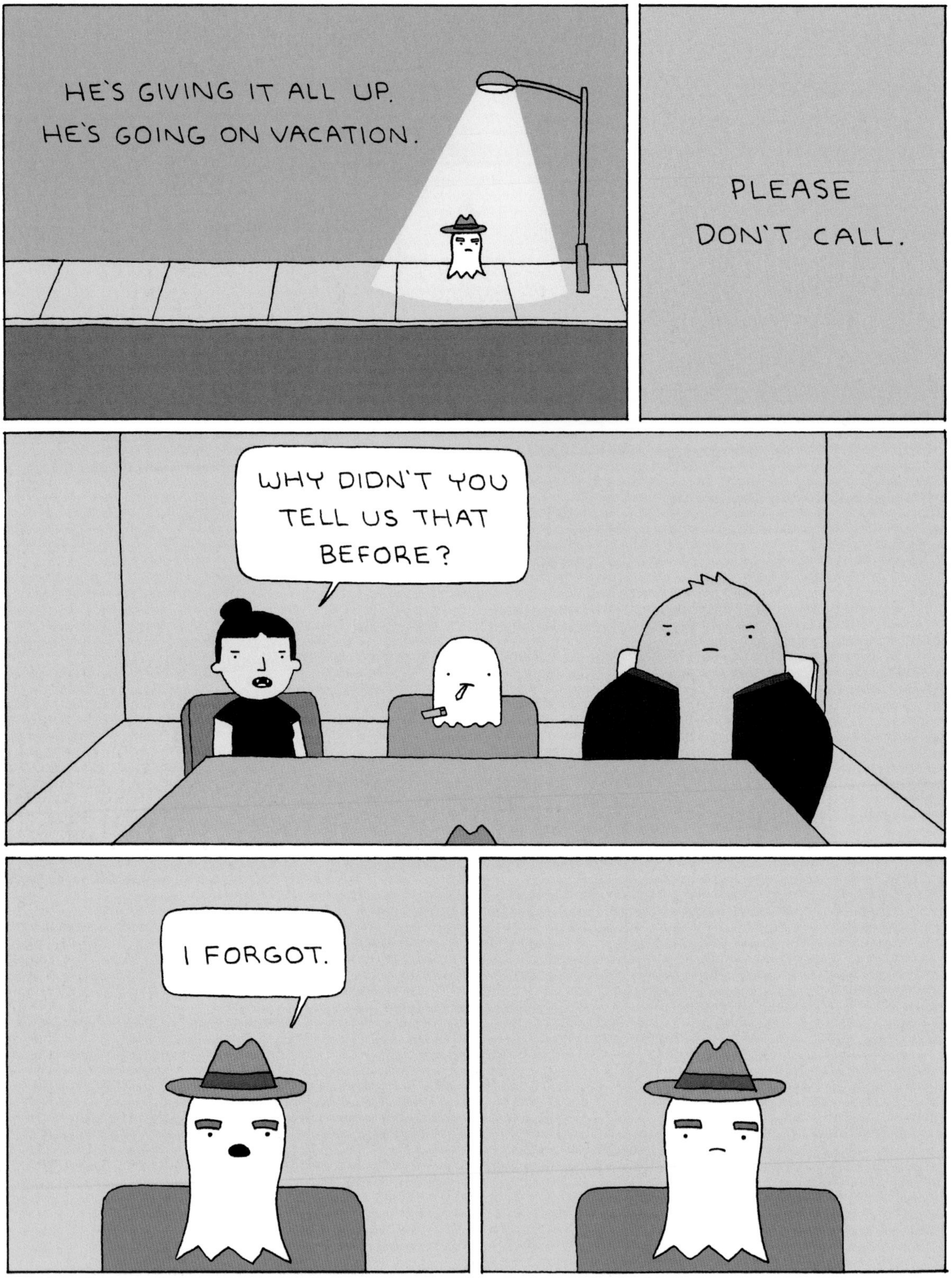
HE'S GIVING IT ALL UP.
HE'S GOING ON VACATION.
PLEASE DON'T CALL.
WHY DIDN'T YOU TELL US THAT BEFORE?
I FORGOT.

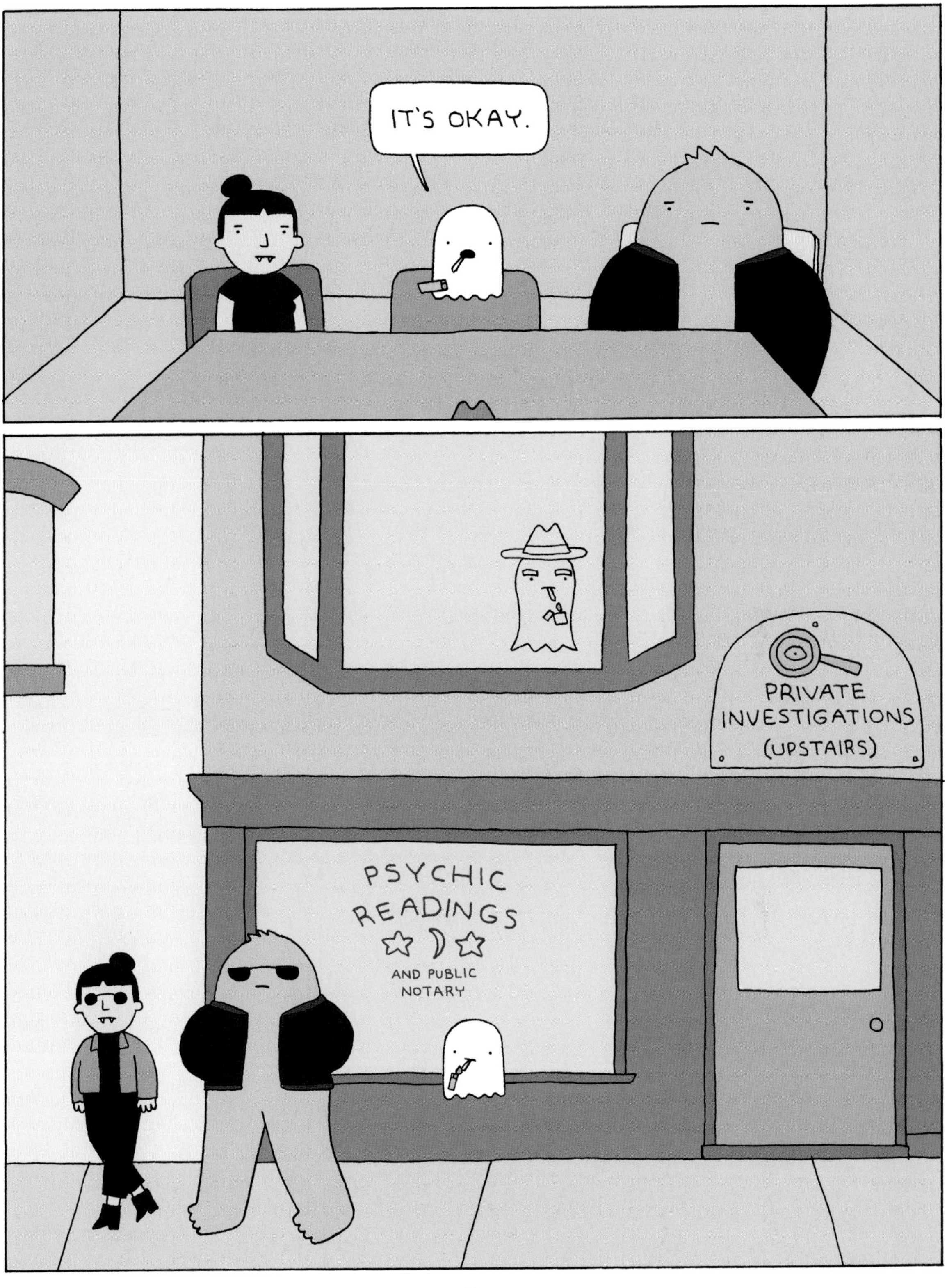
IT'S OKAY.
PRIVATE INVESTIGATIONS (UPSTAIRS)
PSYCHIC READINGS
AND PUBLIC NOTARY

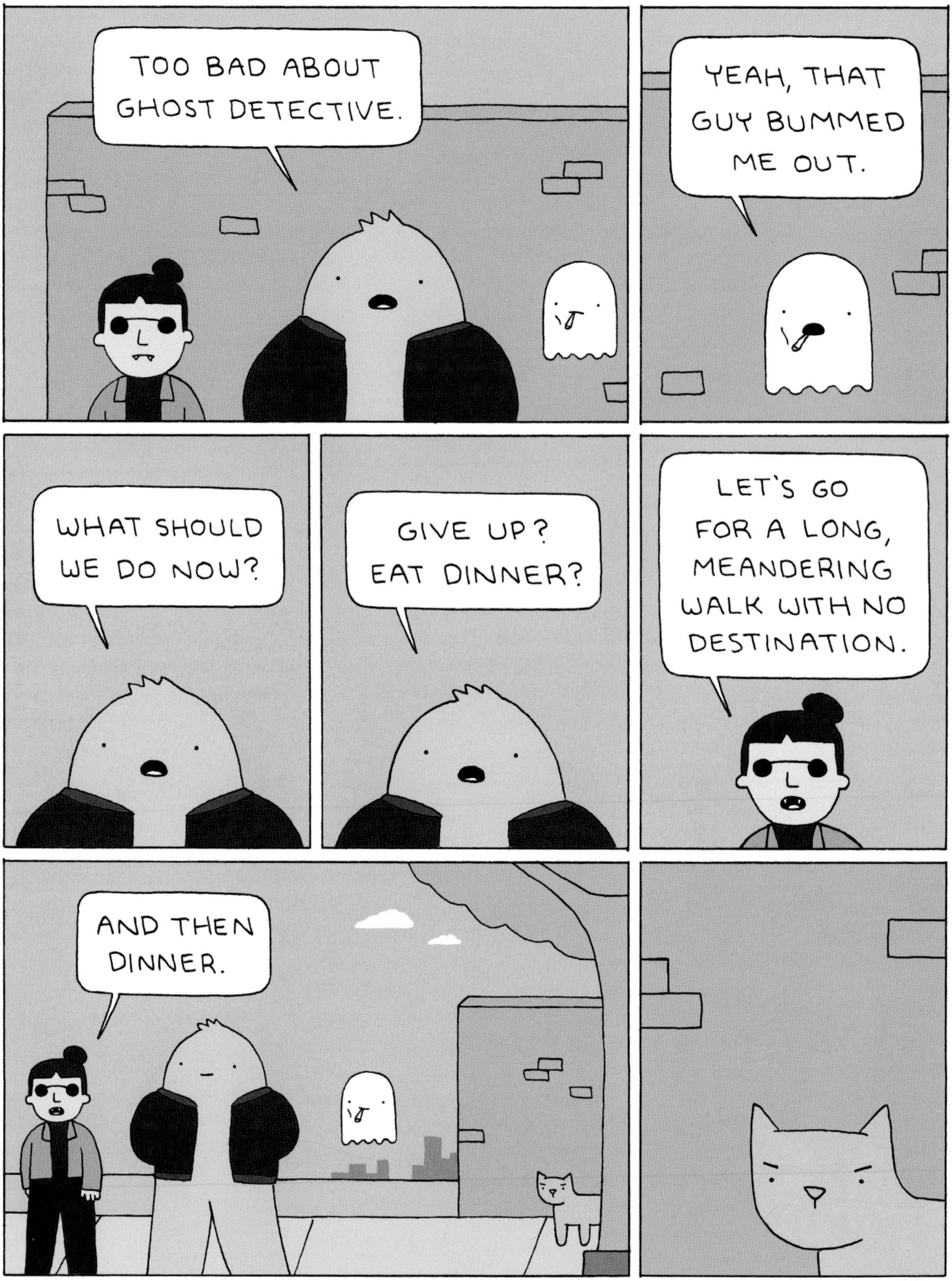
TOO BAD ABOUT GHOST DETECTIVE.
YEAH, THAT GUY BUMMED ME OUT.
WHAT SHOULD WE DO NOW?
GIVE UP? EAT DINNER?
LET'S GO FOR A LONG, MEANDERING WALK WITH NO DESTINATION.
AND THEN DINNER.

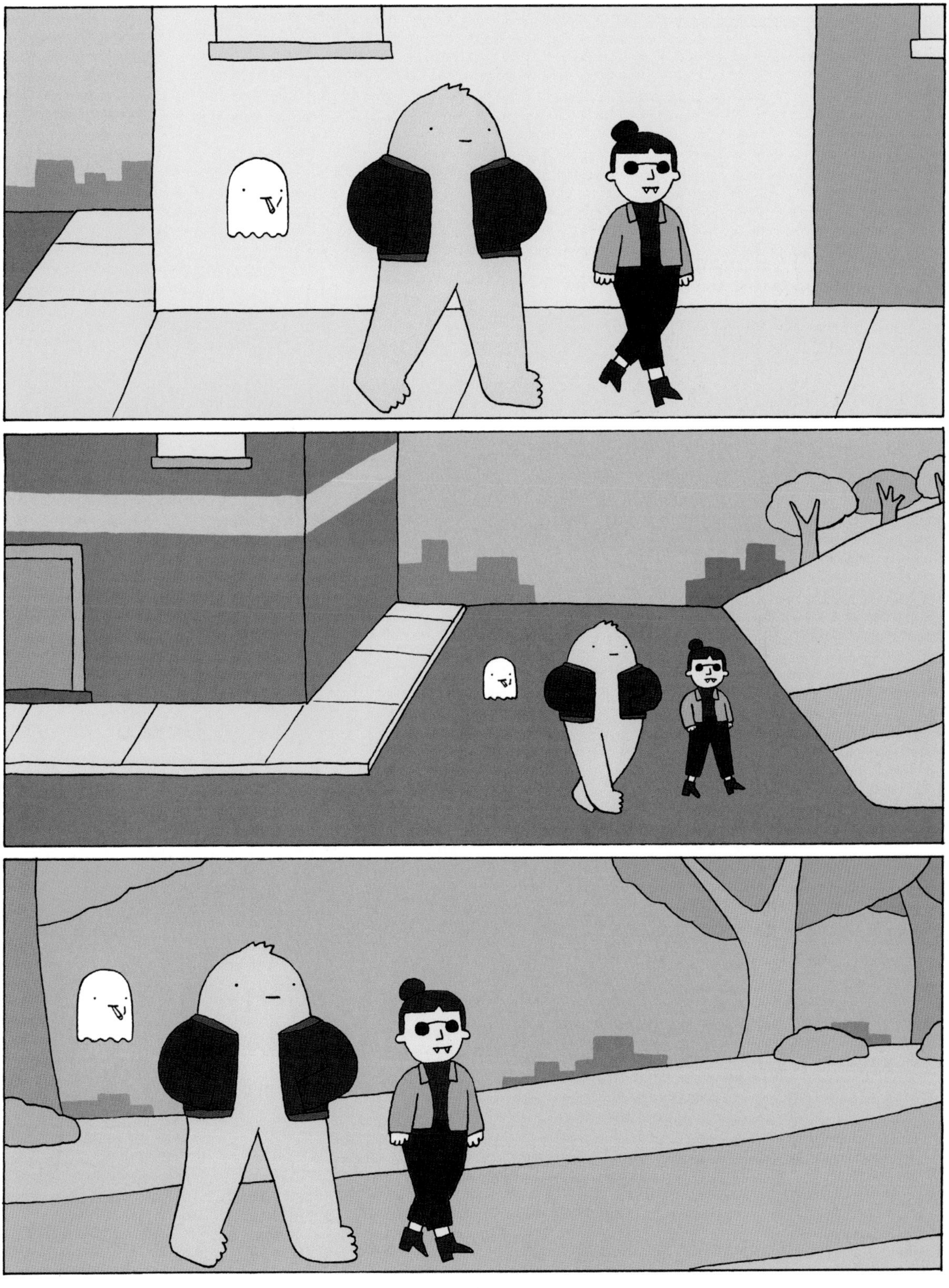

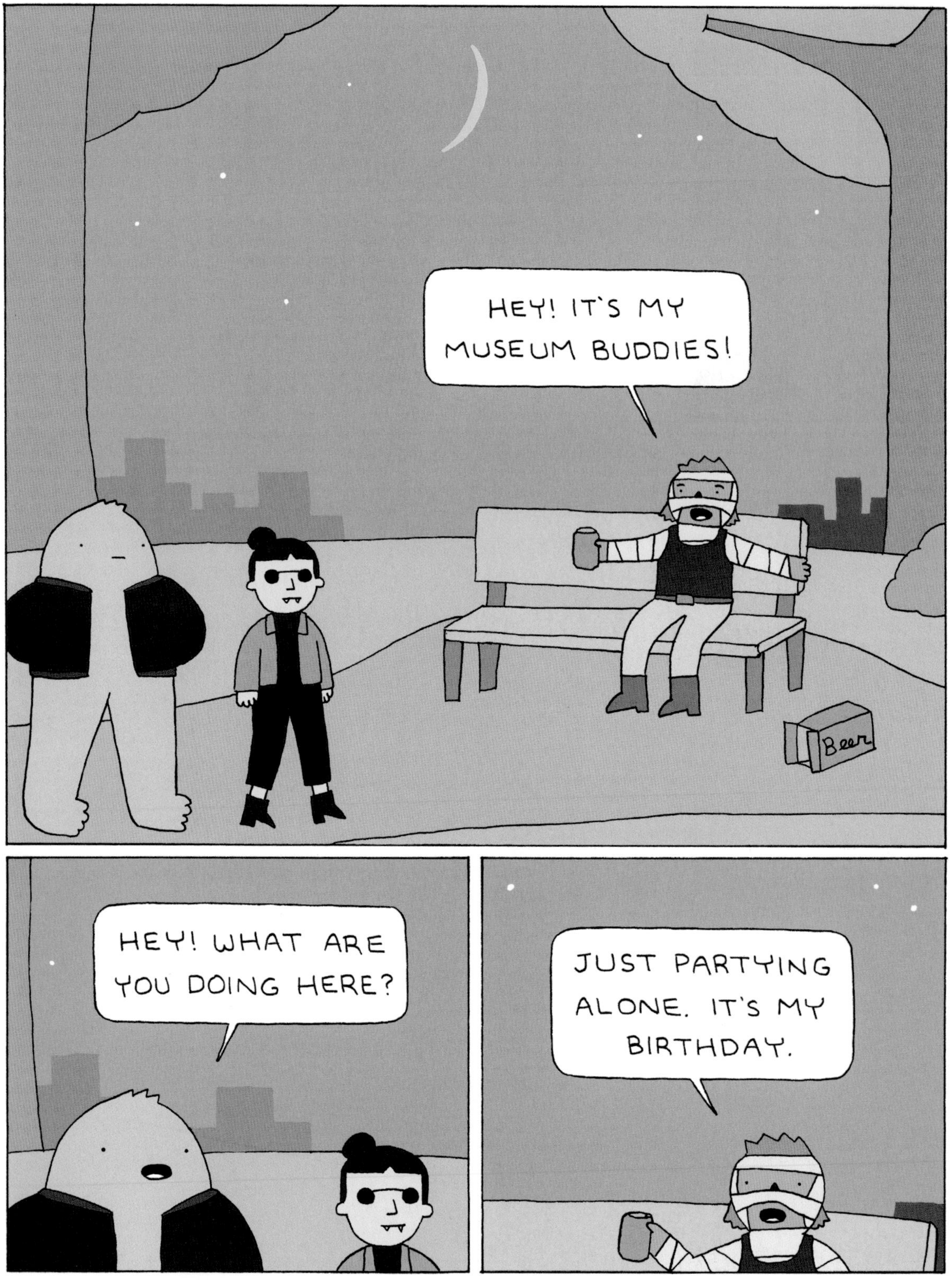
HEY! IT'S MY MUSEUM BUDDIES!
Beer
HEY! WHAT ARE YOU DOING HERE?
JUST PARTYING ALONE. IT'S MY BIRTHDAY.

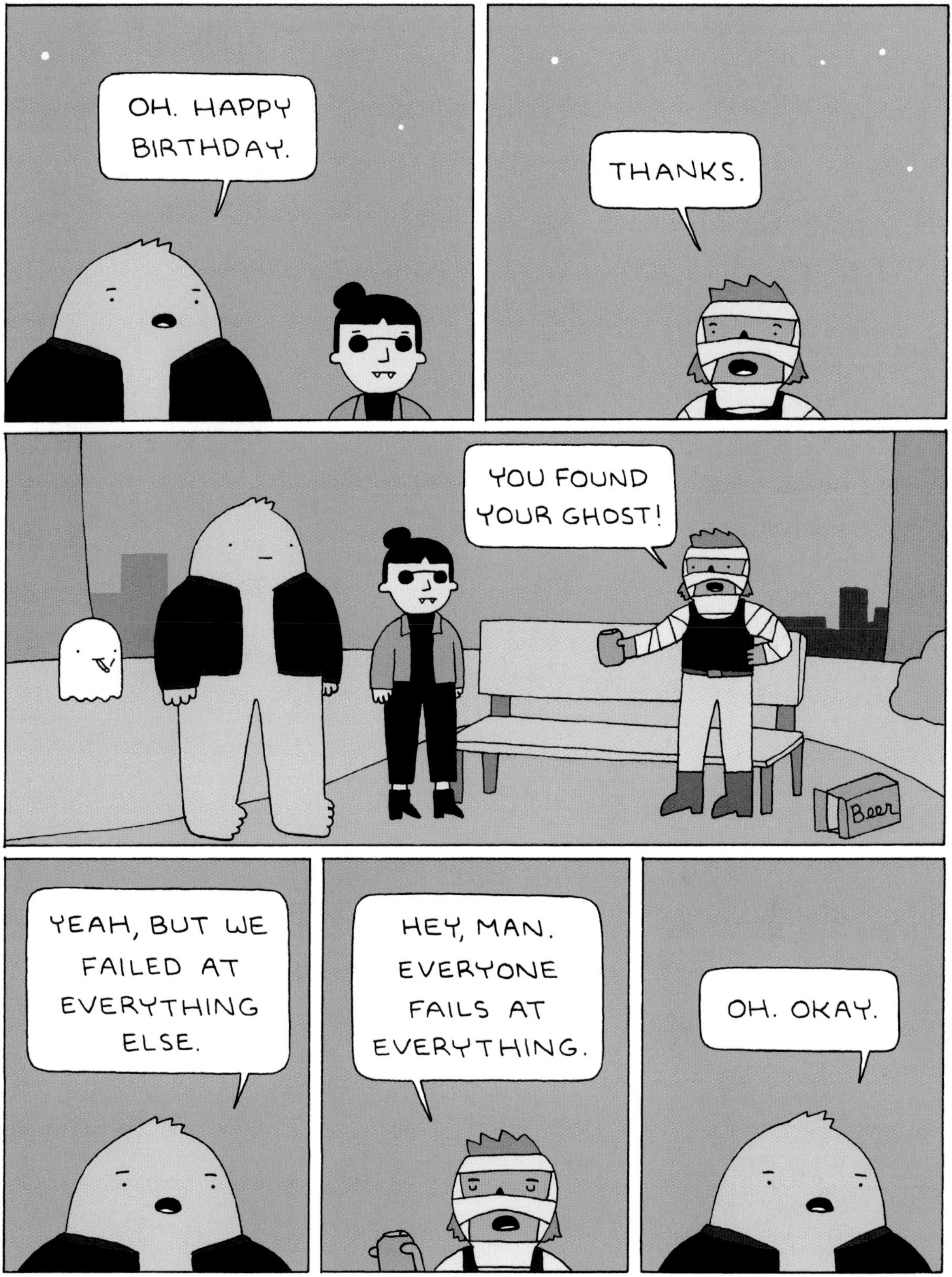
OH. HAPPY BIRTHDAY.
THANKS.
YOU FOUND YOUR GHOST!
Beer
YEAH, BUT WE FAILED AT EVERYTHING ELSE.
HEY, MAN. EVERYONE FAILS AT EVERYTHING.
OH. OKAY.

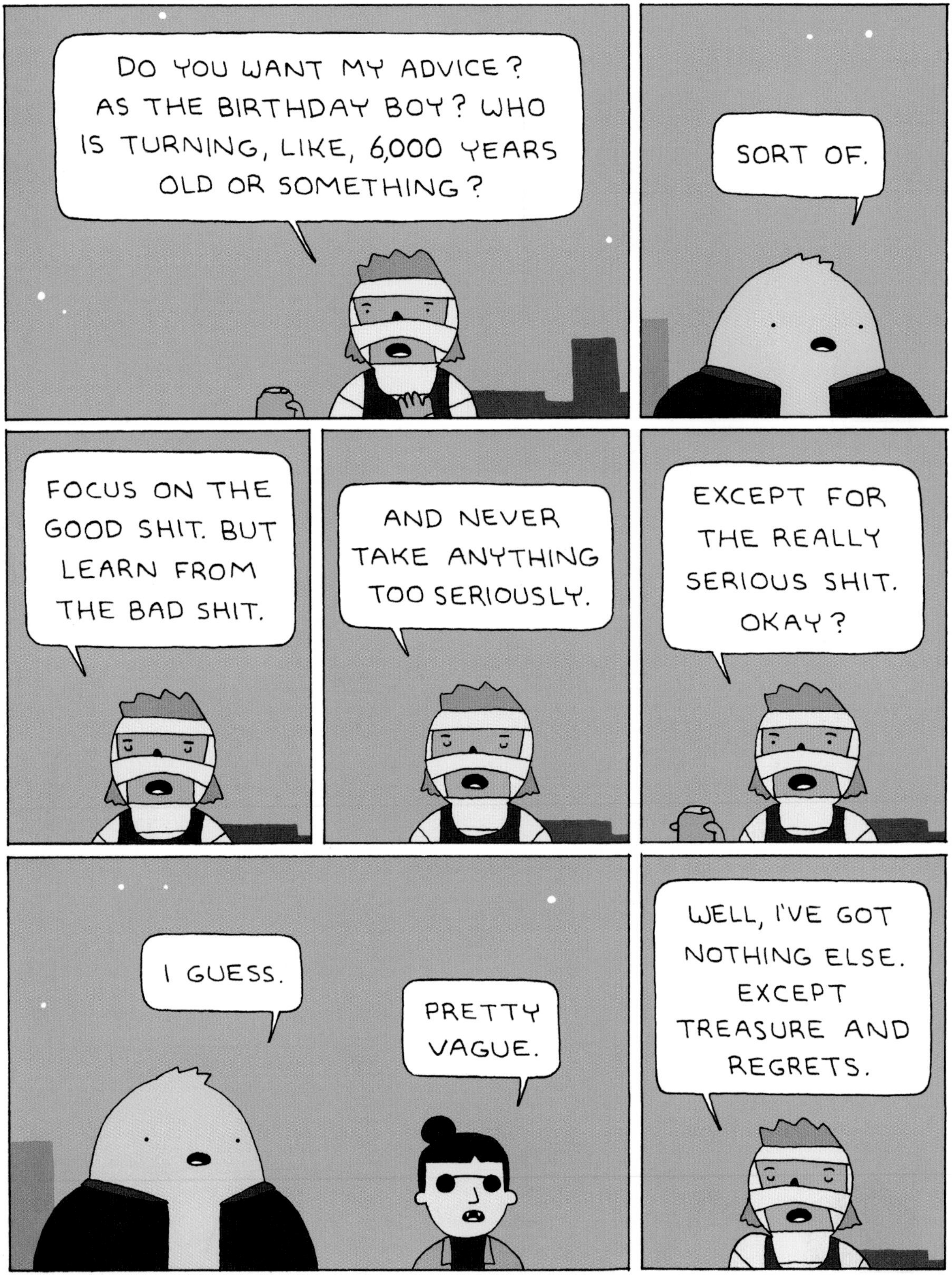
DO YOU WANT MY ADVICE? AS THE BIRTHDAY BOY? WHO IS TURNING, LIKE, 6,000 YEARS OLD OR SOMETHING?
SORT OF.
FOCUS ON THE GOOD SHIT. BUT LEARN FROM THE BAD SHIT.
AND NEVER TAKE ANYTHING TOO SERIOUSLY.
EXCEPT FOR THE REALLY SERIOUS SHIT. OKAY?
I GUESS.
PRETTY VAGUE.
WELL, I'VE GOT NOTHING ELSE. EXCEPT TREASURE AND REGRETS.

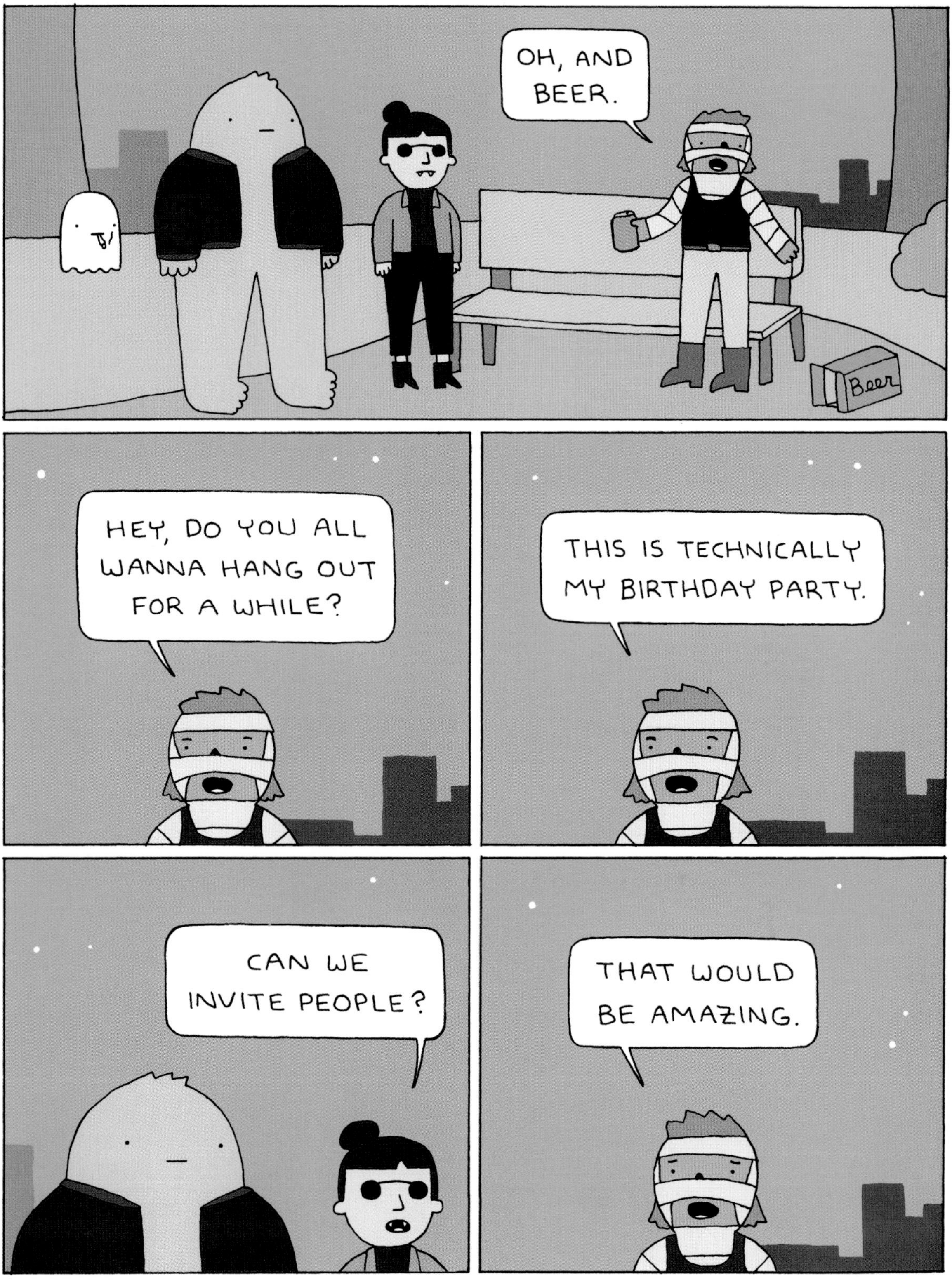
OH, AND BEER.
Beer
HEY, DO YOU ALL WANNA HANG OUT FOR A WHILE?
THIS IS TECHNICALLY MY BIRTHDAY PARTY.
CAN WE INVITE PEOPLE?
THAT WOULD BE AMAZING.

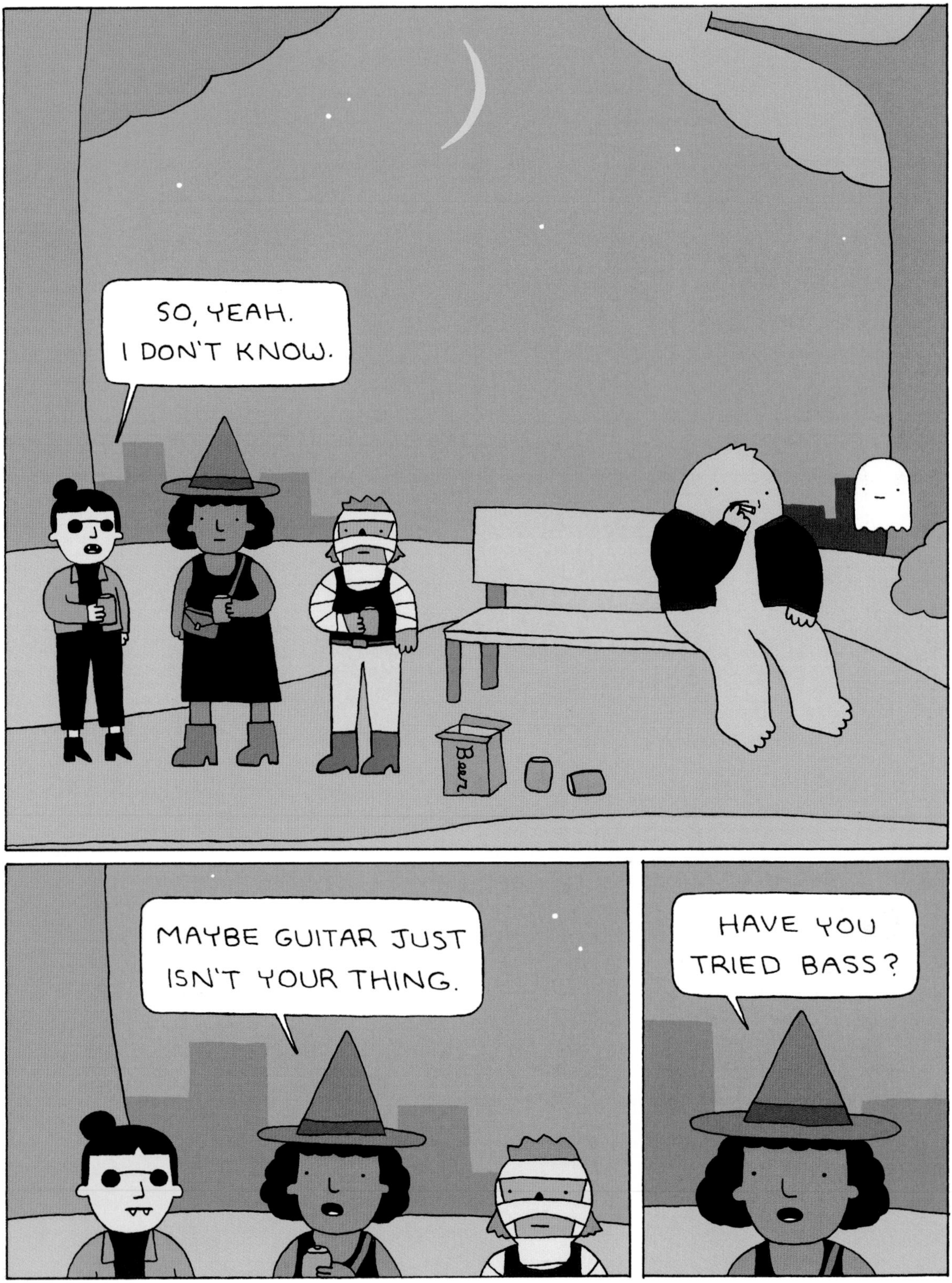
SO, YEAH. I DON'T KNOW.
MAYBE GUITAR JUST ISN'T YOUR THING.
HAVE YOU TRIED BASS?

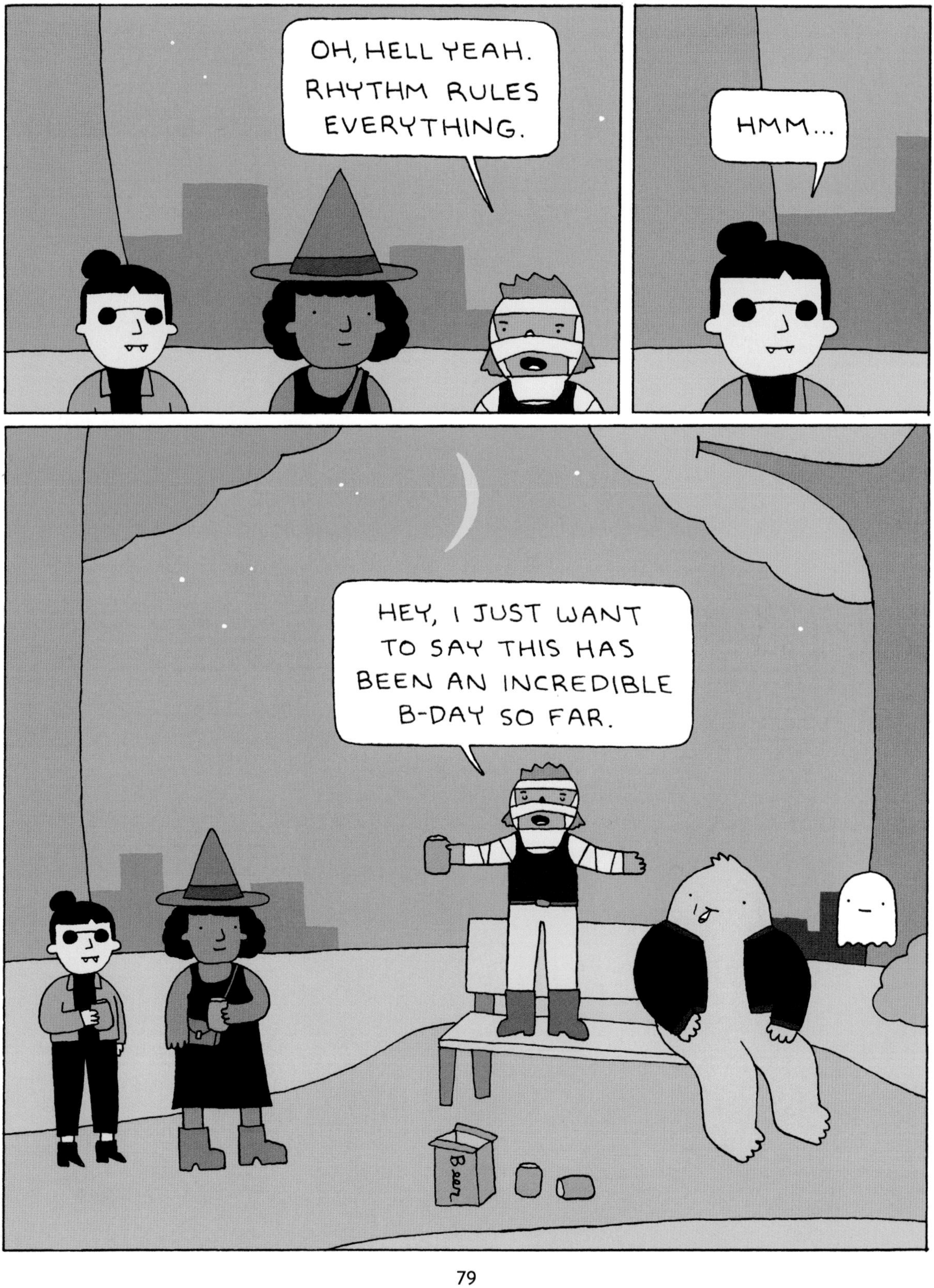
OH, HELL YEAH. RHYTHM RULES EVERYTHING.
HMM...
HEY, I JUST WANT TO SAY THIS HAS BEEN AN INCREDIBLE B-DAY SO FAR.
BEER

AND THOUGH I'VE ONLY KNOWN YOU ALL A SHORT TIME, I...

I CAN HONESTLY SAY YOU MIGHT BE THE BEST FRIENDS I'VE—

MUMMY!

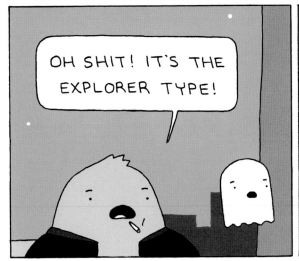

OH SHIT! IT'S THE EXPLORER TYPE!

I'VE COME FOR YOUR TREASURE, YOU ANCIENT FIEND!

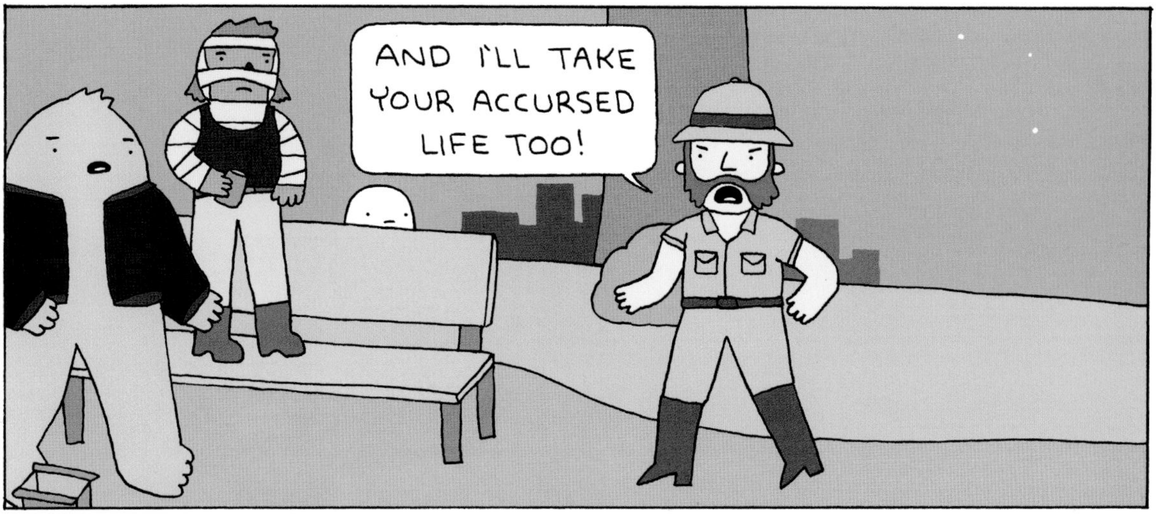
AND I'LL TAKE YOUR ACCURSED LIFE TOO!

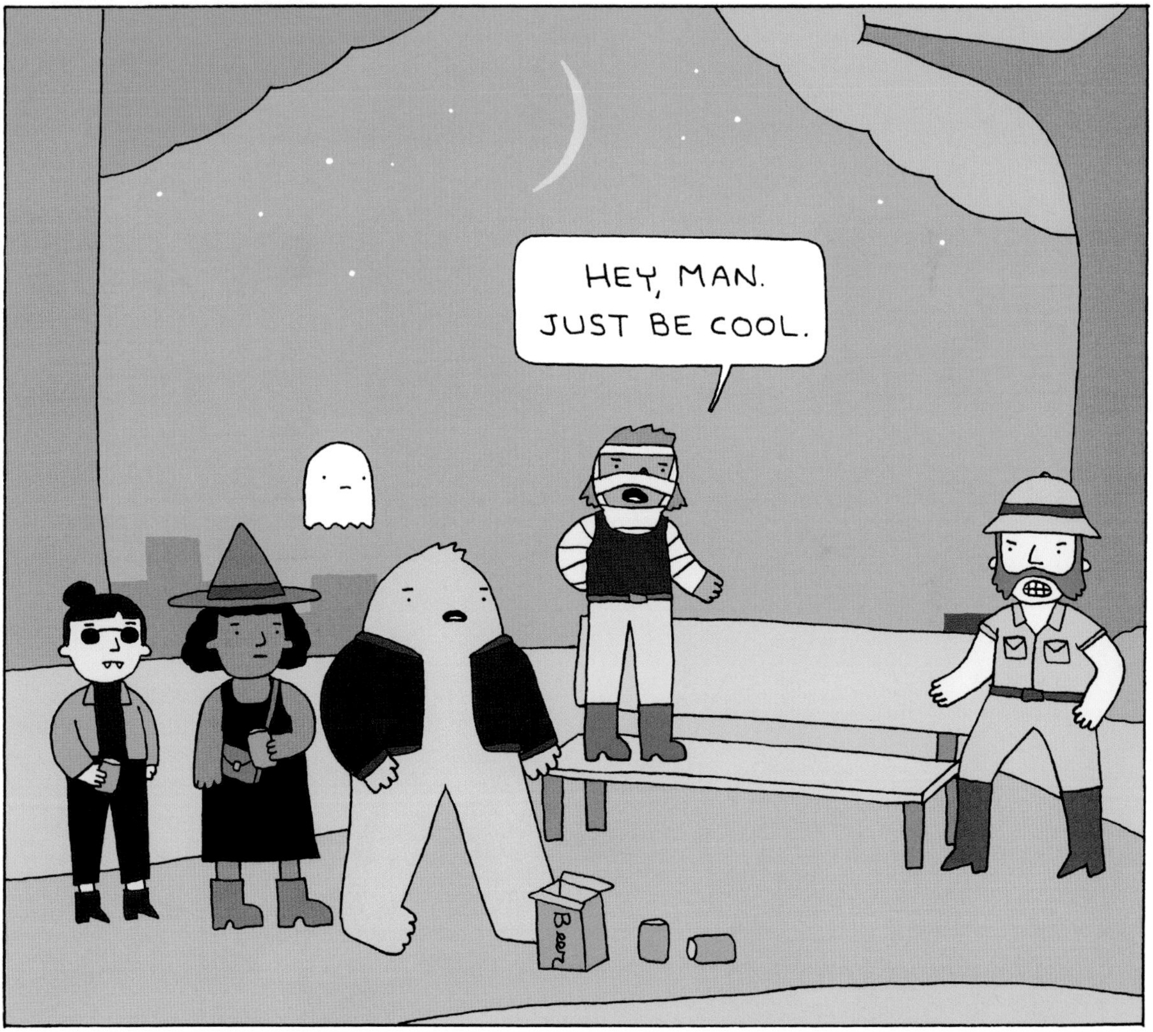
HEY, MAN. JUST BE COOL.
Beer

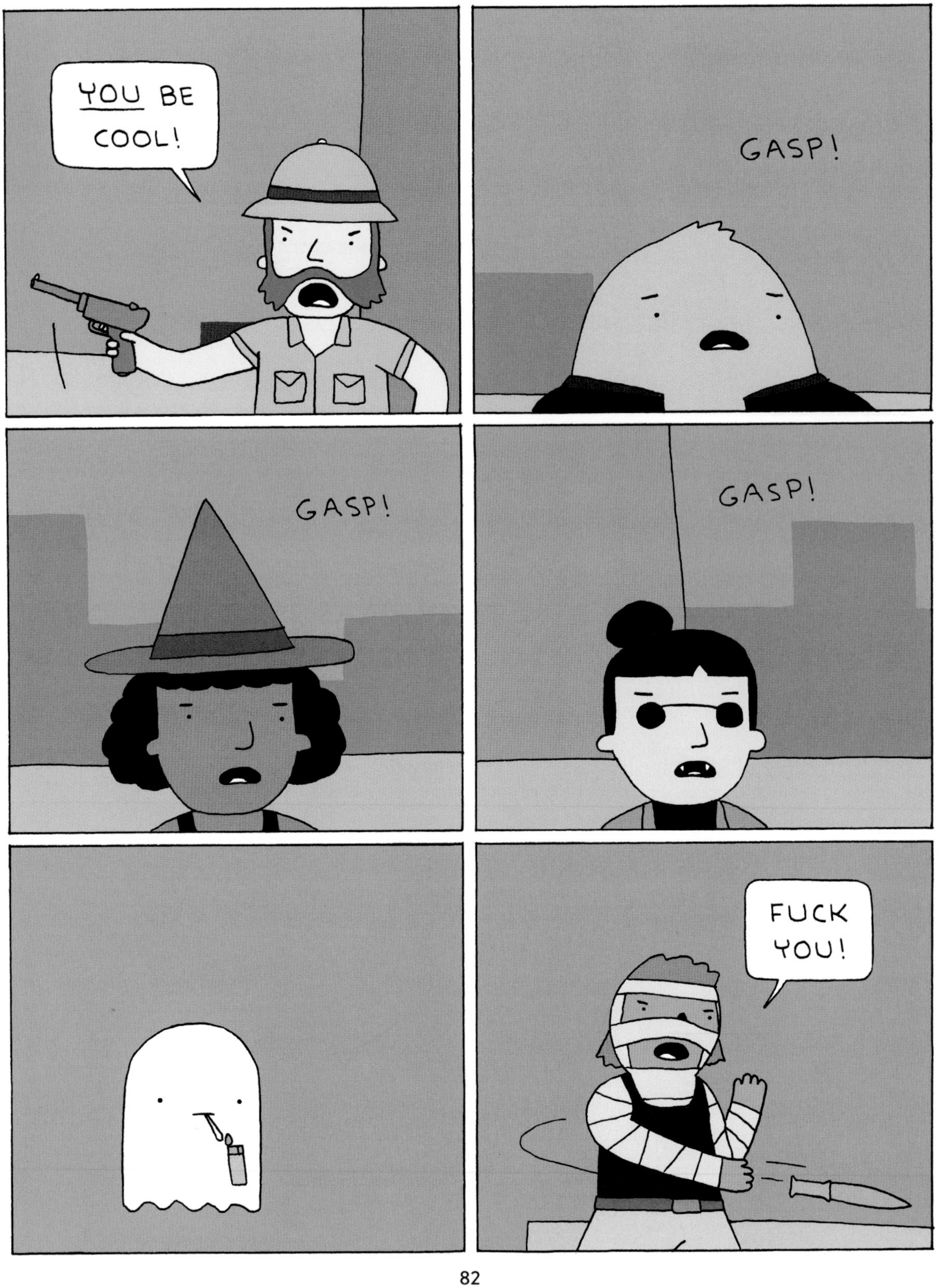
YOU BE COOL!
GASP!
GASP!
GASP!
FUCK YOU!

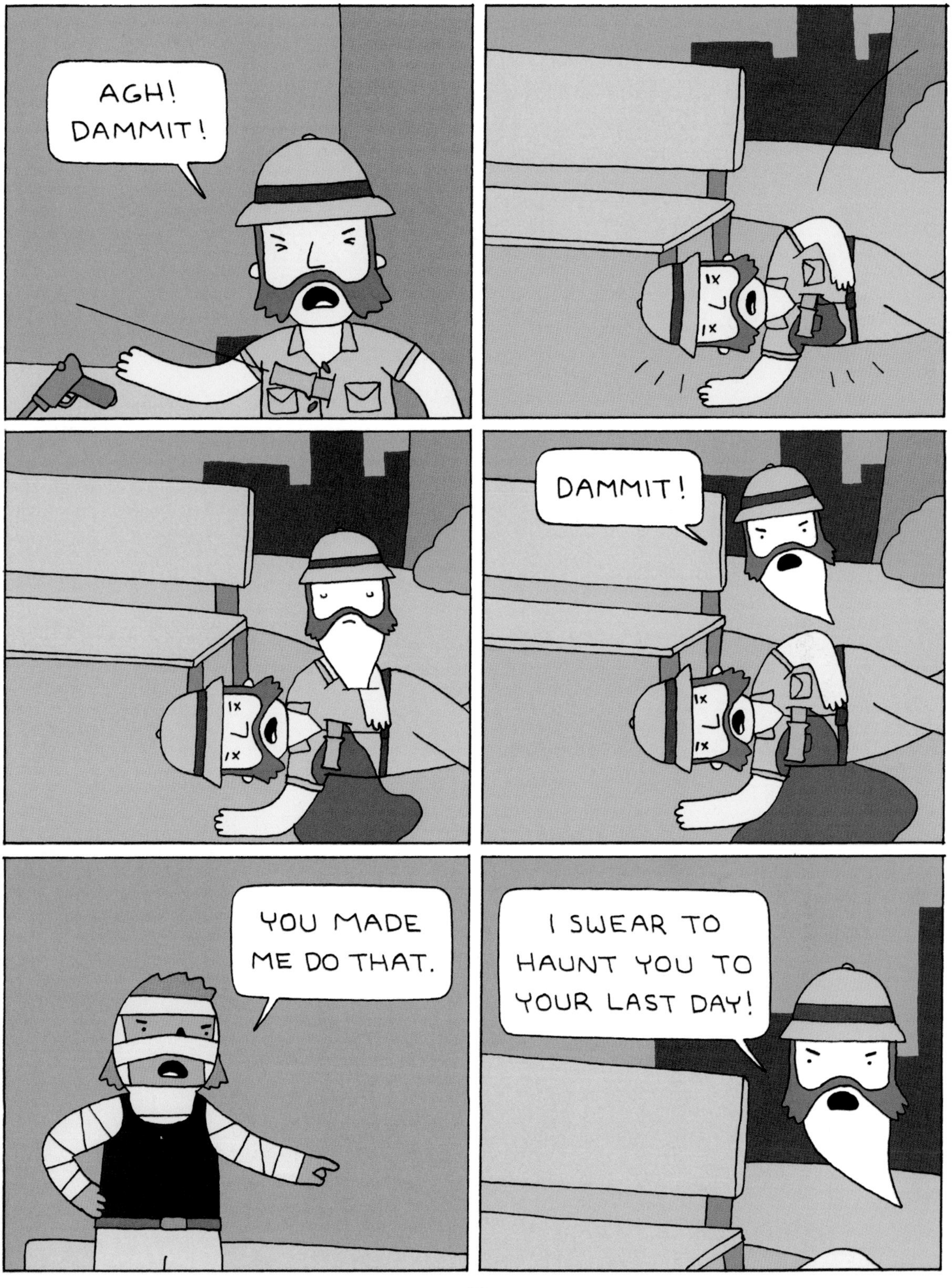
AGH! DAMMIT!
DAMMIT!
YOU MADE ME DO THAT.
I SWEAR TO HAUNT YOU TO YOUR LAST DAY!

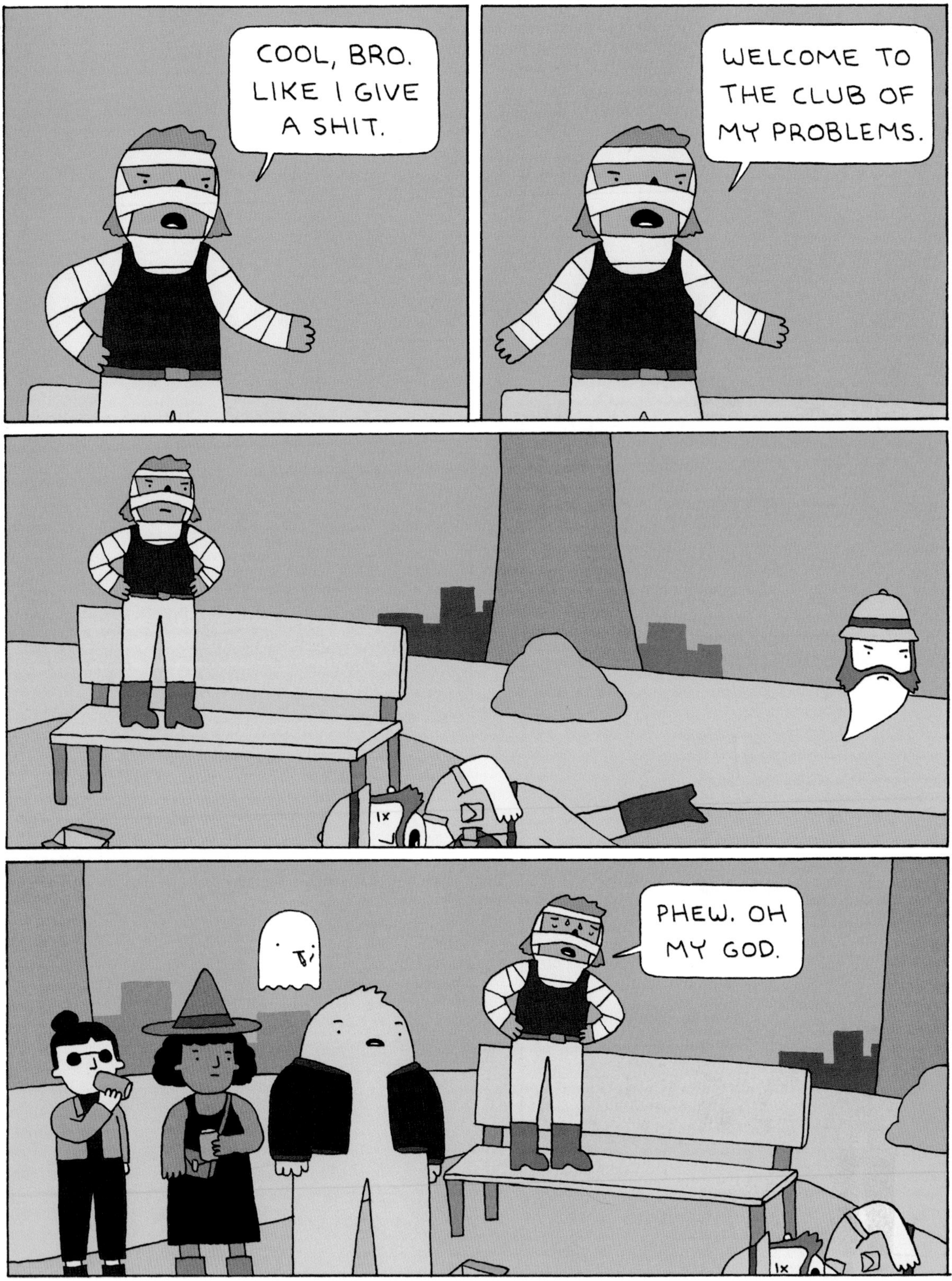
COOL, BRO. LIKE I GIVE A SHIT.
WELCOME TO THE CLUB OF MY PROBLEMS.
PHEW. OH MY GOD.

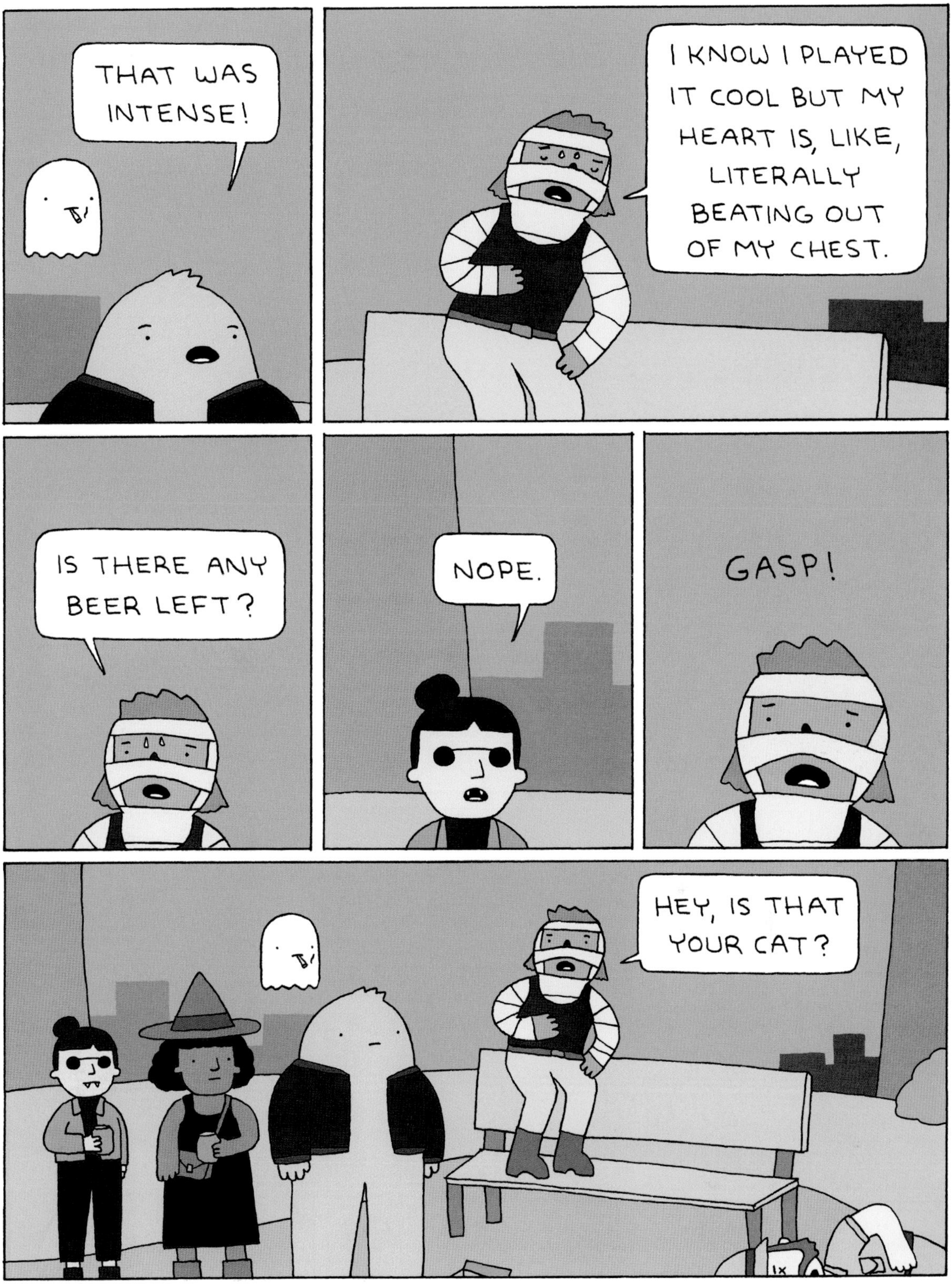
THAT WAS INTENSE!
I KNOW I PLAYED IT COOL BUT MY HEART IS, LIKE, LITERALLY BEATING OUT OF MY CHEST.
IS THERE ANY BEER LEFT?
NOPE.
GASP!
HEY, IS THAT YOUR CAT?

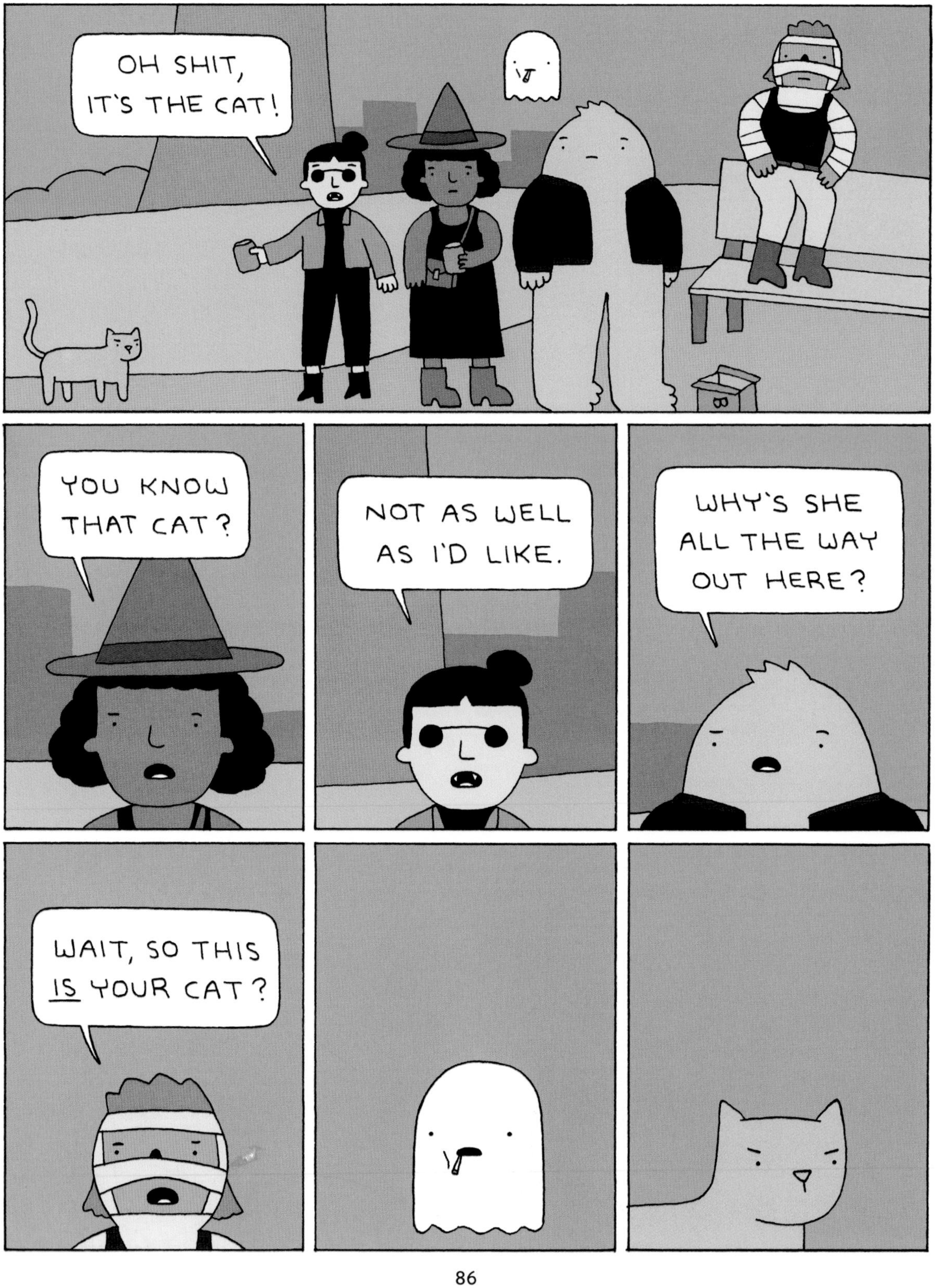
OH SHIT, IT'S THE CAT!
YOU KNOW THAT CAT?
NOT AS WELL AS I'D LIKE.
WHY'S SHE ALL THE WAY OUT HERE?
WAIT, SO THIS IS YOUR CAT?

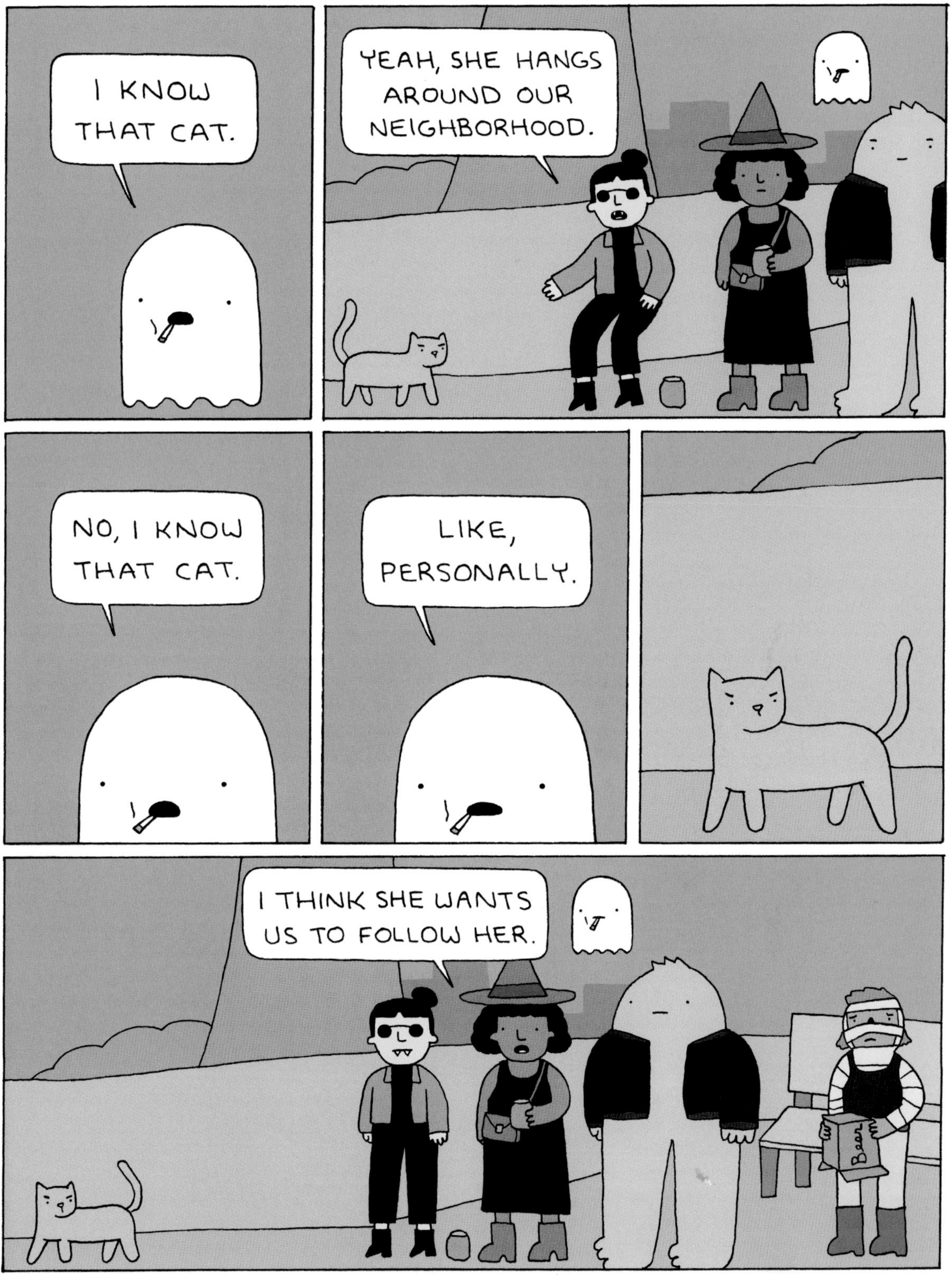
I KNOW THAT CAT.
YEAH, SHE HANGS AROUND OUR NEIGHBORHOOD.
NO, I KNOW THAT CAT.
LIKE, PERSONALLY.
I THINK SHE WANTS US TO FOLLOW HER.
Beer

The Cat

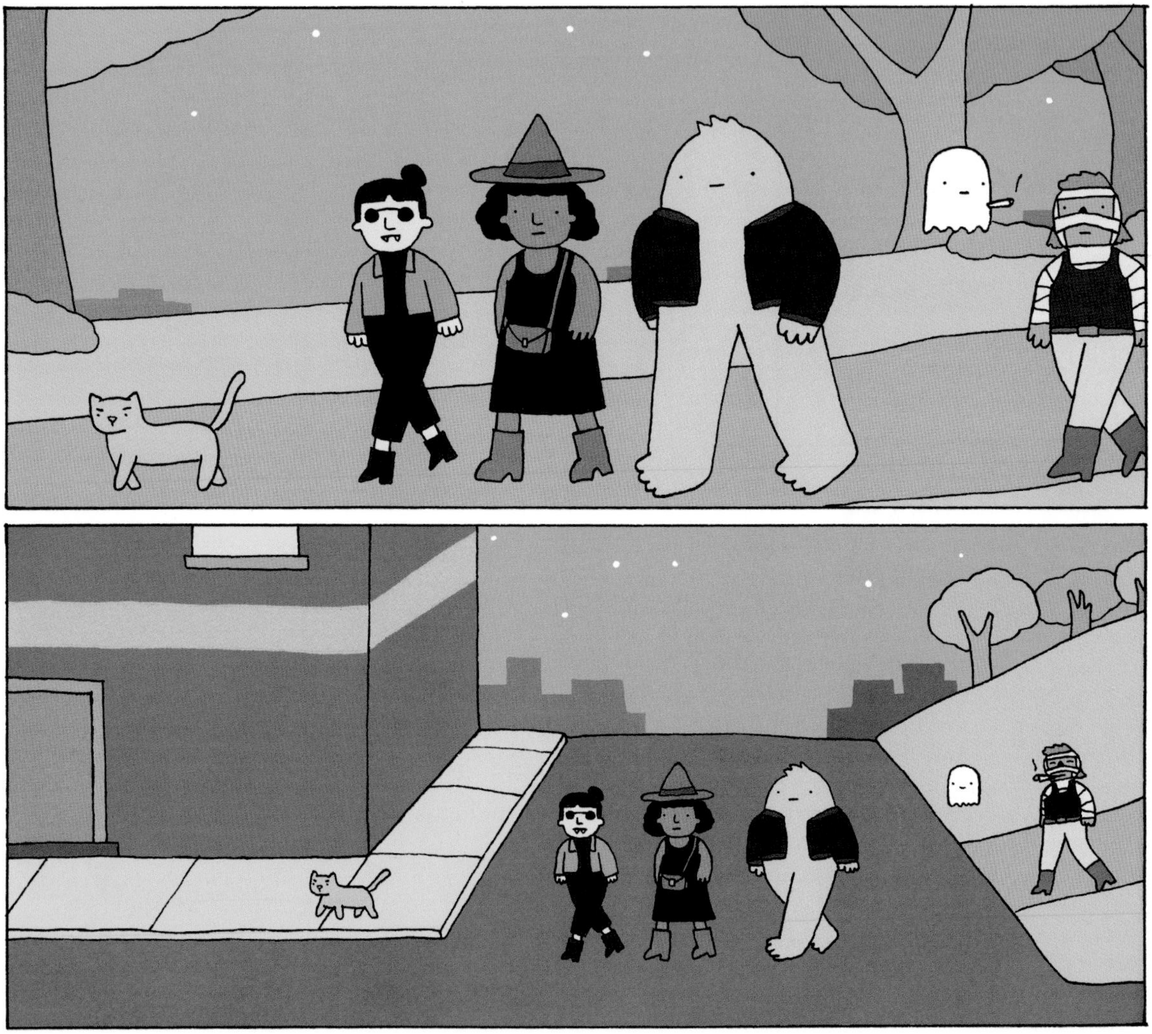

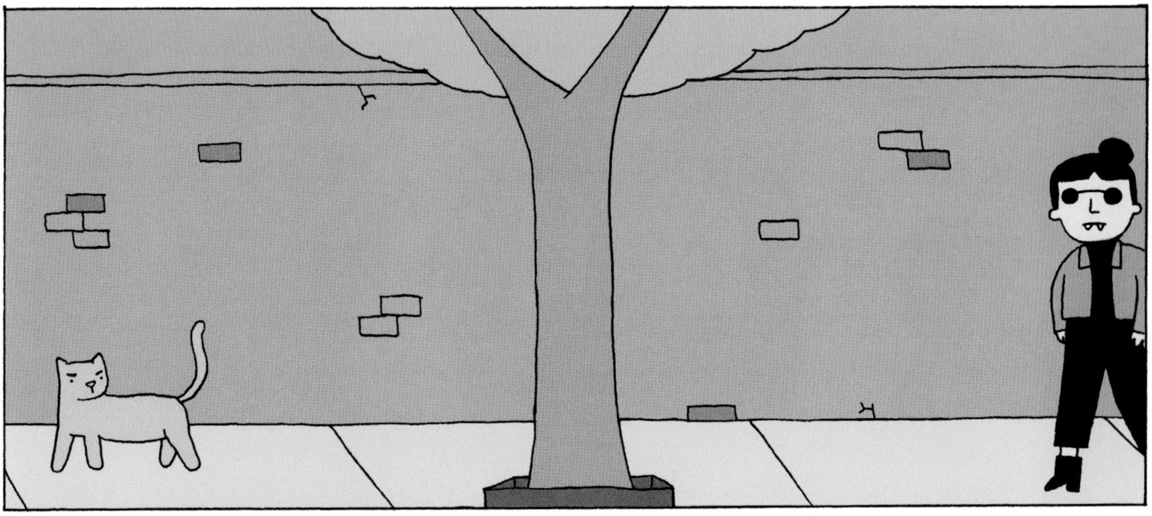

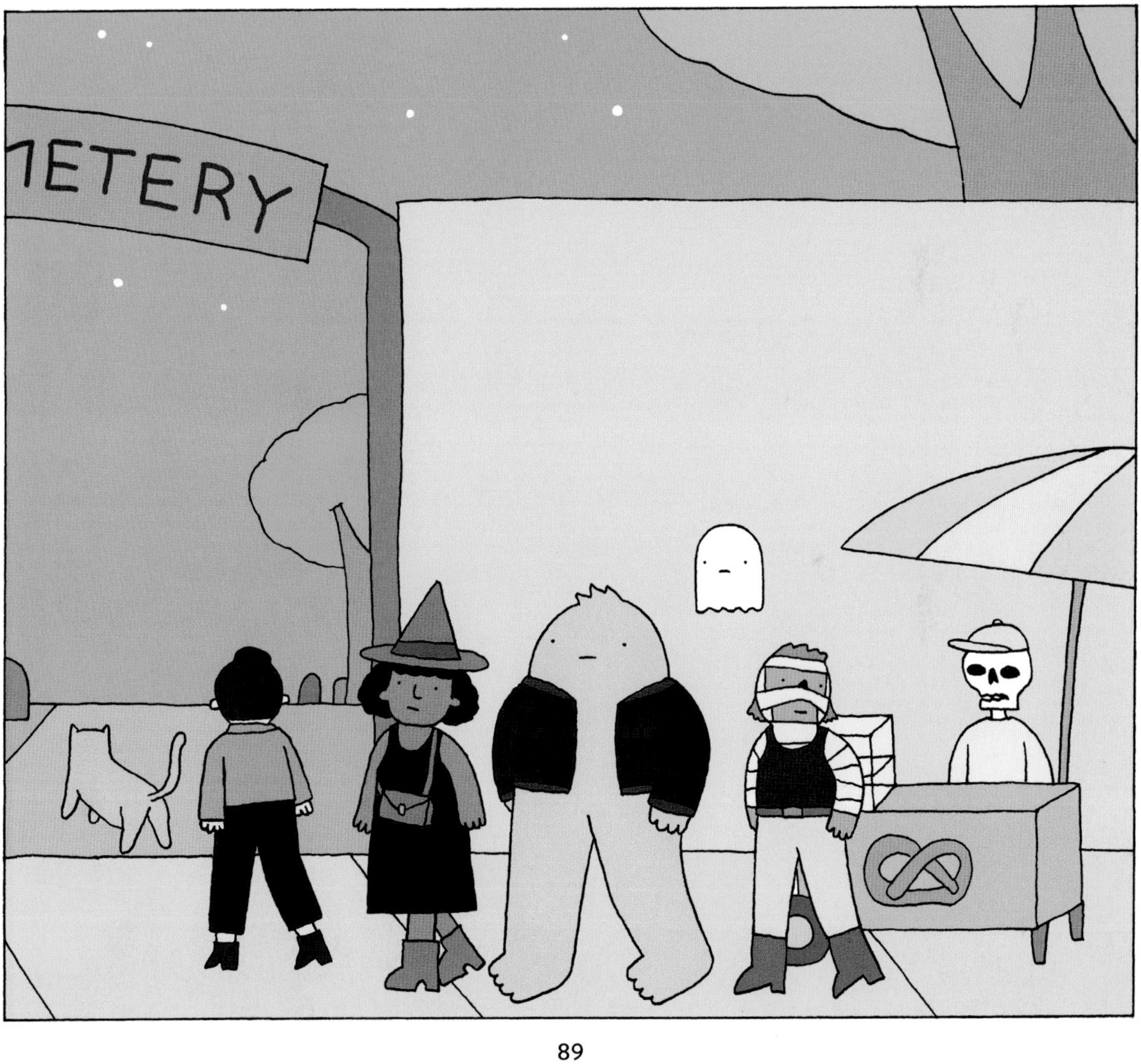
METERY

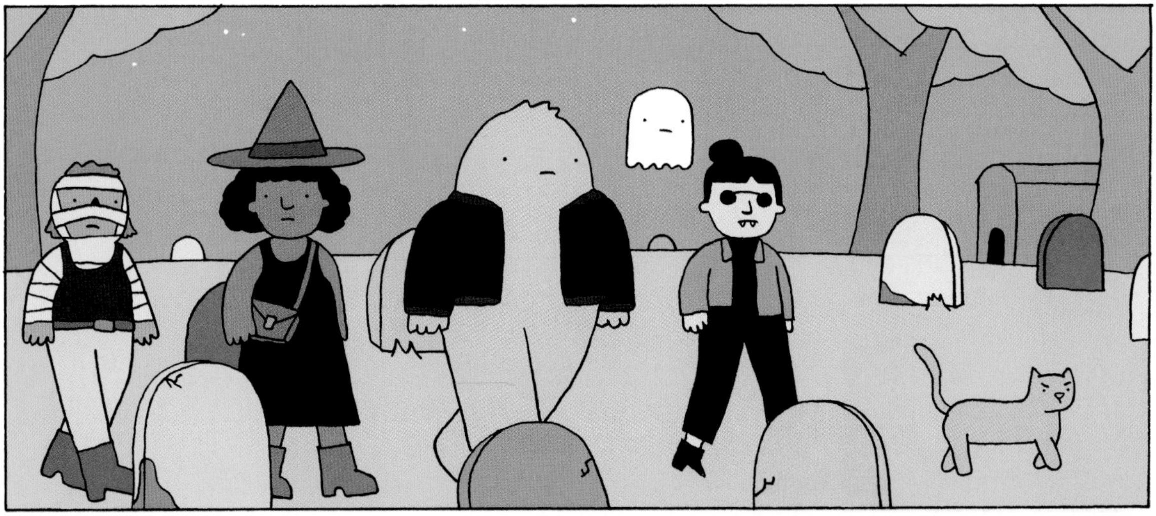

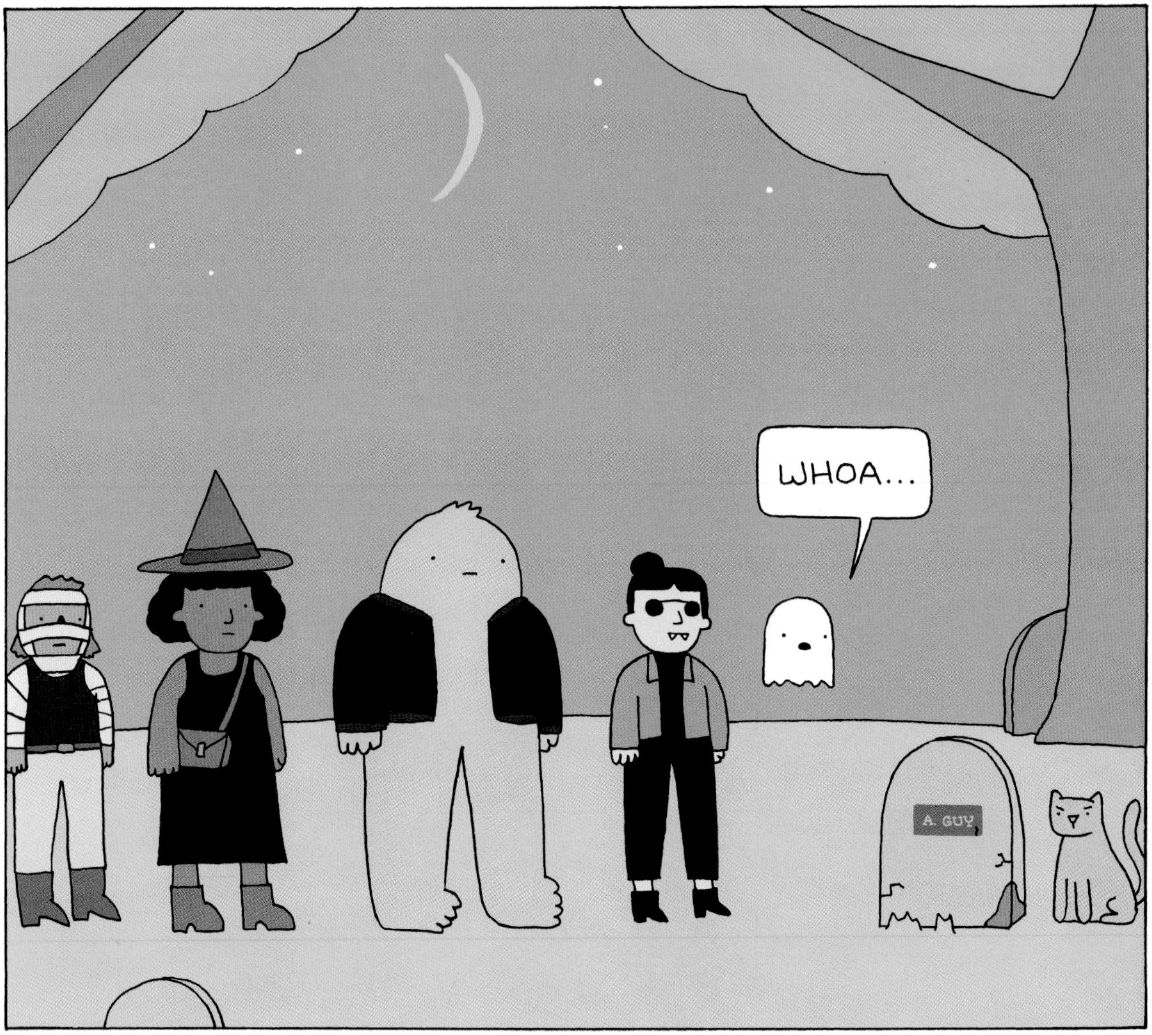
WHOA...
A. GUY

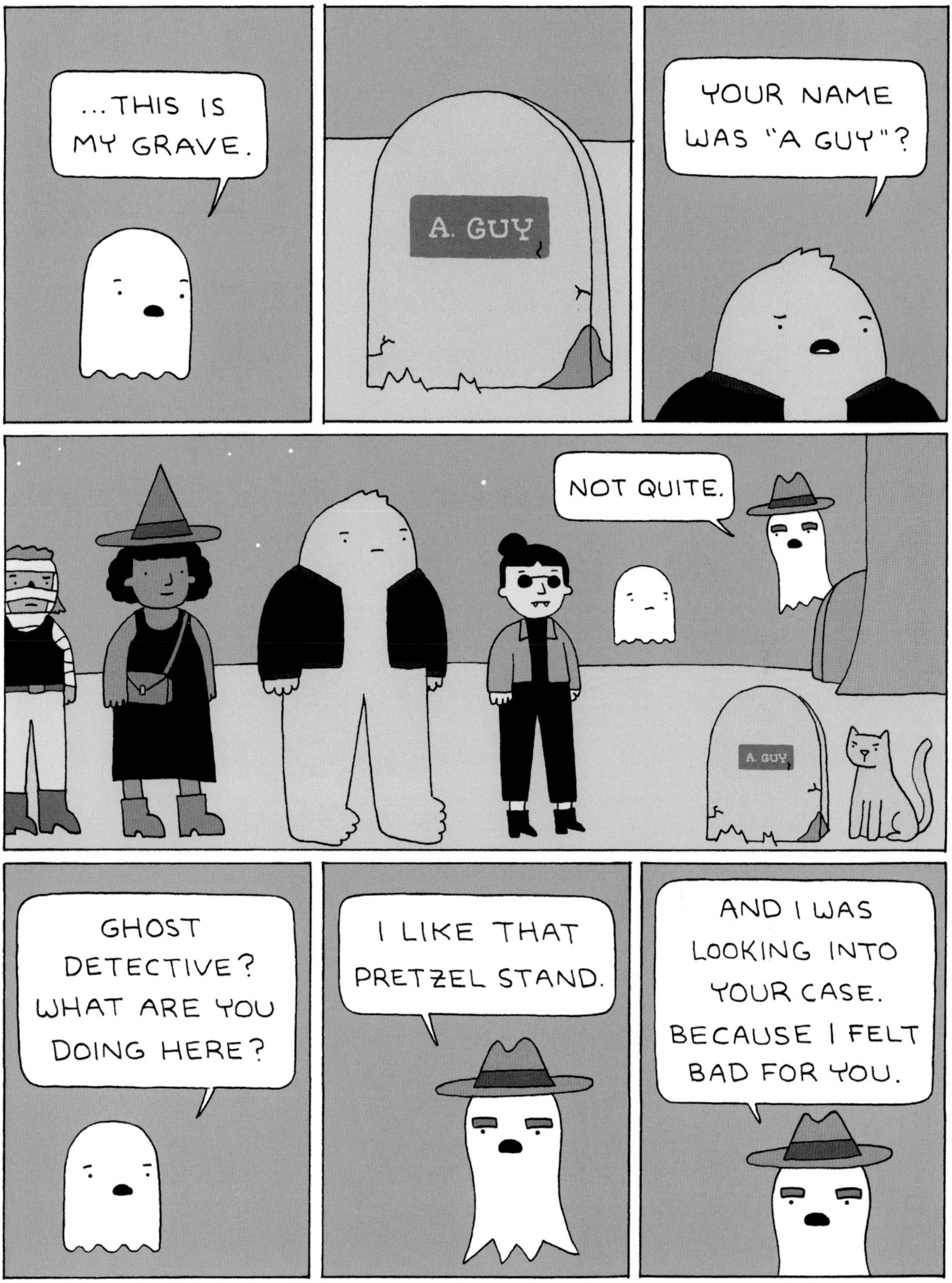
...THIS IS MY GRAVE.
A. GUY
YOUR NAME WAS "A GUY"?
NOT QUITE.
A. GUY
GHOST DETECTIVE? WHAT ARE YOU DOING HERE?
I LIKE THAT PRETZEL STAND.
AND I WAS LOOKING INTO YOUR CASE. BECAUSE I FELT BAD FOR YOU.

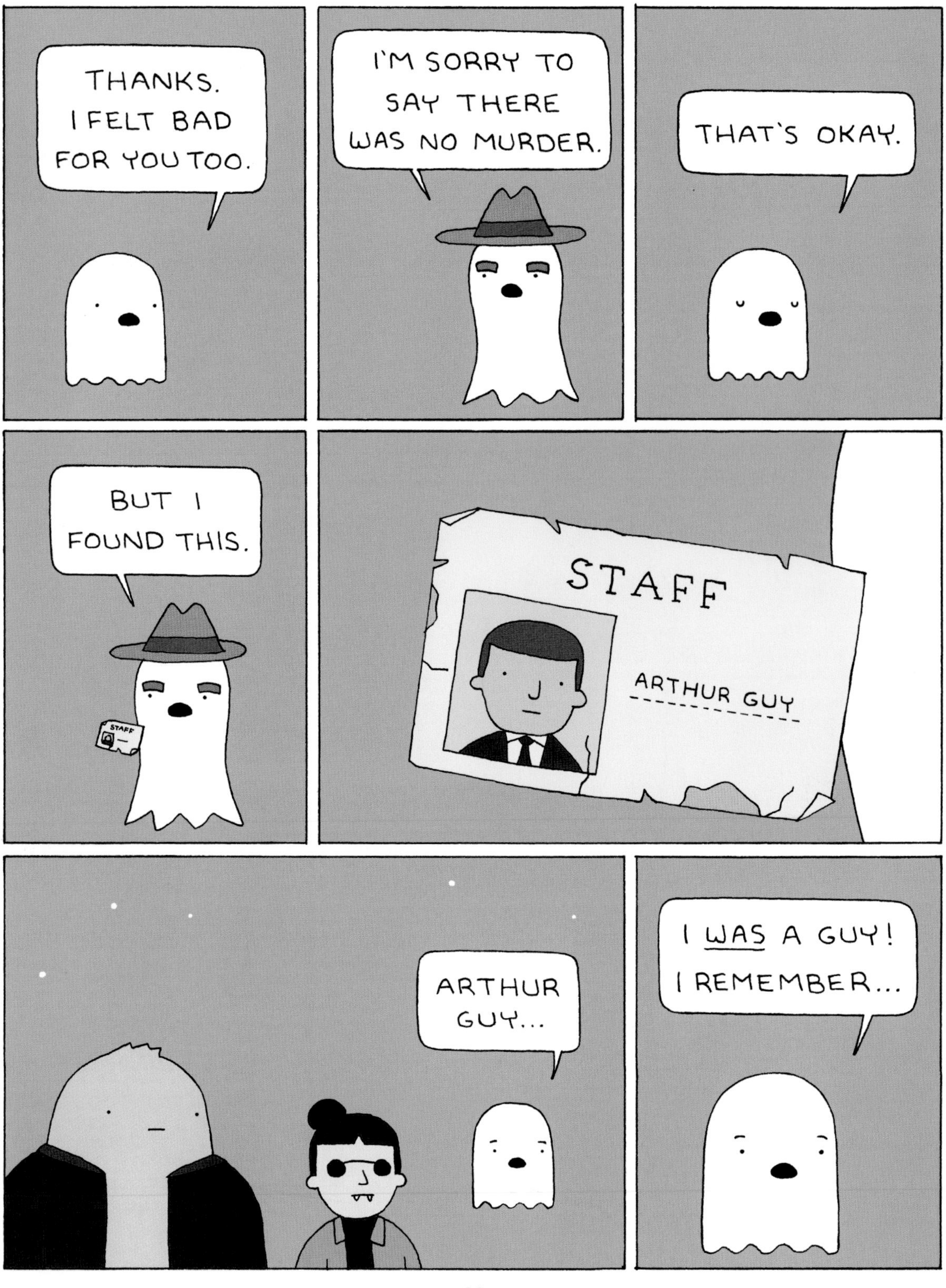
THANKS. I FELT BAD FOR YOU TOO.
I'M SORRY TO SAY THERE WAS NO MURDER.
THAT'S OKAY.
BUT I FOUND THIS.
STAFF
STAFF
ARTHUR GUY
ARTHUR GUY...
I WAS A GUY! I REMEMBER...

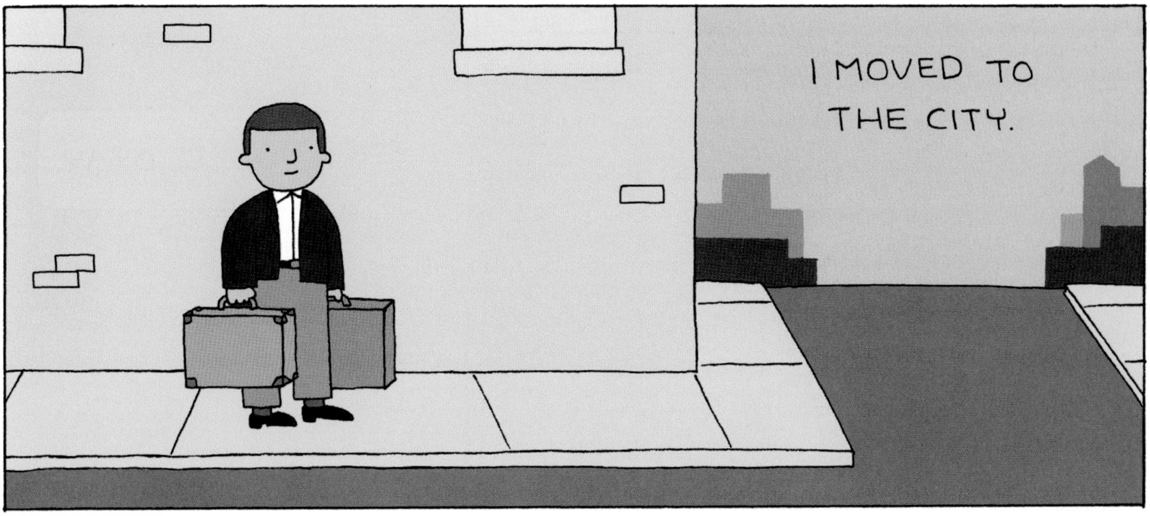
I MOVED TO
THE CITY.

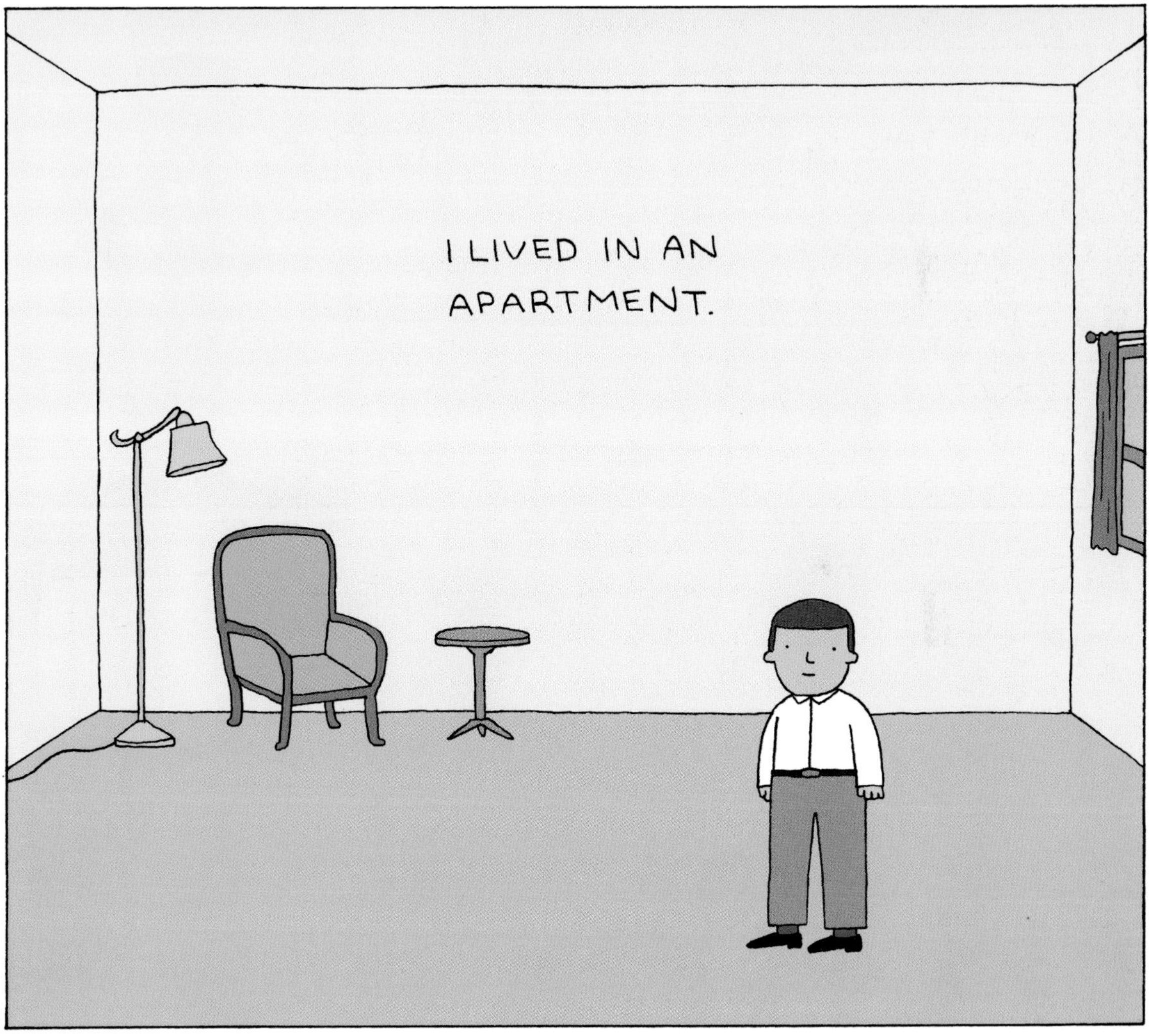
I LIVED IN AN
APARTMENT.

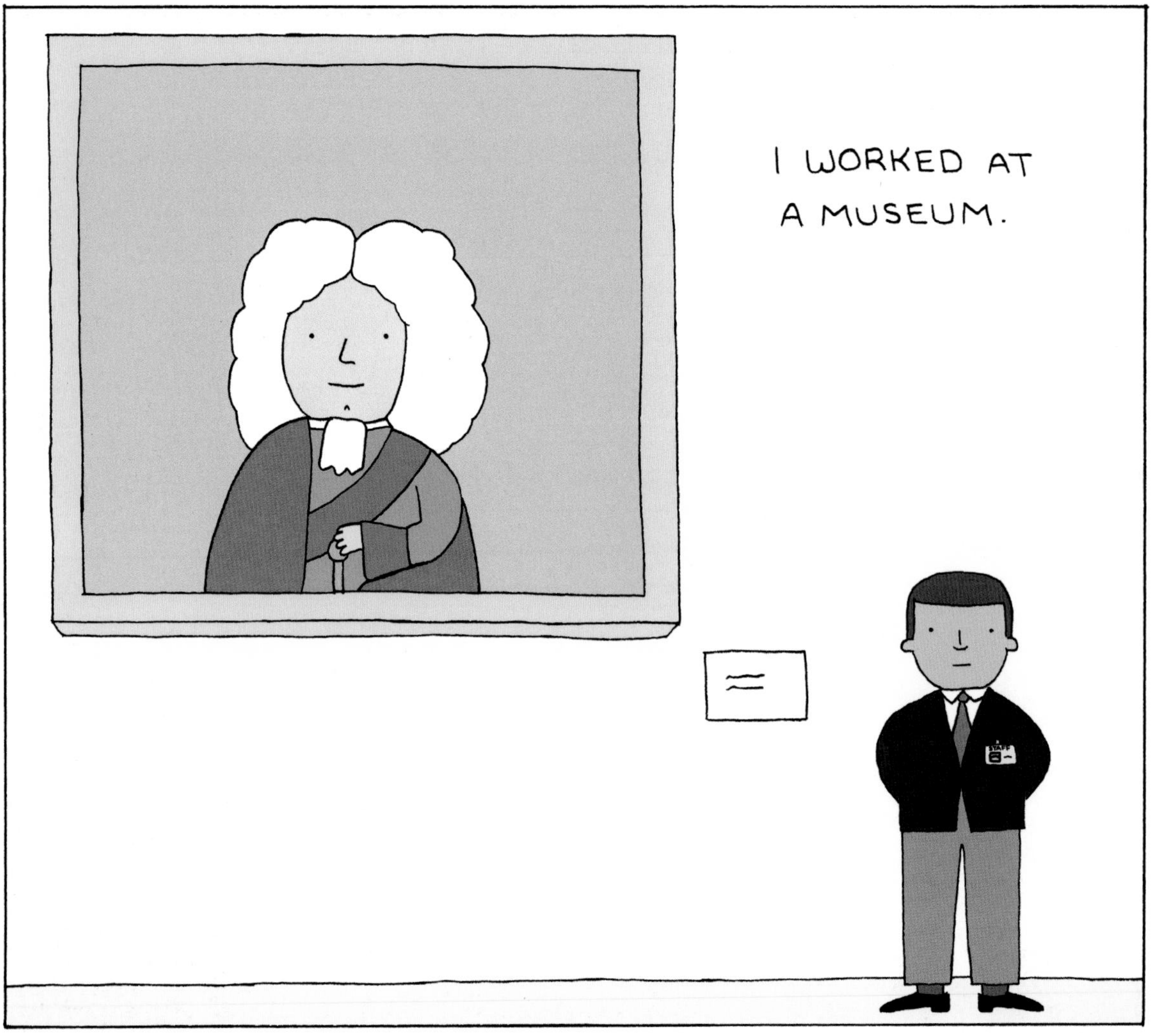
I WORKED AT
A MUSEUM.
STAFF

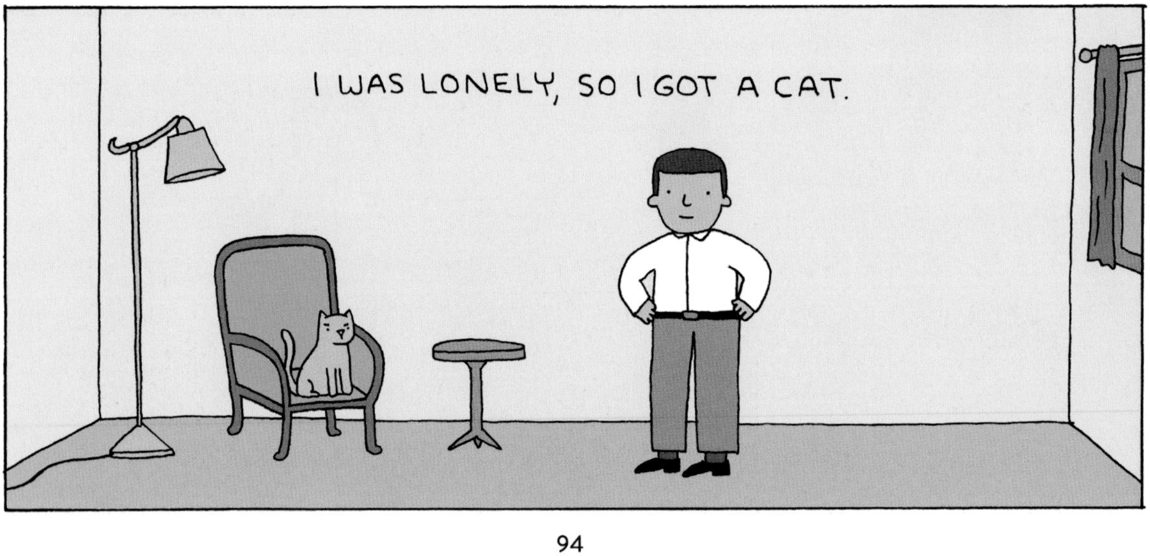
I WAS LONELY, SO I GOT A CAT.

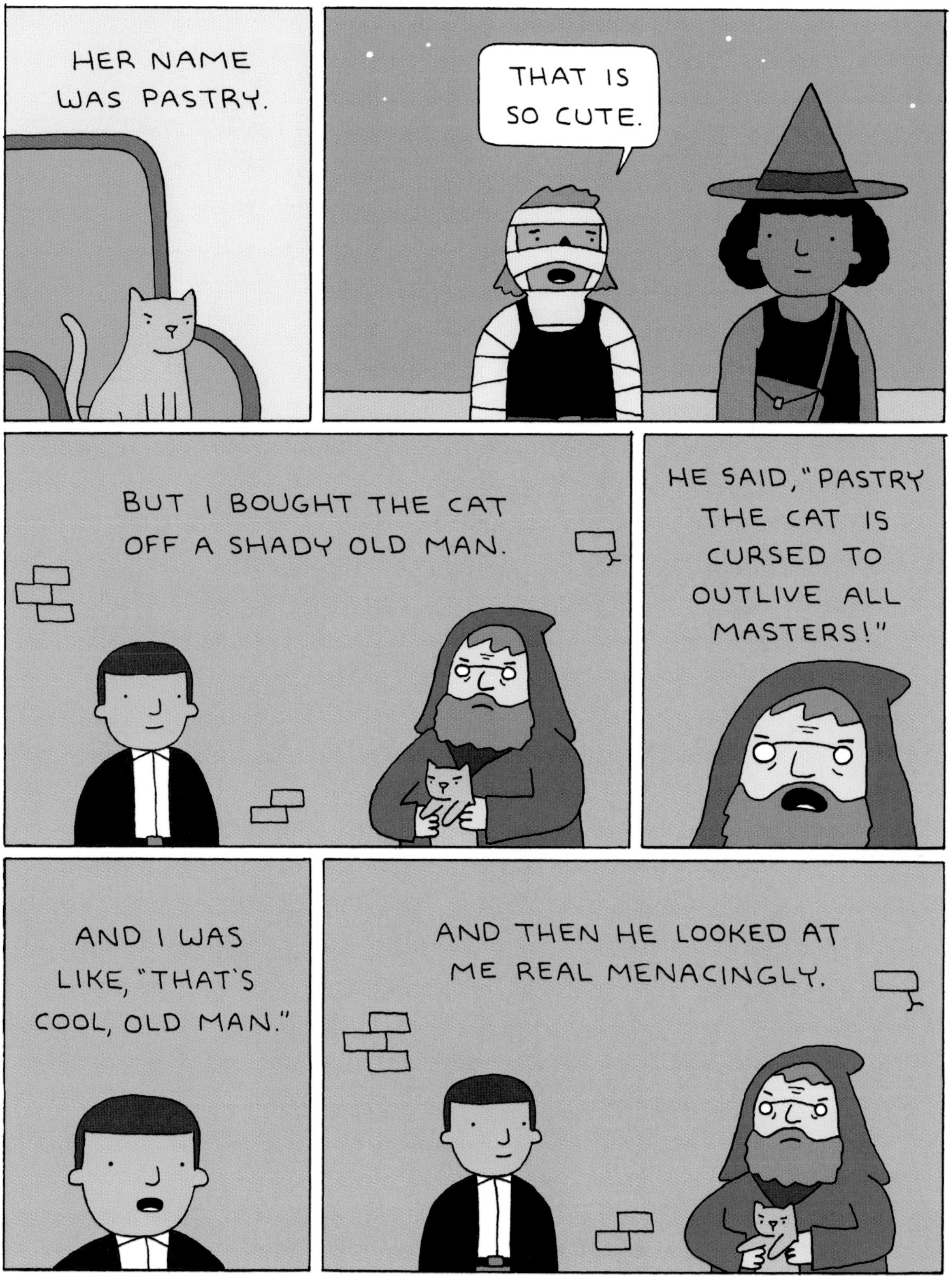
HER NAME WAS PASTRY.
THAT IS SO CUTE.
BUT I BOUGHT THE CAT OFF A SHADY OLD MAN.
HE SAID, "PASTRY THE CAT IS CURSED TO OUTLIVE ALL MASTERS!"
AND I WAS LIKE, "THAT'S COOL, OLD MAN."
AND THEN HE LOOKED AT ME REAL MENACINGLY.

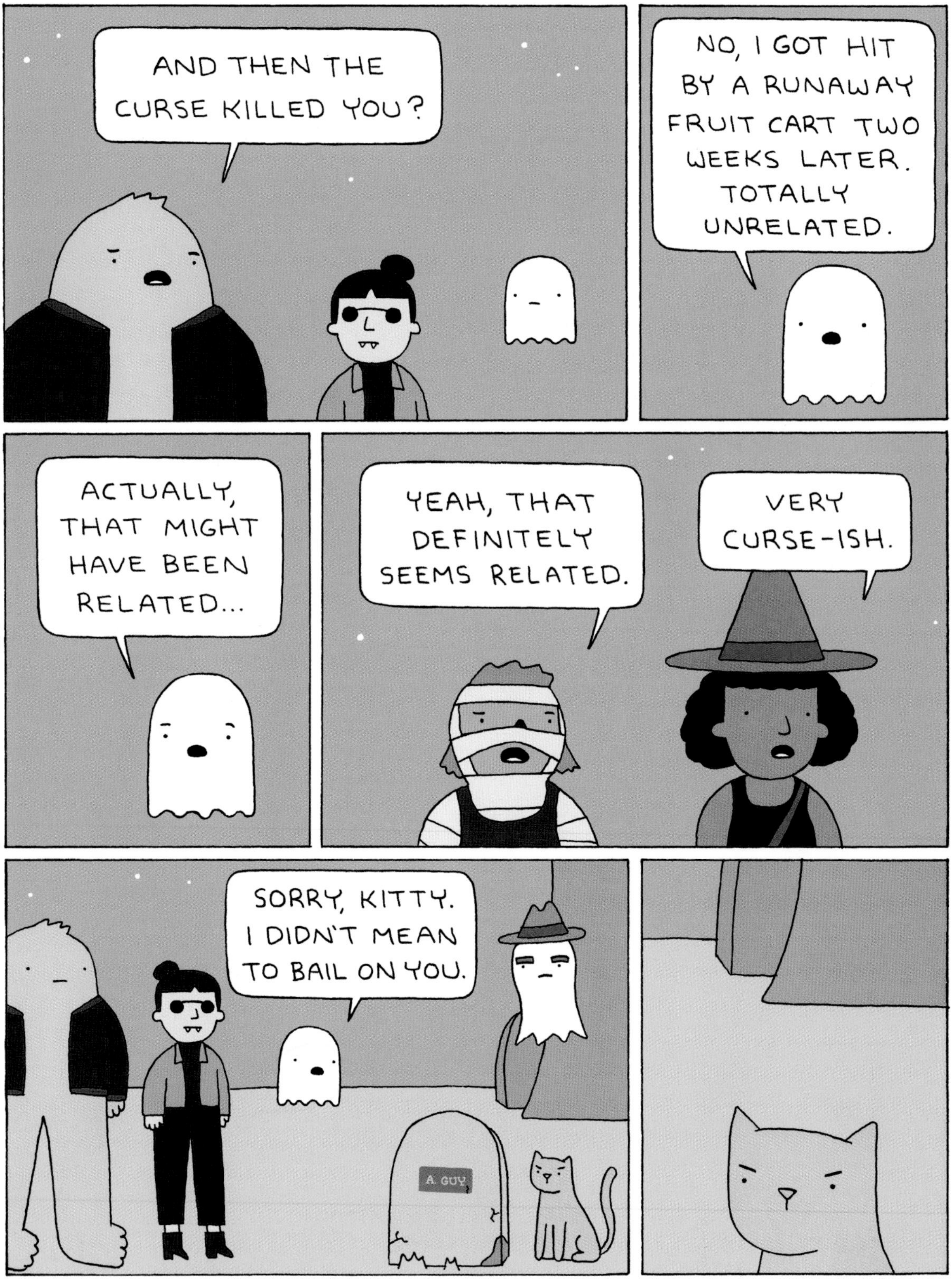
AND THEN THE CURSE KILLED YOU?
NO, I GOT HIT BY A RUNAWAY FRUIT CART TWO WEEKS LATER. TOTALLY UNRELATED.
ACTUALLY, THAT MIGHT HAVE BEEN RELATED...
YEAH, THAT DEFINITELY SEEMS RELATED.
VERY CURSE-ISH.
SORRY, KITTY. I DIDN'T MEAN TO BAIL ON YOU.
A GUY

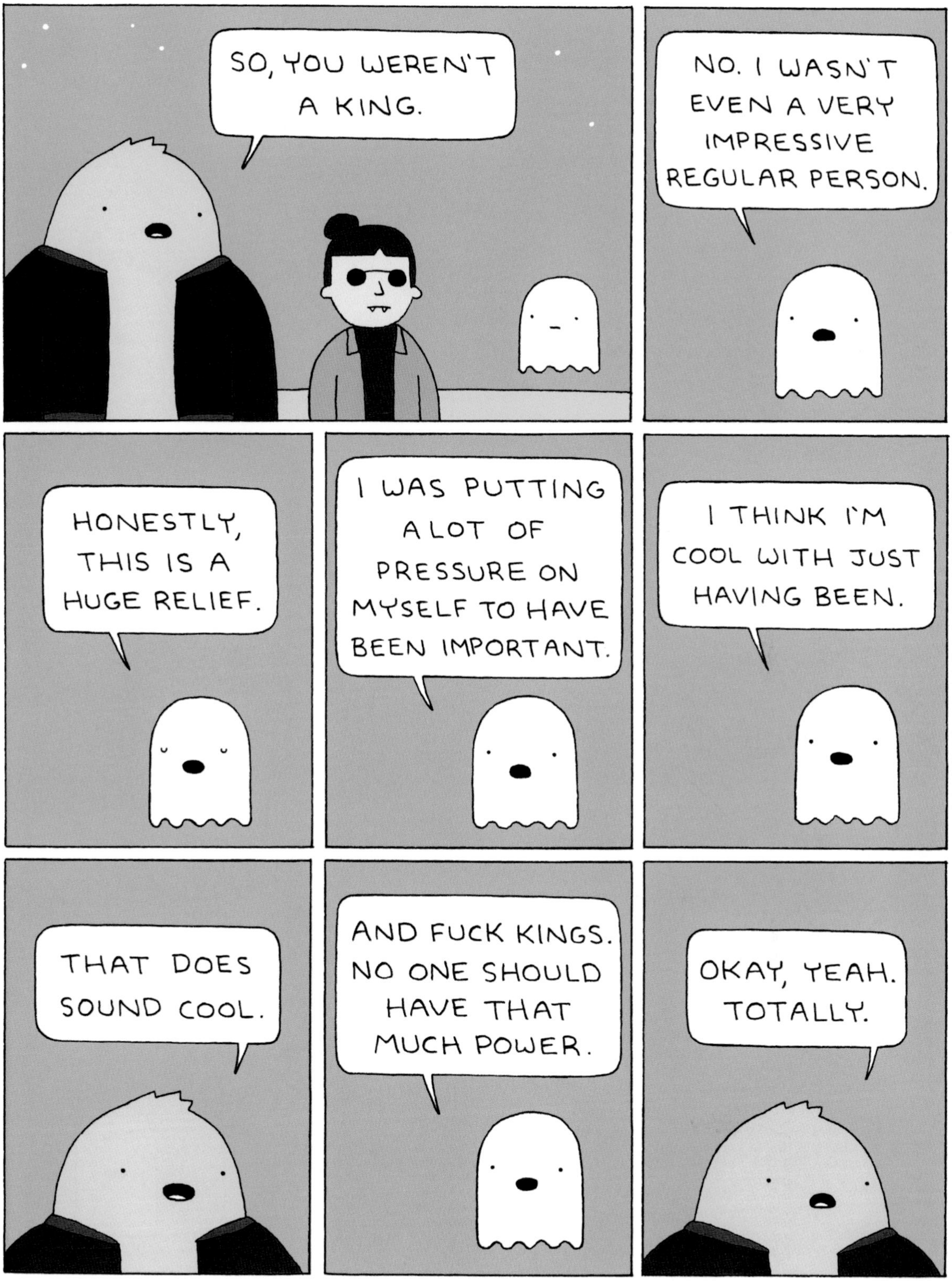
SO, YOU WEREN'T A KING.
NO. I WASN'T EVEN A VERY IMPRESSIVE REGULAR PERSON.
HONESTLY, THIS IS A HUGE RELIEF.
I WAS PUTTING A LOT OF PRESSURE ON MYSELF TO HAVE BEEN IMPORTANT.
I THINK I'M COOL WITH JUST HAVING BEEN.
THAT DOES SOUND COOL.
AND FUCK KINGS. NO ONE SHOULD HAVE THAT MUCH POWER.
OKAY, YEAH. TOTALLY.

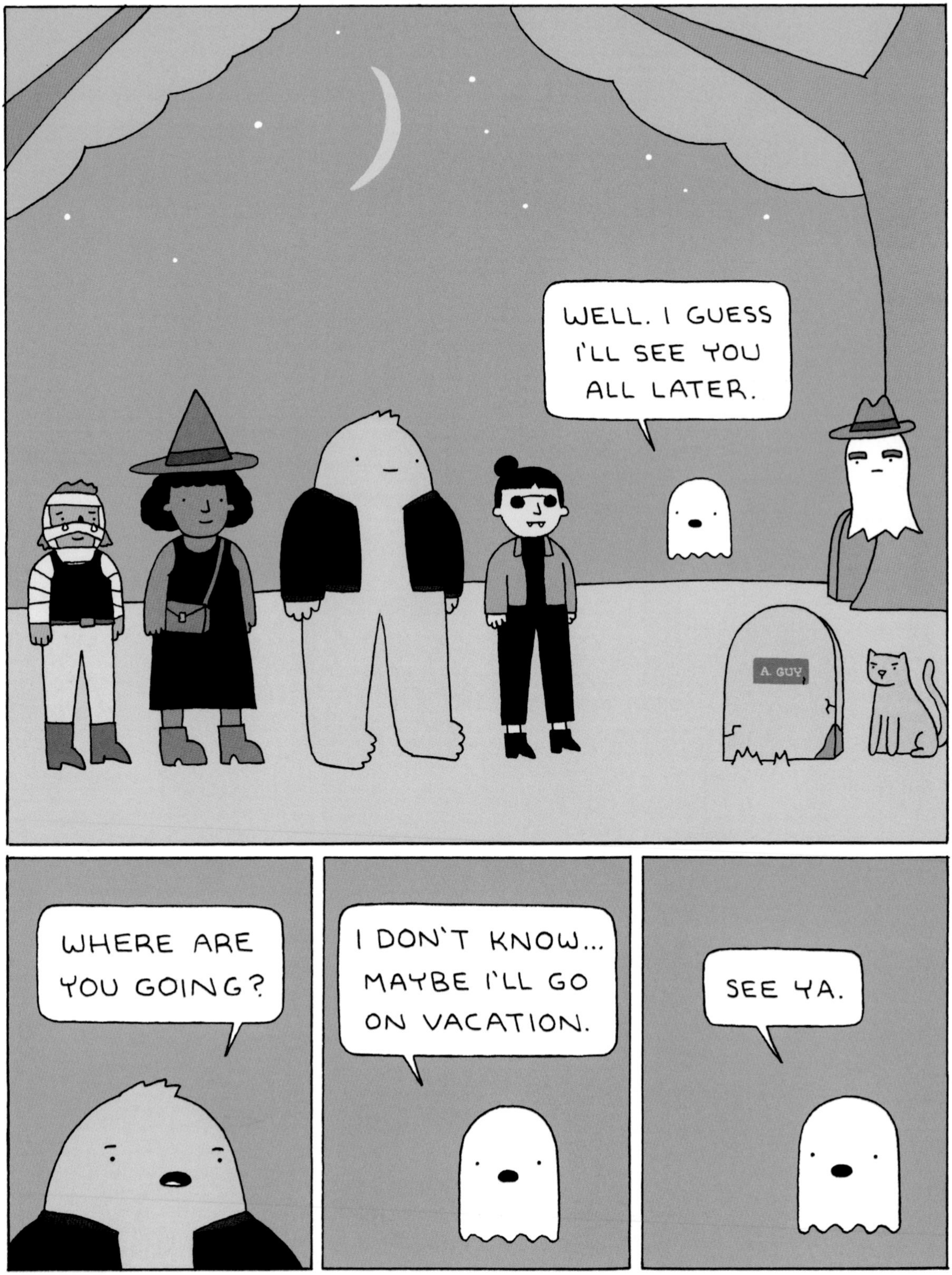
WELL. I GUESS I'LL SEE YOU ALL LATER.
A. GUY
WHERE ARE YOU GOING?
I DON'T KNOW... MAYBE I'LL GO ON VACATION.
SEE YA.

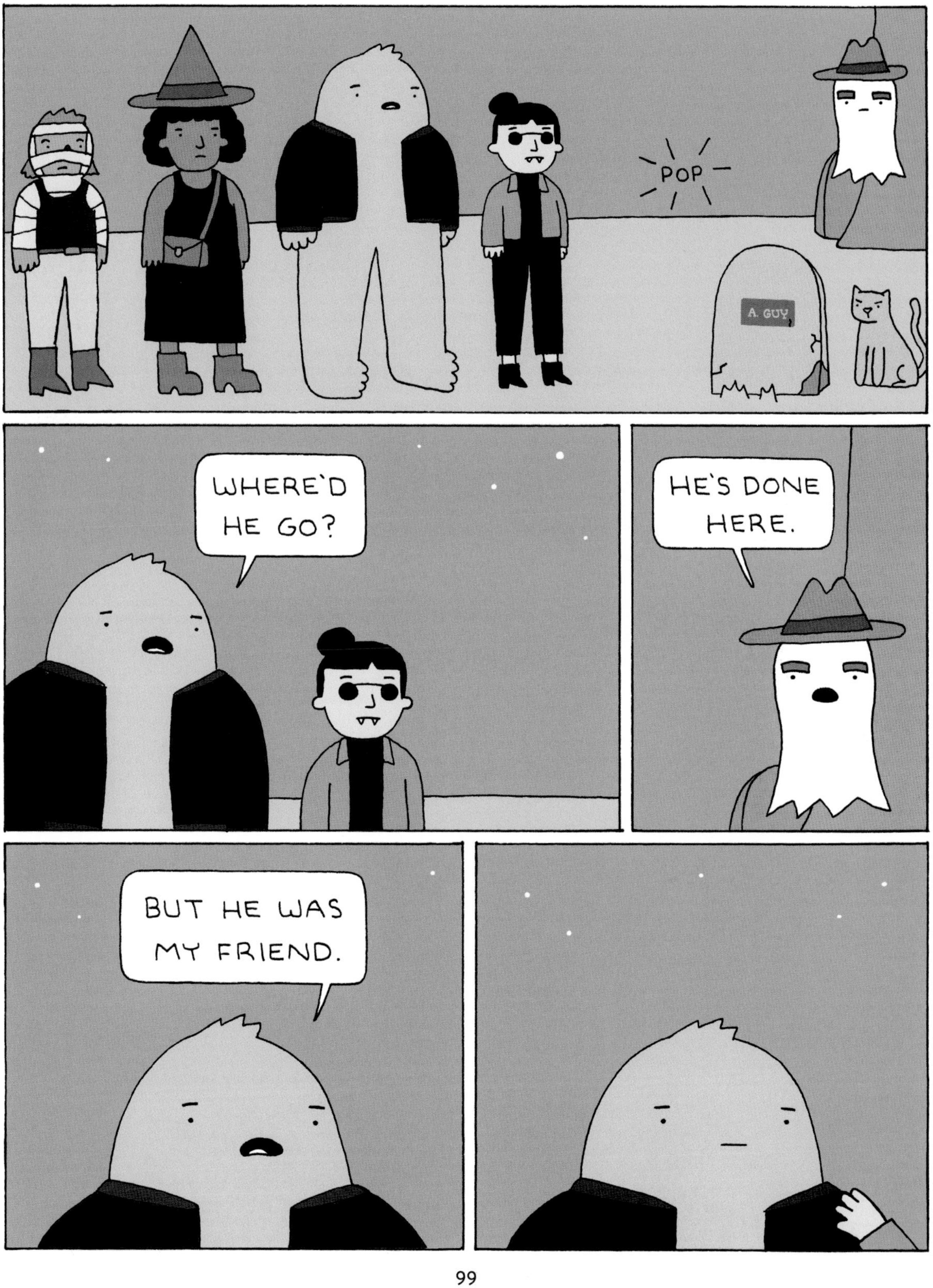
POP
A GUY
WHERE'D HE GO?
HE'S DONE HERE.
BUT HE WAS MY FRIEND.

OH, HEY.
THIS CAT IS
STILL HERE.

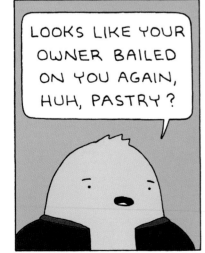

LOOKS LIKE YOUR
OWNER BAILED
ON YOU AGAIN,
HUH, PASTRY?

I GUESS SHE
CAN COME
WITH US...

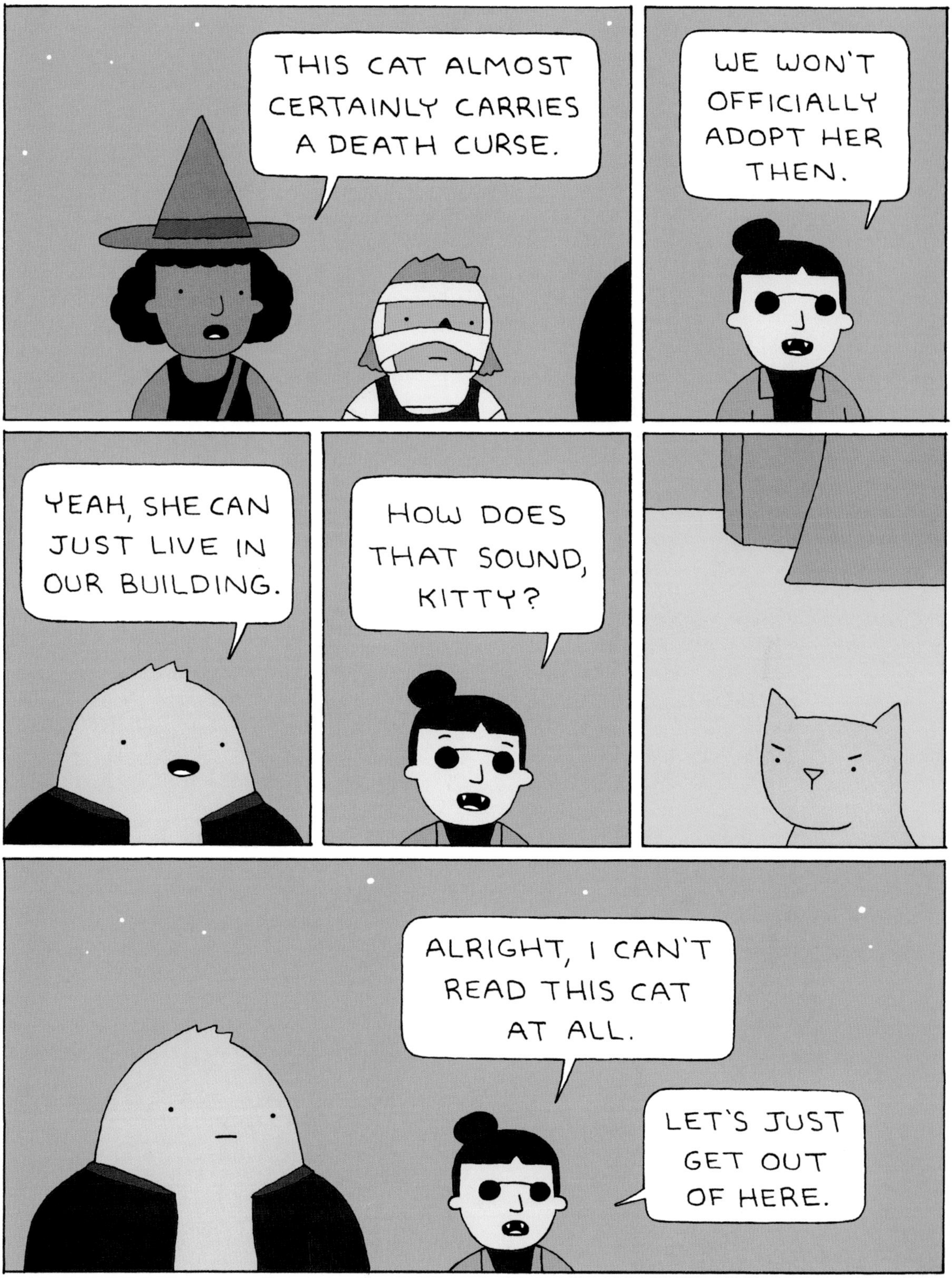
THIS CAT ALMOST CERTAINLY CARRIES A DEATH CURSE.
WE WON'T OFFICIALLY ADOPT HER THEN.
YEAH, SHE CAN JUST LIVE IN OUR BUILDING.
HOW DOES THAT SOUND, KITTY?
ALRIGHT, I CAN'T READ THIS CAT AT ALL.
LET'S JUST GET OUT OF HERE.

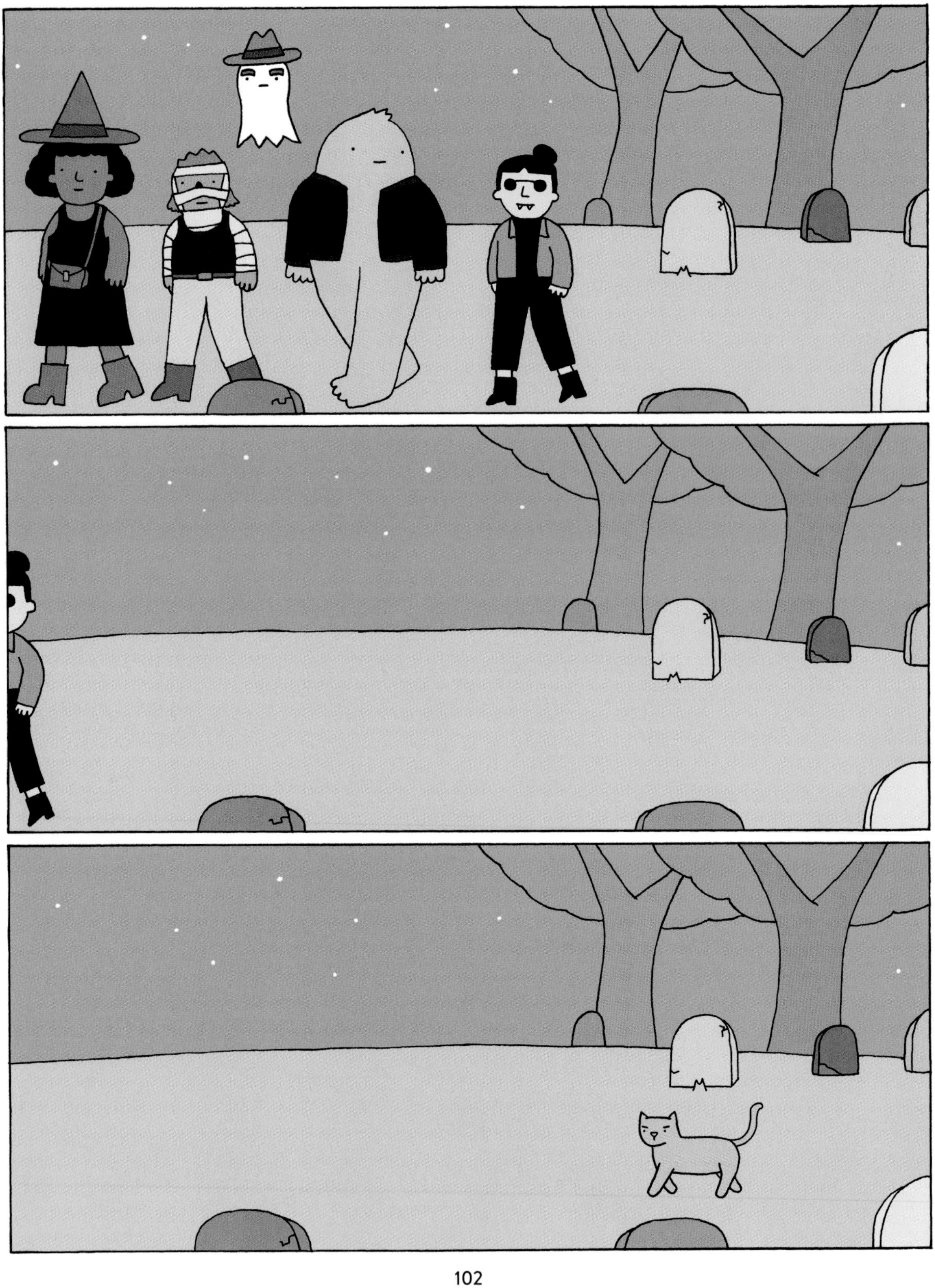

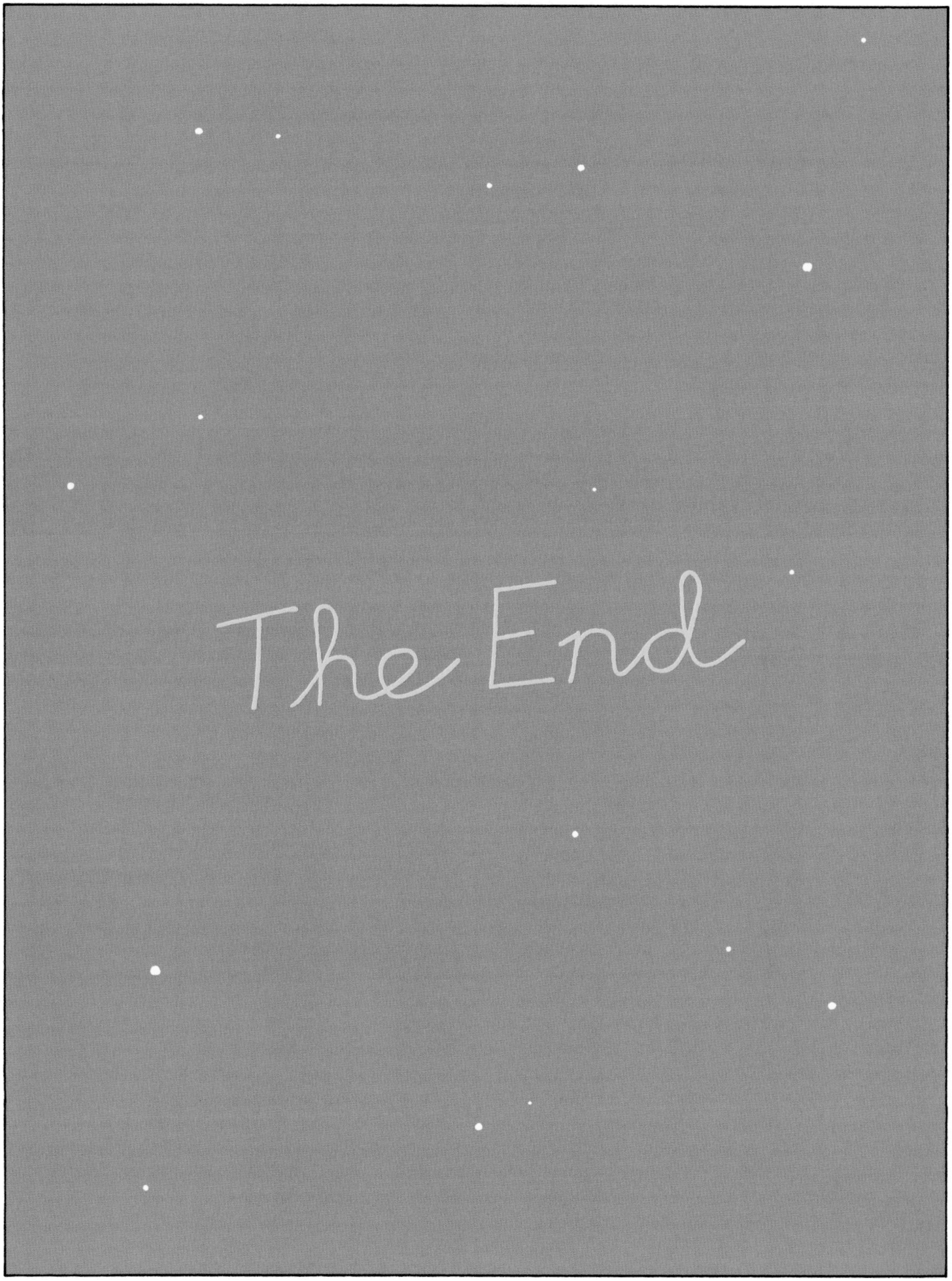
The End

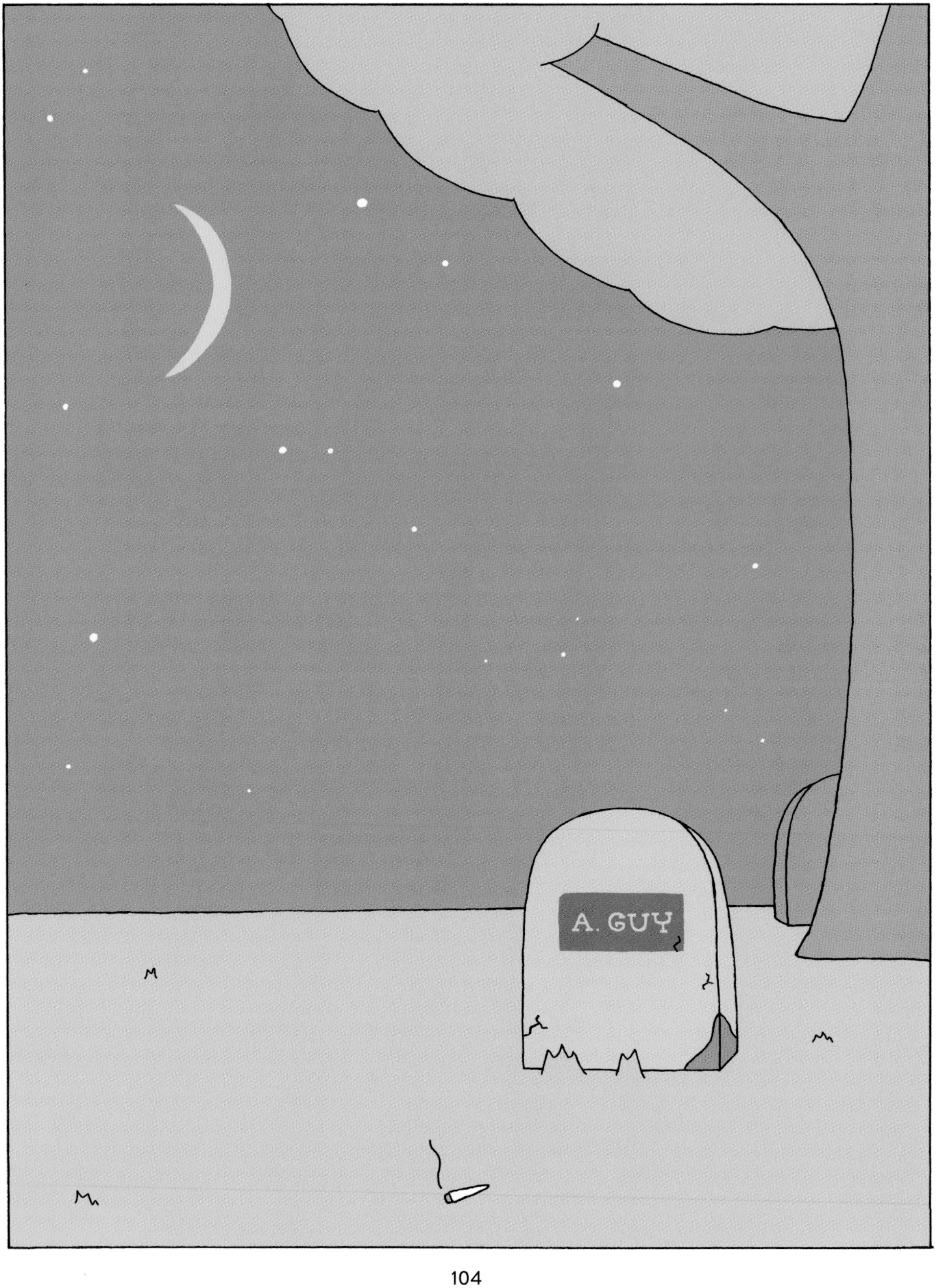
A. GUY

Reza Farazmand is a cartoonist who lives inside the internet. He's best known for his comic series Poorly Drawn Lines, which he started drawing while in school. His work has since appeared on bookshelves, televisions, and websites. It's also been translated into several different languages, which Reza thinks is really cool.